FLANNERY
O'CONNOR
IN THE
AGE OF
TERRORISM

FLANNERY O'CONNOR IN THE AGE OF TERRORISM

Essays on Violence and Grace

Edited by Avis Hewitt
and Robert Donahoo

THE UNIVERSITY OF
TENNESSEE PRESS

KNOXVILLE

ᛠ

Copyright © 2010 by The University of Tennessee Press / Knoxville.
All Rights Reserved. Manufactured in the United States of America.
First Edition.

The paper in this book meets the requirements of American National Standards Institute /
National Information Standards Organization specification Z39.48-1992 (Permanence of
Paper). It contains 30 percent post-consumer waste and is certified by the Forest Steward-
ship Council.

Library of Congress Cataloging-in-Publication Data

Flannery O'Connor in the age of terrorism: essays on violence and grace / edited by Avis
Hewitt and Robert Donahoo.
    p. cm.
Includes bibliographical references and index.
ISBN-13: 978-1-57233-698-8
ISBN-10: 1-57233-698-6

1. O'Connor, Flannery—Criticism and interpretation.
2. Violence in literature.
I. Hewitt, Avis.
II. Donahoo, Robert.

PS3565.C57Z66788 2010
813'.54—dc22
2009045368

CONTENTS

INTRODUCTION

Avis Hewitt

I

The Trappist monk Thomas Merton once wrote that Flannery O'Connor does not belong in the company of Ernest Hemingway and Katherine Anne Porter but in the company of Sophocles because her work "serves to teach man his dishonor." Our current cultural moment deals in clear ways with issues of dishonor, with issues of the place of the United States in the world community after the terrorist attack on New York City in 2001 and the nation's response to it evolving into the Iraq War. If we look to our literature to explain our lives, then among American writers, Flannery O'Connor has shown herself one of the most adept at addressing our urgent yearning for literature to mirror lived experience—not only as an analogue to its particulars, but also to its principles. Never in recent times has O'Connor's classic apology for the relentlessly recurring and seemingly arbitrary violence of her fiction—"To the hard of hearing you have to shout; for the almost blind you must draw large and startling figures" (*MM* 34)—been more readily acceptable or seemed more apt than as our nation stood stunned in the aftermath of 9/11. Few could miss, regardless of their level of religiosity, sensing that a great evil had been loosed on the world—again.

And, of course, O'Connor assented to the notion of evil: her "subject in fiction is the action of grace in territory held largely by the devil" (*MM* 118). Then, too, O'Connor's era was itself a time of terror, spanning World War II, the Cold War, and the conflict in Korea. As several writers in this volume remind us, she wrote in her letters: "at night I dream of radiated bulls and peacocks and swans" (*CW* 1152). Yet she also asserted that grace is central to her vision, even though most of her characters and scenes stop short of providing illustrations of gracious living. Those few that do pray, "Jesus, stab me in the heart!" along with Mrs. Greenleaf, who in her corpulence lies upon the ground waving her arms and attempting to suffer empathetically with those whose troubles unfold in the newspaper clippings beneath her (*CW* 506). In fact, her prayer might be taken as a mantra for O'Connor's project. To O'Connor, the fiction writer does not work with the goal of "uplift," of demonstrating to a tired but eager populace how well they are doing, how "successful" they are. When *Life* magazine asked a group of promising young novelists in 1957, "Who speaks for America today?" she wrote that evidently it was the advertising agencies, a salty answer to *Life*'s complaint, woven between pages of commodity paradise, that the young Cold War writers in ascendance were not capturing "the joy of life itself" (*MM* 26). How true. For O'Connor, the joy of life could not be found in accelerated acquisitiveness. She makes plain—as plain as the winter and the winter-woman in Lucette Carmody's sermon (*CW* 413)—her approach. She testifies in her essays that she "see[s] from the standpoint of Christian orthodoxy . . . [with] the meaning of life centered in our Redemption in Christ" (*MM* 32)—a circumstance that renders problematic any paramount connections between the material acquisitiveness of the 1950s, the narcissism and hedonism of more recent decades, and "the joy of living."

For O'Connor, deepest joy lies in engagement with the Real. William Sessions explains the focus of O'Connor's Catholic theology to be the Real Presence, which juxtaposes powerfully with the Lacanian notion of the Real as a terrifying exposure to nothingness—resulting perhaps in "no pleasure but meanness" (*CW* 152). O'Connor dramatically supersedes Lacan's limited thinking as she depicts our quotidian scrapes against ultimate reality. Her stories privilege the use of force and fearsome sundering as a means of moving characters—and readers—beyond mundane and stifling perceptions. Her truck is with New Testament paradox: we must be broken to be made whole. O'Connor famously confessed that nihilism is "the gas" we moderns "breathe" and that without the church, she would be the "stinkingest logical positivist you ever saw" (*HB* 97). But she did not stop with nihilism or positivism just because they were the most readily accessible informants for the self in modern culture. Her perceptions persisted depth upon depth into the Real until she struck upon "the almost imperceptible intrusions of grace" (*MM* 112). The contemporary reader often feels somewhat scared and insignificant in a world where school massacres or shootings in a random McDonald's outlet or at any local mall or on a college campus have replaced fears of traditional warfare and of pestilence and famine. These days our pestilence comes from staving off our "famine" through the use of pesticides lavishly spread to produce our daily bread, of which we suffer more from having too much than having too little. We are the era that has elevated Ruby Turpin's extra pounds to a level-red crisis. In short, we have made vague anxiety our enveloping milieu and, in doing so, readied ourselves to engage with an author who acknowledges our angst over random but pervasive violence—who, in fact, is evidently fascinated with it—but sees something beyond it. We situate our contemporary readings of O'Connor in "the age of terrorism," not because we forget that every age is in some ways an age of terror, but because our contemporary moment, these postmillennial times, call for the wisdom that still inheres in O'Connor work as we construe ourselves susceptible to terrors on divers fronts—without, within, global, quotidian.

To O'Connor the violence of this world may often be arbitrary, but that does not make it the ultimate arbiter of meaning. On the college lecture circuit, she contextualized the palpable fears of the Cold War by making suffering purposeful: "in my own stories I have found that violence is strangely capable of returning my characters to reality and preparing them to accept their moment of grace" (*MM* 112). Faulkner had written in his Nobel Prize acceptance speech of 1954 that one question in the 1950s overshadowed all other considerations: "When will I be blown up?" Citizens spent decades learning to live with that issue until the failure of the Soviet bloc ushered in a new era of human hopefulness in the 1990s. But it did not last. The precipitant attack on New York City's World Trade Center became "the large and startling figure" reminding us that we are never safe, that, as the 1662 Book of Common Prayer has it, "in the midst of life we are in death." And O'Connor "does" death. It may well be one of the reasons that, after the initial stunned reaction of critics to *Wise Blood* (Kreyling 12), she has maintained steady readerly and critical interest. From the small boy who drowns himself to reenact the baptismal moment that made him "count" to a bigger boy who hangs himself in his own attic in order to get closer to his mother in heaven; from Haze Motes killing with his car an alter ego who brings him no "solace" to Frankie Tarwater murdering by baptism his mentally challenged little cousin Bishop; from the grandmother's imprudent revelation of The Misfit's newspaper notoriety to Thomas's finding "the comforts of home" so insulating that he inadvertently (?) shoots his own mother—O'Connor does not cower from taking our vanities and self-absorptions to the limits they would generally warrant, except for the "almost imperceptible intrusions of grace."

Astute readers of O'Connor recognize that with almost every one of her ego-driven, fatuous characters—which is almost every one of her characters—we muse "there but for the grace of God" . . . goes someone we know. We recognize the deep truth of O'Connor's portraits but hope heartily that we are the exception to such foibles, surely. Did she anticipate as much? Thinking that we have "heads so hard" that little else will work, she aimed in her stories to return readers to reality, even though the goal is accomplished only at "considerable cost." Given the nature and degree of violence in our time, with a new and dramatically increased sense of daily palpable fear tainting our quotidian rounds since 9/11, we seem cognizant of that cost in new ways. In October 2006, just as a group of one hundred O'Connor scholars were preparing to converge in Grand Rapids, Michigan, to consider ways in which this new age of terrorism resonates with O'Connor's use of violence and grace, news of a horrific, devastating event intruded in a shocking, painful way on the congenial academic event: on Tuesday, October 2, Charles Carl Roberts IV, a thirty-two-year-old milk-tank driver, entered an Amish schoolhouse in Lancaster County, Pennsylvania, to shoot and kill five girls, ages seven to thirteen, and seriously wound several others. We discovered that as a society we are not yet inured to violence where the random, arbitrary murder of schoolchildren is concerned—especially when the targets are an explicitly peace-loving, devout element of American culture that exempts itself from "mainstream madness" in favor of a less worldly and a godlier way of life. The O'Connor conjunction of violence and grace took on anagogical dimensions when the families of the slain innocent girls chose to pray for the slayer and his relatives and to attend his funeral.

II

Not all O'Connorites read her to find confirmation of Jesus as "a unique intervention in human history." In fact, in 2004 at the annual gathering of the American Literature Association in San Francisco, Tim Caron, a scholar specializing in notions of the sacred in southern literature and convicted that current criticism is "segregationist" in its division of American literature into particularized threads, such as African American literature, argued that the O'Connor "camp" also harbors a crippling bifurcation of its own—into True Believers and Apostates (138). True Believers, akin to Eric Hoffer's 1951 assessment of the mentality or mode by which the masses sometimes embrace an idea or cause, take O'Connor at her nonfiction word and read her stories and novels according to the meticulous reception control that she attempted in *Mystery and Manners*. They opt for this relationship to her work because they are, in Caron's view, also "true believers" in their desire to "see from the standpoint of our Redemption in Christ." Apostates, on the other hand, share neither O'Connor's fervent Christian conviction nor the readerly goal of discerning the anagogical revelations of her stories along with the material ones. Yet they find her telling compelling truths about the nature of lived experience. Apostates admit that as she shocks us into perceptions of underlying reality, she makes us laugh out loud, a sure sign that she has hit a vein that serves as a lifeline.

The split pushes forward heedlessly between readers who champion O'Connor because she reinforces a Christ-imbued worldview and those who choose to read her because she is shocking and funny apart from her anagogical goals. An articulate segment of the O'Connor scholarly community wants to lay to rest O'Connor's religiosity in a "take it or leave it" manner. We live in an era of "truth claims" where pluralism has muddied our conviction that convictions are even acceptable. Mark Eaton argues that "belief in anything seems precarious at best, provisional or untenable at worst" (144). Not so for O'Connor. To receptive readers, she illuminates a world beyond the physical one, a world that even with its evidently necessary violence is also, as Gerard Manley Hopkins puts it, "charged with the grandeur of God" ("Pied Beauty"). From the beginning, such secularists as John Hawkes, Josephine Hendin, and Martha Stephens have produced criticism to counter that of Sister Bernetta Quinn, Sister Kathleen Feeley, and John Desmond. Theological readings of O'Connor persist to the present, especially in Christina Bieber Lake's *The Incarnational Art of Flannery O'Connor* (2005), Ralph Wood's *Flannery O'Connor and the Christ-Haunted South* (2004), Susan Srigley's *Flannery O'Connor's Sacramental Art* (2004), and Richard Giannone's *Flannery O'Connor: Hermit Novelist* (2000) and *Flannery O'Connor and the Mystery of Love* (1999). Even a preliminary list must also include Regis Martin's *Unmasking the Devil* (2005), Farrell O'Gorman's *Peculiar Crossroads: Flannery O'Connor, Walker Percy, and Catholic Vision in Postwar Southern Fiction* (2004), Henry Edmondson III's *Return to Good and Evil: Flannery O'Connor's Response to Nihilism* (2002), and George Kilcourse's *Flannery O'Connor's Religious Imagination: A World with Everything Off Balance* (2001). The scales tip so clearly in favor of theological approaches—even four decades after O'Connor's death—that strong, useful feminist and new historicist studies, like Katherine Hemple Prown's *Revising Flannery O'Connor: Southern Literary Culture and the Problem of Female Authorship* (2001) and Jon Lance Bacon's *Flannery O'Connor and Cold War Culture* (1993) stand out for having created much resonant new knowledge apart from anagogical considerations, while works like Sarah Gordon's *Flannery O'Connor: The Obedient Imagination* (2000) investigate the intersection of the author's identity as mid-century Catholic Christian and southern female.

Work continues apace in every direction. The field of O'Connor studies has grown exponentially since the author's death in 1964. The *Flannery O'Connor Bulletin/Review,* established just a few years after her death, is now distinguished as the longest continually published journal devoted to the work of a woman writer among all scholarly publications. The current Modern Language

Association's bibliography cites 1,329 entries on her. Books and articles on her work rank her twentieth among the entire array of U.S. authors of the last four centuries about whom critics might chose to write. Moreover, her reputation has become dramatically international. Of the twenty latest articles devoted to O'Connor, two are in French and one is in Spanish. Just a bit farther down the list are publications in Japanese and Norwegian. The 2007 American Literature Association featured as one of its two annual panels on O'Connor a focus on her international readership. In spite of this global attention, surprisingly few—only six or so—collections of Anglophone essays on O'Connor's work have been a part of this trajectory.

Still, these volumes collecting innovative perspectives on O'Connor, her work, and her times have become a significant element of O'Connor studies. In 1966, Melvin J. Friedman and Lewis A. Lawson published *The Added Dimension: The Art and Mind of Flannery O'Connor* (Fordham University Press), with necessary lag time from composition to print denying interpretive coverage to the stories from O'Connor's posthumous collection, *Everything That Rises Must Converge* (1965). In 1985, Melvin Friedman and Beverly Lyon Clark published *Critical Essays on Flannery O'Connor* with G. K. Hall of Boston, a work that included twelve reviews of her books, four tributes, and twelve scholarly essays—all reprinted works. In 1996, Sura P. Rath and Mary Neff Shaw edited for University of South Carolina Press *Flannery O'Connor: New Perspectives*, a collection of ten original essays by a variety of the most prominent scholars in the field at that time. That was well over a decade ago.

Since the turn of the millennium, three more collections have been brought out. In 2004, Teresa Caruso edited for Peter Lang a set of theoretically charged essays titled *"On the Subject of the Feminist Business": Re-Reading Flannery O'Connor.* The nine essays it contains deal with issues of gender and embodiment in O'Connor, an important segment of contemporary O'Connor studies representing a good mix of new and established O'Connor scholars. Then in 2006, University of South Carolina Press brought out *Flannery O'Connor's Radical Reality,* edited by two Danish scholars of American literature, Jan Nordby Gretlund and Karl-Heinz Westarp. This book features several provocative new O'Connor interpretations and several retrospectives. The Mercer University Press collection from 2007, *Inside the Church of Flannery O'Connor: Sacrament, Sacramental, and the Sacred in Her Fiction,* looks at the contestation that surrounds religious interpretations—the aforementioned carefully prescribed reader reception, at which she has proved stunningly persuasive—of O'Connor's work. *Inside* explicitly emphasizes the "voices of sharp dissent" among critics who find her Christian perspective at odds with the "social policies" implicit in her fiction.

Our collection attempts a more overarching task than arguing retrospection or religion. The fifteen authors reread O'Connor, and whether they mention them or not, they also reread the collapsing towers, Abu Ghraib, and the relentless discussions in the media—of which the Internet now constitutes an overwhelming and unregulated element—of our perceptions of international terrorism and national security. Much of what concerns us in the world, including the potential for violence that inheres in it, is now electrified with an urgency to forge connections and arrive at new levels of peaceful, harmonious, mutually enhancing relationship among individuals and among cultures, rather than letting the forces of destruction hold sway. The essays here implicitly address that urgency.

III

In the opening section of the collection, the essayists focus directly on the issue of violence. Anthony Di Renzo (*American Gargoyles: Flannery O'Connor and the Medieval Grotesque,* 1993) addresses explicitly a significant element of our collection: how the murders and mayhem O'Connor freely portrays illuminate our fears of fundamentalism by paralleling the medieval madness of religious cabals, treachery, and warfare that portended an apocalyptic mysticism akin to the irrational fundamentalism of our own time. Christina Bieber Lake (*The Incarnational Art of Flannery O'Connor,* 2005) remembers the timely work of Jacques Ellul, whose 1960 critique of *The Technological Society* prophesied our treating one another mechanistically, as abstractions and instruments. Lake demonstrates that O'Connor's sensitivity to valuing her characters' personhood, not their "usefulness," increased dramatically over the years of her work by comparing an MFA story, "The Crop," with a story that O'Connor completed on her deathbed, "Parker's Back."

Ralph C. Wood (*Flannery O'Connor and the Christ-Haunted South,* 2004) explicates the efficacy of bodily misery—lupus, in O'Connor's case, and anorexia brought on by religious fasting, in the case of the French mystic Simone Weil. In both cases, corporeal "violence" wrought an awareness of *malheur,* which Wood defines as affliction mingled with "inevitability" and "doom." Both of these women—and Weil's life and writings were of great interest to O'Connor—saw that the rightful relation to one's affliction allows her or him to live "in accord with the true grain of the universe." Ramsey Michaels contrasts the explicitly violent images that abound in O'Connor's second novel with the muted images of the Eucharist—O'Connor called this book "a minor hymn to the Eucharist"—and demonstrates the extent to which those analogues inform the novel's action and indicate Francis Tarwater's pilgrim's progress toward Christian conversion, regardless of prophet status. Like Michaels, Linda Naranjo-Huebl selects a narrow focus, reviewing the critical context that surrounds "A Stroke of Good Fortune" and finding an inconsistent ethic of life. However, she argues that such an evoked critical context, if brought into dialogue, articulates the limited and polarized visions of womanhood and motherhood and the preclusion of mutually life-affirming alternatives for women and children that marked the American 1950s.

The middle segment of essays contextualizes O'Connor's mid-twentieth-century experience as a Cold War observer and, to some extent, participant in popular culture through comics and books that she would inevitably have witnessed in play around her, as well as the mechanist man-as-machine tendencies of Henry Ford's mass production techné that dominated that century. Two of the authors in this section compare O'Connor's use of violence to other authors with whom she shares affinities. Jon Lance Bacon (*Flannery O'Connor and Cold War Culture,* 1993) earned an invaluable place in O'Connor studies fifteen years ago with his groundbreaking examination of O'Connor in her time—politically, religiously, intellectually, and culturally. Now he provides an arresting New Historicist reading of the parallels between popular culture expressions of dread in the "gory stories" told by horror comics of the day and the national angst that knowledge of the Holocaust and effects of the atomic bombs dropped on Japan created in the populace in general and in O'Connor's fictional images and plots in particular.

William Brevda compares two prominent writers of noir—James Ross and Jim Thompson—to O'Connor's project in "A Good Man Is Hard to Find" and discovers that while the satanic ironies of the suffering doubters in what Kierkegaard calls "the sphere of infinite resignation" laugh themselves sick inside, the freaks in O'Connor make a leap of faith from irony to prophecy and laugh themselves well. John Sykes (*Flannery O'Connor, Walker Percy, and the Aesthetic of Revelation,* 2007) turns our attention to that farmer-screenwriter-turned-Nobel-Prize-winning-novelist William Faulkner. He investigates the connection between the enigmatic response of Benjy in the closing scene of *The Sound and the Fury* and the yard statue of a jockey with "a wild look of misery" that serves as the focal point and closing symbol of "The Artificial Nigger." His project involves giving proper credit to the Confederate statue as a parallel force with regard to Christian iconography, finding the South's Lost Cause to engage the Christian drama, if such a drama could forego the elements of resurrection and redemption.

With Cormac McCarthy's recent Pulitzer Prize for *The Road,* Farrell O'Gorman (*Peculiar Crossroads: Flannery O'Connor, Walker Percy and Catholic Vision in Postwar Southern Fiction,* 2004) reminds us of the connection between these two writers both once southern, pointing out their mutual penchant for prodigal prophets and the connection between the violence of nature and nature's God. Doug Davis argues the profound relationship between Americans and their cars. As Brian Abel Ragen and J. O. Tate have argued previously, O'Connor characters manifest that national obsession, but Davis demonstrates that they do not simply love their vehicles but become extensions of them, "deeply alienated image[s] of the emergent postwar hybrids," which reveals themselves as participants in "an era of machinic coupling and desire."

The third segment of the collection blasts any notion that O'Connor writes formulaic stories of easy orthodoxy (Gordon 247). The writers here uncover her depths, revealing the extent to which she has anticipated our millennial world with its politics that have eclipsed the color line, its penchant for creating icons, its tendency to hide and to scapegoat uncomfortable truths and people, and its explosions of literary theories that attempt to reduce truth to those truth claims that pluralism promotes. Marshall Bruce Gentry (*Flannery O'Connor's Religion of the Grotesque,* 1986) looks at the myriad manifestations of "color" in O'Connor's work to discover that she evidently saw race-mixing as both inevitable and desirable, even if she was socially conditioned to be uncomfortable with it. He also finds that her characters frequently experience more than one racial status and that being "mixed" promotes integrity.

William Sessions, known as "Billy" in Flannery O'Connor's award-winning collection of letters, *The Habit of Being* (1979) and a Renaissance scholar currently working on the authorized biography of O'Connor, reflects on the mythic and legendary qualities O'Connor has taken on in recent decades. He demonstrates her steadily increasing global popularity and international reputation as he muses on how it is and what it means that O'Connor has become a cultural icon.

William Monroe labels the excision that incarceration enacts on "the distempered parts" of society (T. S. Eliot's "East Coker") a selective violence that O'Connor understood intuitively, anticipating the work of Michel Foucault, as a purification system for maintaining arrangements, structures, and hierarchies that are resistant to revelation and reform similar to Rene Girard's notion of the scapegoat as inevitable to mimetic desire. Thomas Haddox (*Fears and Fascinations: Representing Catholicism in the American South,* 2005) assesses the current debates in literary circles as lacking a lesson from O'Connor studies, given that identity politics too often reveals multiple subjectivities, inviting critics to take a stand for its novelty, rather than for its truth value. Without bringing our core beliefs into play, we cannot make literary critiques as valuable to life experience as the genius of our fiction writers warrants. That O'Connor critics have traditionally followed O'Connor's own bold lead in making their deepest convictions a bedrock of their writing lives bodes well for our relearning in terrorist times that the art of persuasion can be more valuable than the art of evasion.

The concluding essay in this collection is Robert Donahoo's survey of the current state of O'Connor criticism after several decades of steady and impassioned productivity. He recognizes the sometimes "violent" diversity of readings that she attracts as a crucial reason that the field stays such a vital element of American literary studies. He also points to significant gaps in the scholarship as it currently stands and suggests that not only does O'Connor reward readings informed by every sort of contemporary theory but is so dynamic a writer that her work can serve as the basis for new theoretical constructs.

Finally, these essays serve only as a truncated sampling of the astonishing number of ways in which a writer whose time among us was so short—only thirty-nine years—yet whose literary output—two novels, two short story collections, a set of essays, and a collection of letters—was so dynamic that we cannot help but attribute the fanfare to a deep genius, a genius apparent even to undergraduates and high schoolers who encounter her in fleeting anthology interludes. Whether we know her from only a short story or spend years in the analysis of her prose, we readers recognize that in *any* age when human exigencies wrestle with apparently inexorable forces, O'Connor's work opens worlds to her readers that are depth upon depth worth continuing to explore.

Acknowledgments

I would like to join Bob in thanking Sura, Bruce, and Virginia, each of whom has promoted my involvement in O'Connor work. I especially thank Ralph Wood, who relentlessly mentors me by his generosity of spirit, by his example, and by his work not only in literature but in that life in Christ that all believers share.

For their friendship, for their relentless passion for all things O'Connor and literary, and for their crucial roles in the 2006 event that served as the impetus for this book, "Flannery O'Connor in the Age of Terrorism: A Conference on Violence and Grace," I thank my then students: Becky Karnes, Ruth Reiniche, and Chris Triezenberg.

At Grand Valley State University I thank Gayle Davis, Jill VanAntwerp, and Ben Lockerd for their strong, ongoing support of O'Connor work and projects on our campus. To each of them I am most grateful and realize how powerfully their generosity and good will "underwrite" my unflagging zeal for O'Connor studies.

As this project becomes a wrap, I thank my co-editor, the gracious and savvy Bob Donahoo, who has been steadily splendid at shaping the evolving manuscript. I have much enjoyed our learning bookmaking together. At University of Tennessee Press, I thank Scot Danforth for saying yes to our project and Thomas Wells for seeing us through it. And here at the homestead, I thank John Hewitt for letting me get away with loving O'Connor studies lots and for proofing every line of this manuscript.

Works Cited

Caron, Tim. "'The Bottom Rail Is on the Top': Race and 'Theological Whiteness' in Flannery O'Connor's Short Fiction." *Inside the Church of Flannery O'Connor: Sacrament, Sacramental, and the Sacred in Her Fiction.* Ed. Joanne Halleran McMullen and Jon Parrish Peede. Macon: Mercer UP, 2007. 138–64.

———. "Theological Whiteness: Flannery O'Connor and Her Critics. Flannery O'Connor's Universality." American Literature Association, San Francisco, 29 May 2004.

Eaton, Mark. "Inventing Hope: The Question of Belief in *White Noise* and *Mao II*." *Approaches to Teaching* White Noise. Ed. Tim Engles and John N. Duvall. New York: MLA, 2006. 144–57.

Gordon, Sarah. *Flannery O'Conner: The Obedient Imagination.* Athens: U of Georgia P, 2000.

Kreyling, Michael. "Introduction." *New Essays on* Wise Blood. Ed. Michael Kreyling. Cambridge: Cambridge UP, 1995. 1–24.

O'Connor, Flannery. *Collected Works.* New York: Library of America, 1988.

———. *The Habit of Being.* Ed. Sally Fitzgerald. New York: Farrar, 1979.

———. *Mystery and Manners: Occasional Prose.* Ed. Sally and Robert Fitzgerald. New York: Farrar, 1969.

Part One

READING O'CONNOR'S VIOLENCE

AND THE VIOLENT BEAR IT AWAY: O'CONNOR AND THE MENACE OF APOCALYPTIC TERRORISM

Anthony Di Renzo

> Mankind can't endure the thought that the world was born by chance, by mistake, just because four brainless atoms bumped into one another on a slippery highway. So a cosmic plot has to be found—God, angels, devils. . . . People put bombs on trains because they're looking for God.
>
> —Umberto Eco, *Foucault's Pendulum*

I

"For [the fiction writer]," Flannery O'Connor said, "the bomb that was dropped on Hiroshima affects life on the Oconee River, and there's not anything he can do about it" (*MM* 77). A devout Catholic living in the Cold War, when Manichean politics brought the world to the brink of Armageddon, O'Connor often commented on the atomic bomb's fallout on her imagination. Given her knowledge of the liturgical calendar and her eye for ghastly coincidence, she knew that 6 August, the date of the Hiroshima bombing, coincided with the Feast of the Transfiguration, the day Christ on Mount Tabor revealed his divine nature to his most intimate apostles in a flash of blinding light. At the Los Alamos test site, several Catholic physicists had compared the first atomic blast to Matthias Grünewald's altar piece *The Resurrection*. Like her friend Thomas Merton, O'Connor considered the bomb a satanic parody of God's power and a harbinger of a possible apocalypse.

Today O'Connor scholars work under the shadow of another bomb. Ever since 9/11 revealed the murderous fury of apocalyptic terrorism, we have been forced to reexamine our assumptions about and approaches to her fiction. "Historical events have once again confirmed 'what goes around comes around,'" declares Michael Kreyling, who believes the War on Terror has returned us to "a Cold War culture of official dread, anxiety, and suspicion" (2). The fall of the Twin Towers marked the collapse of an old paradigm. Until then, we tended to see O'Connor's work within its original context: a postwar America coming to terms with militant secularism, where the arrogance of science had marginalized orthodoxy, Christian charity had been replaced by welfare, and liberals pre-served evangelicals in formaldehyde. That context no longer exists. Instead, we live in a post-9/11 America of militant fundamentalism, where the arrogance of orthodoxy has marginalized science, the Gospel of Prosperity sanctifies a Darwinian economy, and evangelicals have placed liberals on the endangered species list.

Flannery O'Connor's fear that the Bible Belt would resemble the rest of the country was premature. If anything, as shown in a political cartoon popular after the 2000 presidential election, a map dividing North America into the United States of Canada and Jesus Land, the rest of the country has become the Bible Belt. Whether in the Ozarks or the Washington Beltway, a frightening number of Americans believe in the literal meaning of the Bible and consider the global war on terrorism a holy crusade, a cosmic battle that will end in the Second Coming. Once again, the world is in flames, and O'Connor scholars must have the courage to draw new circles in the fire.

How do we interpret O'Connor's disturbing and often violent work in these tragic times? What can her rabid preachers, berserk prophets, and eschatological visions teach us about religious fanaticism, political resentment, and apocalyptic terrorism? Too often we have treated O'Connor's works as allegory or homily rather than fiction dealing with the problem of belief in the postmodern world. Neither a theologian nor an apologist, she was keenly aware how her grotesque characters are "afflicted in both mind and body" and possess "little—or at best a distorted—sense of spiritual purpose" (*MM* 32). "They seem to carry an invisible burden," she admitted; "their fanaticism is a reproach, not merely an eccentricity" (*MM* 44).

But a reproach against what? "Against the emptiness of secular humanism!" religious critics will reply. But O'Connor more often reproaches the pride, resentment, and vindictiveness passing for religion, the paranoia, xenophobia, and will-to-power fueling fundamentalism, here and abroad. We forget that fact at our peril if we insist her stories are hermeneutically sealed parables. As human remains continue to be removed from Ground Zero, we must go beyond even O'Connor's advice to concentrate on "the actions of grace" in her fiction and ignore "the dead bodies" (*MM* 113). The dead bodies are equally important and will increase in significance as the death toll mounts in a war of religious terrorism.

Here I speak from bitter personal experience. Having lost students and parishioners in the bombing of Pan Am Flight 103, and classmates, colleagues, and clients in the World Trade Center attacks, I have come to reevaluate Flannery O'Connor's prophetic art. I am not alone. At "Flannery O'Connor in the Age of Terrorism: An Academic Conference on Violence and Grace," held in Grand Rapids, Michigan, 5–7 October 2006, many presenters challenged participants to reconsider the bloodshed and mayhem so prevalent in O'Connor's fiction. What do they mean in a post-9/11 world? Old interpretations, the product of old critical approaches, have been, if not invalidated, permanently damaged. No longer can we take O'Connor's theological defense of her work as Gospel: "The novelist with Christian concerns," she once explained, "will find in modern life distortions which are repugnant to him, and his problem will be to make these distortions appear as distortions to an audience which is used to seeing them as natural, and he may well be forced to use more violent means to get his vision across to this hostile audience" (*MM* 33–34).

As Claire Katz challenged over twenty years ago, we should question our readiness to accept O'Connor's anagogic intent as critically definitive. For although she claimed that "violence is strangely capable of returning my characters to reality and preparing them for their moment of grace" (*MM* 112), she often unleashes "a whirlwind of destructive forces more profound than her Christian theme would seem to justify—murder, rape, mutilation—for ostensibly religious purposes" (Katz 55). Religious violence is not simply "a rhetoric demanded by a secular audience"; it expresses, at least partly, Flannery O'Connor's vision and values (56). If O'Connor studies is to remain vital, relevant, and honest, it must rethink fundamental questions about the violent fundamentalism at the heart of O'Connor's work. To do so, we must confront the shadow of orthodox Christianity and the potential madness in apocalyptic mysticism—two things we have denied or explained away for the past forty years.

As a lector who has recited passages from Revelation at funerals, a Eucharistic minister who has brought the viaticum to the dying, I am pained to say these things. But given national events, O'Connor scholars cannot remain blind to or blasé about the horrific underside of O'Connor's traditional Christian symbolism. Left unexamined, symbols become idols, and idols always demand human sacrifice. As the Gospel of Matthew reminds us, ours is not the first age of religious terrorism: "From the days of John the Baptist until now, the Kingdom of Heaven suffers violence, and the violent bear it away" (11:12). But "suffers" not only means "endures" but also "permits," "allows." The church itself, history shows, spawned the Dragon of the Apocalypse.

To understand how, we must return to the ancient controversy surrounding the Book of Revelation's inclusion in the Bible, the subsequent rise of violent millenarian sects, and their brutal repression. The "pervasive blood symbolism" of early Christian rhetoric and art is "grounded" in this history of apocalyptic bloodshed (Thörnqvst 85). The same eschatology, the same war between terrorism and counterterrorism also informs Flannery O'Connor's harrowing fiction, particularly *The Violent Bear It Away*, where an apprentice prophet learns at a terrible cost to distinguish between holy and unholy apocalypse. We must learn to do the same, if we are to survive in a world of jihads and crusades.

Flannery O'Connor's attitude toward the Book of Revelation was complex. Writing to Ted Spivey on 16 November 1958, she echoes Boris Pasternak's verdict in *Dr. Zhivago:* "All great, genuine art resembles and continues the Revelation of St. John" (*HB* 305). But she tempered this aesthetic enthusiasm with critical distance. As Sister Kathleen Feeley notes, O'Connor possessed "one of the finest private theological libraries in the country" (xvii). Arthur Kinney and Lorine M. Getz have documented her extensive reading in church history and sophisticated hermeneutics. She was, therefore, no Mason Tarwater, a naïve fundamentalist, but a Catholic intellectual and an amateur biblical scholar familiar with Revelation's troubling textual history. Indeed, when surveying the carnage leading to the Synod of Hippo, the church council that determined the canonical Scriptures, she may have felt as appalled as Rayber, caught in "an undertow" of blood "dragging [her] backwards" to "some ancient source, some desert prophet or polesitter" (*VBA* 192)

Despite its present centrality to Christian art and eschatology, the Book of Revelation was almost excluded from the Bible because it seemed to justify mass destruction. No message could be more disturbing to the early church. When the Synod of Hippo met in 393 A.D., it faced a world burdened by slavery and oppression, threatened by invasion and revolt, and yearning to purify itself through annihilation. With his usual erudition, W. H. Auden discusses the mass hysteria and palpable death wish that haunted Late Antiquity:

> Even during the prosperous years of the Antonine peace, radically dualistic theories, which were neither Platonic nor Christian, began to be propounded and their influence grew stronger as the political and economic conditions of the Empire grew worse. Some held that the Cosmos had been created by an Evil Spirit, or by an ignorant one, or by bodiless intelligences

who become bored with contemplating God and turned to the inferior; others concluded that it had somehow or other fallen into the power of star-demons. The incarnation of the human soul in fleshly body, living and dying on earth, was felt by many to be a curse, not a blessing, and accounted for as being either the punishment for an earlier sin committed in Heaven or the result of a false choice made by the soul itself. (42–43)

Disgusted by the physical world, the Gnostics urged people to transcend or abolish the flesh. Marcion described man as "a sack of excrement," begotten by "an obscene act," thrown into the world by "grotesque convulsions," and "doomed to be dissolved by death"; Valentinus considered birth "every bit as absurd as death," "the entry into a condition that would be true damnation if death and Jesus did not deliver us from it" (Guitton 61–62). Even Ruby Hill in "A Stroke of Good Fortune," who considers human fertility "poisonous," never hated conception with the same intensity (*CS* 95). As Flannery O'Connor knew, early Christian ascetics often succumbed to "the notion that you can worship [God] in pure spirit," a situation she slyly satirizes in "Parker's Back" (*HB* 594). Such heresy often leads to violence. To show contempt for the body, Origen castrated himself and Simeon Stylites allowed himself to rot. Not content to harm themselves, these fanatics often harmed others. Sarah Ruth Cates beats her husband for tattooing a Byzantine Christ on his back, but this is nothing compared to the Marcionite riots that nearly destroyed Alexandria.

Because of the Gnostic threat, the Apocalypse of St. John became a lightning rod of contention at the Synod of Hippo. Written three centuries earlier, Revelation was a provocative and hallucinatory allegory of Rome's persecution of the early church. Western clerics considered the text a political embarrassment, a relic from a time when Christianity was a fringe sect rather than the official religion of the empire. If anything, they argued, Revelation's apocalyptic thinking had prolonged the church's persecution by creating lunatic cults like the Circoncellions, a radical wing of the anticlerical Donatists. Armed with clubs, the Circoncellions attacked the imperial troops and assassinated priests and bishops. Like Asa Hawks, the evil street preacher in *Wise Blood,* they blinded themselves and their enemies with mixtures of lime and vinegar. Panting for martyrdom, they accosted and murdered wayfarers who refused to kill them. When that failed, they organized "sumptuous funeral banquets" and leapt off cliffs (Eco, *Travels* 98).

Obsessed with Christ's Second Coming, the Circoncellions had been enemies of the state and heretics of the church. With church and state united against the common threat of barbarian invasion, civil order should be preserved and apocalyptic thinking discouraged. Once Christians became Roman citizens and the emperor God's chosen servant, the Book of Revelation became invalid, some Western theologians concluded. As Rosemary Gallagher, professor of Religious Studies at Connecticut College, observes: "When the Beast [of the Apocalypse] converts, it's no fun playing pin the tail on the anti-Christ."

Eastern clerics' objections were more ethical than political. Revelation's militarism deeply troubled them, perhaps because they descended from the conquered rather than the conquerors. Like Mary Maud in "Why Do the Heathen Rage?" they were shocked to see the Prince of Peace depicted as "the General with the sword in his mouth, marching to do violence" (*CS* 487). Christ rode into Jerusalem on a donkey, they retorted, not a white charger. Furthermore, Revelation's entire tone—solitary, visionary, misanthropic—contradicted Christian fellowship and set a dangerous precedent. Any mad hermit succumbing to the temptations of isolation could become convinced he had received a direct revelation from God.

Consider the arch-heretic Montanus. One hundred thirty years before the Synod of Hippo, this charismatic ascetic had declared himself the incarnation of the Holy Spirit. Flocking to him, ecstatics surrendered themselves to hallucinations that supposedly signaled Christ's imminent return. The Montanists expected the New Jerusalem to literally descend on Phrygia. Like wildfire, their cult spread across the Mediterranean, leaving death and chaos in its wake. Seduced by the flickering flames of fanaticism, even "the great master" Tertullian had "lapsed" (Jerome). Once, Tertullian had encouraged believers to flee from persecution; after his conversion to Montanism, he "demanded that they expose themselves to it" (Guitton 70). The sect desired its own martyrs, and its wish came true.

To avoid future conflagrations, the Eastern fathers warned, the synod should not stuff the Scriptures with tinder. After Montanus, the church needed to emphasize "its *institutional* rather than its prophetic function" and "could no longer consider herself the receptacle of pure souls only" (Guitton 71). The danger of that notion had become all too clear. Instead, the church "should accept being a mixture" of good and bad and "teach charity to the laity" (71). Where was the charity in Revelation's spiteful curses and gloating delight in bloodshed?

Despite these objections, Revelation became the last book of the Christian Bible, thanks to St. Augustine—whose influence on Flannery O'Connor, Debra Romanick Baldwin and Richard Giannone have shown, cannot be overstated.

A former Manichean, Augustine was drawn to Revelation's duality, its cosmic battle between good and evil; but that battle, he insisted at the Synod of Hippo, occurred in every believer's soul here and now, not at the end of time. For Augustine, Revelation was "symbolism, not literal history," less a coded commentary on the persecution of the early martyrs than an allegory on the pilgrim church on earth (White). The sheer extremism of the book's imagery, he argued, militated against a literal interpretation. Just as the Gospel's injunction to pluck out one's eye or cut off one's hand did not sanction self-mutilation, Revelation's violent imagery, seen through the eyes of grace, did not sanction bloodshed. Proper instruction and a humble awareness of human frailty would protect the faithful. Indeed, the final chapter of the Book of Revelation warns against adding or subtracting anything to the text. By placing that injunction at the end of the Christian Bible, the church would discourage future heresies.

A pioneer of the Quadriga, the fourfold interpretive method O'Connor employs in her essay "The Nature and Aim of Fiction," Augustine expected readers to go beyond a text's literal meaning and consider its "allegorical," "moral," and "anagogical" meaning (*MM* 72). Unfortunately, he underestimated the power of the literal, as well as the political and theological, abuses inherent in fundamentalism. "Christianity's real strength, its world-conquering force," notes depth psychologist James Hillman, "lies not with its sophisticated theology, sophisticated interpretations. It succeeds because it mobilizes the [human] will, and the will needs fundamentalism or it doesn't know what to do. Fundamentalism serves the hero myth. It gives you fundamental principles—words, truth, directions. It builds a strong ego" (81).

Augustine himself had called this propensity *libido dominandi*, the will to dominate or domineer others, the very opposite of Christian charity. Ironically, by persuading his fellow theologians to include Revelation in the Bible, Augustine had made it tempting for Christians to mistake the City of Man for the City of God. In a passage worthy of Gibbon, D. H. Lawrence discusses the historical implications for the church:

> And so there crept into the New Testament the Grand Christian enemy, the power-spirit. At the very last moment, when the devil had been so beautifully shut out, in he slipped, dressed in apocalyptic disguise, and enthroned himself at the end of the book as Revelation.
>
> For Revelation, be it said once and for all, is the revelation of the undying will-to-power in man, and its sanctification, its final triumph. If you have to suffer martyrdom, and if all the universe has to be destroyed in the

process, still, still, still, O Christian, you shall reign as a king and set your foot on the neck of your old bosses!

This is the message of Revelation.

And just as inevitably as Jesus had to have a Judas Iscariot among his disciples, so did there have to be a Revelation in the New Testament.

Why? Because the nature of man demands it, and it will always demand it. . . .

The power-drive in a man like Judas felt itself betrayed [by Jesus' humility]! So it betrayed back again: with a kiss. And in the same way, Revelation had to be included in the New Testament, to give the death kiss to the Gospels. (14–15, 18)

II

Over the next seven centuries, the church taught a figurative interpretation of the Book of Revelation, its official teaching to this day. Not even the hysteria surrounding the approach of the first millennium made a significant impact. But the church's exegetical monopoly was challenged in the twelfth century when Joachim of Fiore (1135–1202), a Calabrian monk and mystic, interpreted the Apocalypse as a literal timeline. History, Joachim believed, is Trinitarian, consisting of three stages. The first is the Age of the Father, the Old Testament, lasting for forty-two generations. The second is the Age of the Son, the New Testament, also forty-two generations. "Joachim's calculations," explains Bernard McGinn, professor of theological history at the University of Chicago, "led him to believe he was living at the very end of this period. No more than two generations—that is, no more than 60 years, possibly less—remained before the coming of the Antichrist and the Antichrist's persecution." Saladin's reconquest of Jerusalem certainly seemed like an omen of the End Times, but for Joachim, this was not the end of history. A third era, the Age of the Holy Spirit, a time of a contemplative ecclesiastical utopia, would rise like a phoenix from the ashes of a scorched earth.

Joachim had an international reputation in the late twelfth century. Despite living in a remote mountaintop monastery, the prophet's fame had spread wide. He functioned as "an apocalyptic advisor" to a number of the popes, and his predictions determined the course of the later Crusades. On his way to Jerusalem, Richard the Lionheart tarried at Messina and sought Joachim's advice. After his death, the Fourth Lateran Council (1215) criticized his ideas about the nature of the Trinity but took no action. Pope Alexander IV, however, condemned his writings and set up a commission that in 1263 declared his theories heretical. Accordingly, Thomas Aquinas condemned Joachim in the *Summa Theologica*. Nevertheless, Dante placed him in Paradise and, although never officially beatified, Joachim is still considered a saint in the Mezzogiorno.

But Joachim's impact on medieval Italian Catholicism was catastrophic. As Marjorie Reeves reports, the prophet's "fierceness" could prompt the Emperor Henry VI's marshal to remark: "*Quanta mala latent sub cuculla illa!* How much evil is hidden under his cowl!" (11). Combining apocalyptic prophecy and an early form of liberation theology, Joachim's mystical Marxist vision opened the floodgates of revolution, "even within the ranks of the picked troops of orthodoxy" (Christie-Murray 110). John of Parma, a zealous Franciscan, wrote an incendiary preface to the 1254 edition of Joachim's *The Eternal Gospel,* "proclaiming the coming of a new religion to replace Christianity, which, [he] suggested had failed" (110). The result was revolution. John Donne describes the ensuing carnage in his famous Pentecost sermon of 1628: "And so they kindled a Warre in Heaven [*sic*], greater than that in *Revelation*. . . . For here they brought God the Son into the field against God the Holy Ghost, and made the Holy Ghost devest, disseise, and dispossesse the Sonne of his Government [*sic*]" (265).

Violent millenarian sects arose. Ironically, these groups "were stimulated by the renovation of religious ideas produced by the reform program in the Church in the preceding century, and especially by the appeal to the examples of the apostles" (Wakefield and Evans 25). Perhaps the most disturbing were the Fraticelli, Franciscan splinter groups who preached and practiced terrorism in the name of Christ. Gherardo Segarelli (1240–1300), a charismatic workman, founded the Apostoloci or Apostolic Brethren, a radical sect determined to return the church to the poverty and egalitarianism of first-century Christianity—by force, if necessary. After Gherardo was burned at the stake, his successor Fra Dolcino (1250–1307), the bastard son of a priest, adopted more militant tactics. Now called the Dolcinites, the movement increasingly acted like a guerilla army. Cribbing Joachim of Fiore's apocalyptic theology, Dolcino incited his followers to loot and murder to bring about the millennium according to Revelation's blueprint. When the Dolcinites marauded, church and state crushed them. In 1306 Pope Clement V called for a special crusade and on 23 March 1307, troops stormed the Dolcinite fortress on Mount Rubello, massacred the rebels, and turned the Carnasco River red with blood. Dolcino and his co-prophet, Margaret of Trent, were captured alive, tortured, and executed.

Chaos ruled. Brothers of the Free Spirit, itinerant swindlers suspected of Satanism, preyed on credulous burghers. Suicide squads attacked Christian knights, while self-mutilators accosted pilgrims and travelers: "During the Crusades," Umberto Eco reports, "bands of Tafurs, all hairy and dirty, took to sacking, cannibalism, and the massacre of the Jews; insuperable in battle, these Tafurs were feared by the Saracens. In the thirteenth century, flagellant movements spread (the Crucifiers, Brothers of the Cross, the Secret Flagellants of Thuringia), moving from one village to another, lashing themselves until they bled" (*Travels* 98).

But the greatest and most widespread menace came from Catharism, an underground Gnostic sect that had established its own church. Convinced matter was the source of all evil, Cathars denied the Incarnation and the Crucifixion. For them, as for Hazel Motes, Christ is not the Word made Flesh but the "pin point of light" in every believer's soul (*WB* 120). For this reason, they abhorred the sacraments. Water was too impure for baptism, just as bread was unfit for consecration. Most Cathars were peaceful peasants and artisans, but extremists supposedly pillaged, raped, and starved themselves to death to prove they were free from earthly morality. As children of the light, chosen before time, they could experiment with darkness, the same perverse Gospel preached at Jonestown and Waco. "The Catharist crisis in the Middle Ages," argues Jean Guitton,

> is the first form of revolt against the cultural and social aspect of [institutional] Christianity, of the return to a certain gospel, a first attempt to recover radical "purity": the separation from the world carried to the extreme which is the condemnation of the flesh in the function to transmit life. . . . The problems raised by the relations, always so difficult to fix, between spirit and flesh, between the ideal and the real, between the exigencies of perfection and adjustment, between council and precept—they are as much alive today as in the days of the Catharists. (22)

Seeing the resemblance to her own era, Flannery O'Connor wrote: "I don't believe that if God intends for the world to be spared [from Armageddon] He'll have to lead a few select people to start things over again. . . . [Rather,] I believe all this is accomplished in the patience of Christ in history and not with select people but with very ordinary ones—as ordinary as the vacillating children of Israel and the fishermen apostles" (*HB* 337). During a severe social crisis, however, believers are tempted to flee history, separate from the ungodly, and hide in the wilderness to recover some primordial purity. Isolated and defensive, they fall prey to resentment and hatred.

"All heresy," Augustine warns in *De Haeresibus,* "begins with excessive holiness," a desire to transcend human limitations and the necessary compromises and inevitable failings of human society (12). Flannery O'Connor agreed. "Ideal Christianity doesn't exist," she wrote to Sister Mariella Gable, shortly before her death, "because anything the human being touches, even the Christian truth, he deforms slightly in his own image. Even the saints do this" (*HB* 516). On another occasion, defending the church's scandalously mixed nature to Ted Spivey, she quoted the following parable from St. Augustine:

> The church in this world is a threshing floor, and I have often said before and still say now, it is piled high with chaff and grain together. It is no use trying to be rid of all the chaff before the winnowing. Don't leave the threshing floor before that, just because you are not going to put up with sinner. Otherwise you will be gobbled up by the birds before you can be brought into the barn. (*HB* 330)

III

Unfortunately, O'Connor conceded, birds of prey sometimes roost in the barn. Heresy may have threatened medieval society, but the church responded to religious terrorism with religious counterterrorism, also in Christ's name. Formed in the late twelfth century, the Inquisition was charged to restore order and weed out fifth columnists, but its methods, observes Adso of Melk in *The Name of the Rose,* were as self-defeating as they were ghastly: "Often inquisitors created heretics. And not only in the sense that they imagined heretics where these did not exist, but also that inquisitors repressed the heretical putrefaction so vehemently that many were driven to share in it, in their hatred for the judges. Truly, a circle conceived by the Devil" (52).

Rome could have avoided these atrocities if it had stuck to its original policy. At first, the church was reluctant to execute and preferred the power of the Gospel. Indeed, St. Dominic's mass conversion of thousands of Albigensian heretics in Langedoc prompted the founding of the Dominican order. When the secular government persecuted heretics, powerful clerics objected:

> The Archbishop of Milan protested against the actions of the Milanese mob who seized and burned some Cathari. Peter Damian wrote proudly that saints lay down their lives for the faith but do not destroy heretics. . . . Bernard of Clairvaux, that uncompromising enemy of heresy, wrote that

> heretics should be won by reason rather than force. . . . Pope Alexander III
> said of some Cathari sent to him that "it was better to pardon the guilty than
> take the lives of the innocent." (Christie-Murray 104–5)

Even the less saintly wished to avoid public burnings. The Inquisition prided itself on extorting confessions and pardoning repentant heretics, thus strengthening the church's authority. The stake represented the victory of the obdurate "over ecclesiastical authority and its failure in spite of all its power" (109). In the end, however, neither piety nor policy prevailed against anomie.

Political upheaval and social breakdown fueled paranoia and fanaticism. During the Late Middle Ages, every religious order manufactured its dissidents and heresiarchs. Franciscans and Dominicans savaged each other like tonsured Trotskyites and Stalinists. Fearing anarchy, hardliners exercised "a conscious and severe intolerance in theory and practice," but their harsh crackdowns and inflexible policies only courted disaster (Eco, *Travels* 81). The Avignon Papacy (1309–77), which Petrarch compared to the Babylonian Captivity, and the resulting Western Schism (1378–1417) convinced believers they were living in the End Times, when pope and anti-pope excommunicated each other, crucifixes showed Jesus holding a money bag to justify private property, and the pederast and serial killer Gilles de Rais fought side by side with Joan of Arc, a saint burned for witchcraft. Christ and Antichrist, people joked, had become interchangeable. In Luca Signorelli's apocalyptic fresco in Orvieto Cathedral, Lucifer whispers advice into the ear of Christ's evil twin.

Marooned in this topsy-turvy world of conflicting and contradictory signs, how could one distinguish God from Satan, Christian from heretic? Some gave up trying and chose the simplicity of total annihilation. On the eve of the Albigensian Crusade, which exterminated 100,000 Catharists in Provence, the abbot and papal legate Arnold-Aimery instructed: "Kill them all! God will know His own!" (Christie-Murray 108)

IV

This apocalyptic heritage haunted Flannery O'Connor, who wrestled not only with mortal illness but with the possible extinction of the human race. As Michael Kreyling observes, the constant threat of nuclear annihilation "fed" O'Connor's medieval imagination (2). "At night," she confessed, "I dream of radiated bulls and peacocks and swans" (*HB* 449). For O'Connor, therefore, the Apocalypse was not merely symbolic but real. For all the comforts of modern life, the Cold War, O'Connor believed, had returned the world to the hysteria of the Middle Ages; hence her fascination with modern heresies and her affinity for such "medieval" works as Ingmar Bergman's *The Seventh Seal* (1957), which features a doomsday preacher and a procession of freaks and flagellants (*HB* 377). This anxiety was compounded, Jon Lance Bacon explains, by the precarious position from which O'Connor wrote: "She belonged to a church that many Americans perceived as a foreign power, a would-be invader, a threat analogous to the Soviet Union" (76). Like Muslim Americans today, Catholics during the Cold War often were not considered true Americans. Adherents to an absolutist faith, whose exotic hierarchy within memory had denounced secularism, modernity, and democracy, Catholics supposedly sympathized with totalitarianism and were potential traitors.

Flannery O'Connor bristled whenever pundits compared the Kremlin to the Vatican or equated "the Communist idea of community with the Church's and Communist methods [of indoctrination] with Loyola's" (*HB* 362–63). Nevertheless, she criticized Monsignor Romano Guardini, whom she usually admired, for making excuses in his essay on Dostoevsky's "The Legend of the Grand Inquisitor." Responding to the charge that the Catholic Church was "fascistic" (*HB* 97), she conceded: "God never promised [Mother Church] political infallibility and sometimes she doesn't appear to have elementary good sense. She seems always to be on the wrong side politically or simply a couple hundred years behind the world in political thinking" (347).

Usually, O'Connor's tough-minded view of human nature prevented her from being overly scandalized or apologetic about Catholic history. Sparring with Ted Spivey, she even facetiously defends the Vatican's "consorting with gangsters" from Constantine to Mussolini (347). But sometimes in her correspondence with A, the church's awful contradictions pain and fluster her:

> I am wondering why you convict me of believing in the use of force? It must be because you connect the Church with a belief in the use of force; but the Church is a mystical body which cannot, does not, believe in the use of force (in the sense of forcing conscience, denying the rights of conscience, etc.). I know all her hair-raising history, of course, but principle must be separated from policy. Policy and politics generally go contrary to principle. I in principle do not believe in the use of force, but I might find myself using it, in which case I would have to convict myself of sin. (99)

O'Connor's argument is shaky, perhaps because the subject is too raw; but when she treats the same subject artistically, she becomes more confident. Rather than suffer the terrible contradictions of her age, she exploits and embodies them. Claire Katz places O'Connor's method within its particular historical context:

> Certainly the times provided spectacular metaphors for the darkest side of the mind; the violence of Dachau, Hiroshima, Mississippi too easily supported the most primitive fears. But O'Connor does more than assimilate the outer world to her purpose; she also projects her own corresponding impulses onto the microcosm, shaping through her fiction a world which reflects her specific inner vision. For this writer, the inner and outer worlds merge in an imaginatively extended country . . . dominated by a sense of imminent destruction. (54)

Preferring paradox to synthesis, O'Connor dramatized rather than resolved these destructive impulses. "With the serious [religious] writer," she states, "violence is never an end in itself. . . . Violence is a force which can be used for good or evil, and among other things taken by it is the kingdom of heaven. But regardless of what can be taken by it, the man in the violent situation reveals those qualities least dispensable in his personality, those qualities which are all he will have to take into eternity with him" (*MM* 113–14).

Still, as readers in a world menaced by religious terrorism, we must ask: *What kind of violence? What qualities of character?* Perhaps the answer lies in how O'Connor's protagonists wrestle with and waver between literal and figurative interpretations of the Apocalypse.

V

Like the peasants and burghers of late medieval Europe, O'Connor's poor and middle-class Southerners turn to the Apocalypse during times of personal and social crisis, but O'Connor's reactions to and treatments of this habit are ambivalent. On the one hand, she genuinely appreciates the fundamentalist culture in which her fiction is immersed. "The Hebrew genius for making the absolute concrete," she remarked, "has conditioned the Southerner's way of looking at things. That is the one reason why the South is a storytelling section. Our response to life is different if we have been taught only a definition of faith than if we have trembled with Abraham as he held the knife over Isaac" (*MM* 202–3).

On the other hand, she is appalled when her characters ignore the voice of the angel admonishing Abraham to spare the child. Because they read the Bible literally, not figuratively, they are tone-deaf to more life-saving interpretations,

as James Hillman explains. In a dialogue with Michael Ventura, Hillman echoes
Augustine's explanation of the sacrifice of Isaac:

> The next generation, within language, is the second meaning. It's meta-
> phorical, the next way of seeing something. So by killing the child you
> keep the linearism. In other words, killing the child is the maintenance
> of literalism—is the equivalent of literalism—on the language level. That's
> why you have to kill the son, because the son is the second interpretation, he
> generates it further, so you've got to kill that, if you're a literalist, a "fundy."
> (196)

In O'Connor's exegetical world, literalism always kills. Sometimes innocent
misreadings end in tragedy. Harry in "The River" and Norton in "The Lame
Shall Enter First" respectively drown and hang themselves to get to heaven.
More often, corrupt interpretations of biblical prophecy trigger a bloodbath.
Mrs. Shortley in "The Displaced Person" sees Polish refugees as agents of the
Whore of Babylon:

> God save me, she cried silently, from the stinking power of Satan! And she
> started from that day to read her Bible with a new attention. She poured
> over the Apocalypse and began to quote from the Prophets and before long
> she had come to a deeper understanding of her existence. She saw plainly
> that the meaning of the world was a mystery that had been planned and she
> was not surprised to suspect that she had a special part in the plan because
> she was strong. She saw that the Lord God Almighty had created the strong
> people to do what had to be done and she felt that she would be ready when
> she was called. (*CS* 209).

True, before dying, Mrs. Shortley glimpses "the tremendous frontiers of her
true country," but her narrow vision incites Mr. Guizac's murder (214).

Two errors drive O'Connor's fundamentalists to violence. First, since the
literal meaning of Scripture is usually the easiest, their interpretations tend to be
simplistic and self-serving. In "A Circle in the Fire," Powell believes Mrs. Cope's
farm is his personal Zion and feels justified in committing arson when denied
a share in the Promised Land. Mrs. Turpin in "Revelation" is worse. Taken to
its logical conclusion, her dividing the sheep from the goats, good blood from
white trash, ends in "box cars" and "gas ovens" (*CS* 492). Second, O'Connor's
characters are too obsessed with the historical Jesus to see the cosmic Christ in

their neighbors and become nihilists by default. Determined to discredit Jesus, Hazel Motes starts the Church Without Christ and murders his double, Solace Layfield. Because The Misfit never saw Jesus raise the dead in first-century Palestine, he goes on a killing spree in twentieth-century Georgia.

This psychosis is the sign of the Antichrist, a term that occurs in the Second Epistle of John and nowhere else in the New Testament. The Antichrist denies the humanity of God and, conversely, the divinity of humanity, in the name of faith. As William of Baskerville explains in *The Name of the Rose*, he is the father of religious terrorism:

> The Antichrist does not come from the tribe of Judas, as his heralds have it, or from a far country. The Antichrist can be born from piety itself, from excessive love of God or of the truth, as the heretic is born from the saint and the possessed from the seer. Fear prophets, Adso, and those prepared to die for the truth, for as a rule they make many others die with them, often before them, at times instead of them. Jorge [Williams's nemesis, the blind monk responsible for the murders in the abbey] did a diabolical thing because he loved the truth so lewdly that he dared anything in order to destroy falsehood. (598)

Francis Marion Tarwater, the teenaged prophet in *The Violent Bear It Away*, learns to overcome this spirit of denial and destruction. Growing up in a backwoods shack, Tarwater has been trained to be a militant, off-the-grid survivalist. Home-schooled by his great-uncle Mason, the boy believes history begins with Adam's expulsion from Eden, continues down to the presidency of Herbert Hoover, and will end in the Armageddon. "The boy knew," O'Connor jokes, "that escaping school was the surest sign of his calling" (*VBA* 133). But Tarwater's real limitation is spiritual, not intellectual. He romanticizes the visionary at the expense of the ethical. Compared to the warriors and prophets of the Old Testament, the ministry of Christ seems paltry and domestic: "Had the bush flamed for Moses, the sun stood still for Joshua, the lions turned aside before Daniel only to prophesy the bread of life? Jesus? He felt a terrible disappointment" (135). Tarwater has more grandiose ideas about his mission: "When the Lord's call came, he wished it to be a voice from out of a clear empty sky, the trumpet of the Lord God Almighty, untouched by any fleshly hand or breath. He expected to see wheels of fire in the eyes of unearthly beasts" (136).

Tarwater's asceticism, his shunning of "the intimacy of creation," forms the taproot of his pride (*VBA* 135). This affliction affects Tarwater's entire clan, hidden in the bloodline and "flowing from some ancient source, some desert prophet or polesitter" (192). Even Rayber, the secular schoolteacher, suffers from it. Recognizing this hereditary weakness, Mason reminds Francis of his own failures as a prophet. As a young man, Mason like Jonah had called down God's judgment on an evil city, only to be judged instead. "One morning he saw to his joy a finger of fire coming out of [the sun] and before he could turn, before he could shout, the finger had touched him and the destruction he had been waiting for had fallen on his own brain and his own body. His blood had been burned dry and not the blood of the world" (126). Humbled by this private apocalypse, Mason emphasizes that a prophet's true calling is the corporal and spiritual works of mercy. If God ordains the boy to bury an old man and baptize a retarded child, Tarwater must be content.

Tarwater refuses, of course. Deep down he knows "the ways of his prophecy will not be remarkable," but goaded by his evil genius and a thwarted desire to see "burning bushes" and "fiery beasts," he resorts to down-home terrorism (*VBA* 177). He burns Mason's body, hijacks Rayber's sanity, and eventually drowns Bishop. Tarwater considers his rebellion a holy war against the mundane. When sunlight falls on Bishop's head as he plays in a fountain, Tarwater rejects the sign because it is "something that could happen fifty times a day without no one being the wiser" (221). But the would-be prophet's search-and-destroy mission is no better than Herod's massacre of the innocents. Believers secretly sanctioned this pogrom, declares the child evangelist Lucette Carmody, because cupidity, not reverence, inspires most religious worship.

"God was angry with the world because it always wanted more," Lucette explains to her congregation. "It wanted as much as God and it didn't know what God had but it wanted it and more. It wanted God's own breath, it wanted His very Word and God said, 'I'll give them my Word for a king'" (*VBA* 202). Suckled on apocalyptic prophecy, the faithful yearned for a Messiah dressed in "silver and gold and peacock tails," whose mother "will ride on a four-horned white beast and use the sunset for a cape"; instead, it received a "blue-cold child" in a straw-lined manger and a peasant girl "plain as winter" (202–3). Disillusioned and enraged, humanity avenged itself on the Incarnation at the Crucifixion.

The same murderous and blasphemous impulses possess Tarwater, until he himself suffers violence. Purged by his rape, the boy reaches a new understanding of apocalypse. The fire "that had encircled Daniel, that had raised Elijah from the earth, that had spoken to Moses" commands him to warn humanity not of God's judgment but the "terrible speed" of His mercy (*VBA* 267). But the price is high, perhaps too high. Bishop is dead, and Tarwater, O'Connor implies, is doomed. Like all true prophets, he will die at the hands of the children of God.

VI

"What first characterizes a heritage," Jacques Derrida said, "is that one does not choose it; it is what violently elects us" (3). Whether or not we are believers, then, we share the same dilemma as Flannery O'Connor's characters, because we too are children of the Apocalypse. Pondering the Book of Revelation's significance, Paul Boyer, professor of history at the University of Wisconsin, Madison, concludes that the text appeals to a basic human need: "It says that human history has a discernible purpose. History is meaningful. History has a beginning. History will have an end. And history will culminate in a glorious era. Beyond the horrors of the Great Tribulation lies the Millennium." Driven by what O'Connor calls "a violent, impossible vision of a world transfigured" (*VBA* 192), some people hold civil rights rallies and antiwar protests, others bomb abortion clinics and crash jets into skyscrapers.

Hope and desire motivate all human action. Because we are future-seeking creatures, our desire for the end is a desire for new beginning. At its "deepest level," the Apocalypse is "utopian" (Boyer). Even the West's most secular myths— liberation and individualism; scientific and material progress; nationalism and socialism—spring from Revelation and become blind and destructive if taken too literally. Fundamentalism goes beyond the Bible Belt. It exists in the Pentagon and the Stock Exchange, at Raytheon and the Cato Institute, wherever compassion and awe are sacrificed to power and coercion. If Flannery O'Connor is right and human imagination is "not free, but bound," what do we do with the legacy of apocalypse in a world of religious terrorism (*MM* 197)? Perhaps O'Connor's fiction can provide some answers.

O'Connor's work remains so compelling and contemporary, Claire Katz believes, because its conflicts reflect the central dilemma of modern secular society:

> It parallels our subsequent struggle to assert the magnitude of the individual against the engulfing enormity of a technological culture which fragments social roles, shatters community, and splits off those qualities of warmth, intimacy, and mutual dependence which nourish a sense of identity. The violence in American life which punctuates and relieves the tension of that

struggle is like a mirror projection of the violence with which O'Connor's characters respond to frustration. (56)

Globalization has made this an international crisis. As Islamic terrorists wage a holy war on Godless Western materialism, how can a secular democracy with a strong Christian tradition define and defend itself without resorting to a self-destructive crusade? Will fighting for what House Republican leader John A. Boehner calls "our sacred way of life" avert or bring on Armageddon?

Norman O. Brown offers prophetic insight for our time. For Brown, true apocalypse means not the destruction of the world but of human egotism, the pernicious delusion that the cosmos caters to our whims and sanctions our conquests:

> Take but degree away, it is the end of the world. The reality principle is the importance principle, which commands us to be fooled by appearances, to respect the Emperor's New Clothes. Hierarchy is visible; in the invisible kingdom the first are last. Overthrow the reality principle: no respect for persons, not to be fooled by masks; no clothes, no emperors. All power is an impostor; a paper tiger or idol; it is Burnt up the Moment Men [*sic*] cease to behold it. The Last Judgment is the Vision [*sic*]; the political act is the poetical act, the creative vision. (235)

We desperately need this liberating vision in fundamentalist America, where Mel Gibson combs the Prophecies of Malachi for film treatments, Soccer Moms get off on the pornographic violence of the *Left Behind* series, and White House policy follows *The Late Great Planet Earth*. But a call for poetic apocalypse also acknowledges the Rayberesque limitations of liberal humanism. Reason is not the absence of the irrational, any more than peace is the absence of strife. Humanism's true mission, Brown suggests, "is not to abolish war but to find the true war. [As in William Blake's *Jerusalem:*] 'Open the Hidden Heart in Wars of Mutual Benevolence, Wars of Love'" (182).

Love is the violence that bears away the Kingdom of Heaven. Theologian Roberto Grazioto explains how and why: "[The divine] is and remains free to summon and question [us] in a way that appears destructive rather than formative. St. Augustine, for example, declares that 'love kills what we were, so that we can be what we were not.'" Obviously, Augustine does not mean physical destruction. Rather, the holocaust of grace functions as a dialectic. By affirming everything our pride negates, it reunites us to creation. Religious terrorism travesties and reverses this ontological process. By raining literal destruction in God's name, it exalts hatred and dismembers the world.

During the *Götterdämmerung* of the London blitz, T. S. Eliot dared to write these words:

> The dove descending breaks the air
> With flame of incandescent terror
> Of which the tongues declare
> The one discharge from sin and error.
> The only hope, or else despair
>> Lies in the choice of pyre or pyre—
>> To be redeemed from fire by fire. (57)

Teetering on the brink of a Third World War, we too must choose. This is Flannery O'Connor's challenge for our post-9/11 world, a challenge as old as *The City of God*. Witnessing an earlier clash of civilizations and preparing for the worst, Augustine foretold we all will suffer a baptism of fire. "The Word of God is a burning Word to burn you clean!" warns Lucette Carmody. "Burns man and child, man and child the same, you people! Be saved in the Lord's fire or perish in your own!" (*VBA* 205).

Works Cited

Auden, W. H. "Heresies." *Forewords and Afterwords*. New York: Signet, 1973. 40–48.

Augustine, Saint. *De Haeresibus* (Heresies). Translated and with an introduction and commentary by Rev. Liguori C. Muller. Washington, D.C.: Catholic UP, 1956.

Bacon, Jon Lance. *Flannery O'Connor and Cold War Culture*. Cambridge: Cambridge UP, 1993.

Boehner, Rep. John A. "Iraq War Resolution: H. Con. Res. 6.3." *C-Span Congressional Chronicle*, 13 Feb. 2007. http://www.c-spanarchives.org/congress/?q=node/77531&id=7534818.

Boyer, Paul. "The Resilience of Apocalyptic Beliefs." *Frontline: Apocalypse!* http://www.pbs.org/wgbh/pages/frontline/shows/apocalypse/explanation/resilience.html.

Brown, Norman O. *Love's Body*. New York: Vintage, 1966.

Christie-Murray, David. *A History of Heresy*. Oxford: Oxford UP, 1976.

Derrida, Jacques, and Elizabeth Roudinesco. *For What Tomorrow . . . A Dialogue*. Translated by Jeff Ford. Stanford: Stanford UP, 2004.

Donne, John. *The Sermons of John Donne*. Ed. George R. Potter and Evelyn M. Simpson. Berkley: U of California P, 1956.

Eco, Umberto. *Foucault's Pendulum*. Translated by William Weaver. New York: Harcourt, 1989.

———. *The Name of the Rose*. Translated by William Weaver. New York: Warner, 1983.

———. *Travels in Hyperreality*. Translated by William Weaver. New York: Harcourt, 1986.

Eliot, T. S. "Little Gidding." *The Four Quartets*. New York: Harcourt, 1971. 49–59.

Feeley, Sister Kathleen. *Flannery O'Connor: Voice of the Peacock*. New Brunswick: Rutgers UP, 1972.

Gallagher, Rosemary. "The Book of Revelation." *Frontline: Apocalypse!* http://www.pbs.org/wgbh/pages/frontline/shows/apocalypse/explanation/ revelation.html.

Grazioto, Roberto. "Can a Christian Be a Good Democrat in a Time of War?" http://communio-icr.com/articles/PDF/RGraziotto.pdf.

Guitton, Jean. *Great Heresies and Church Councils*. New York: Harper, 1965.

Hillman, James. *Inter Views: Conversations with Laura Pozzo*. With Laura Pozzo. New York: Harper, 1993.

Hillman, James, and Michael Ventura. *We've Had a Hundred Years of Psychotherapy and the World Is Getting Worse*. San Francisco: Harper, 1992.

Jerome, Saint. "Tertullian." In *De Viris Illustribus* (*On Illustrious Men*). Translated by Kevin Knox. Mawah, NJ: New Advent (Paulist Press), 2008. http://www.newadvent.org/fathers/2708.htm.

Katz, Claire. "Flannery O'Connor's Rage of Vision." *American Literature* 46 (1975): 54–67.

Kreyling, Michael. "A Good Monk Is Hard to Find: Thomas Merton, Flannery O'Connor, the American Catholic Writer, and the Cold War." *Flannery O'Connor's Radical Reality*. Ed. Jan Nordby Gretlund and Karl-Heinz Westarp. Columbia: U of South Carolina P, 2006. 85–101.

Lawrence, D. H. *Apocalypse*. Introduction by Richard Aldington. New York: Penguin, 1976.

McGinn, Bernard. "Joachim of Fiore." *Frontline: Apocalypse!* http://www.pbs.org/wgbh/pages/frontline/shows/apocalypse/explanation/joachim.html.

O'Connor, Flannery. *The Complete Stories*. Introduced by Robert Giroux. New York: Farrar, 1971.

————. *The Habit of Being: The Letters of Flannery O'Connor.* Selected and edited by Sally Fitzgerald. New York: Random, 1980.

————. *Mystery and Manners: Occasional Prose.* Selected and edited by Sally and Robert Fitzgerald. New York: Farrar, 1981.

————. *The Violent Bear It Away.* In *Three by Flannery O'Connor.* Introduced by Sally Fitzgerald. New York: Signet, 1983. 125–267.

————. *Wise Blood.* In *Three by Flannery O'Conner.* Introduced by Sally Fitzgerald. New York: Signet, 1983. 1–120.

Reeves, Marjorie. *The Influence of Prophecy in the Latter Middle Ages: A Study in Joachinism.* Oxford: Oxford UP, 1969.

Thörnqvst, Inger. "The Church Historical Origins of Flannery O'Connor's Blood Symbolism." *Flannery O'Connor's Radical Reality.* Ed. Jan Nordby Gretlund and Karl-Heinz Westarp. Columbia: U of South Carolina P, 2006. 85–101.

Wakefield, Walter L., and Austin P. Evans. *Heresies of the High Middle Ages.* 2nd ed. New York: Columbia UP, 1991.

White, L. Michael. "Augustine's Reinterpretation." *Frontline: Apocalypse!* http://www.pbs.org/wgbh/pages/frontline/shows/apocalypse/explanation/brevelation.html.

THE VIOLENCE OF TECHNIQUE AND THE TECHNIQUE OF VIOLENCE

Christina Bieber Lake

Though he did not live to see much of the twenty-first century, Pope John Paul II may have best articulated its core spiritual concerns. The purpose of his work has been to map out and challenge the ways in which contemporary Western culture has devalued human life. In his 1995 encyclical *Evangelium Vitae,* he quoted the second Vatican council's condemnation of a "number of crimes and attacks against human life," which were named in a long list of current practices through which "people are treated as mere instruments of gain rather than as free and responsible persons." After referring to this document, John Paul II goes on to conclude that "unfortunately, this disturbing state of affairs, far from decreasing, is expanding: with the new prospects opened up by scientific and technological progress there arise new forms of attacks on the dignity of the human being" (495).

John Paul II's insistence that scientific and technological progress can create new opportunities for acts of violence against humanity illustrates how, for him, it is the violence that masquerades as good that is most insidious today. That a great deal of harm may be done by those with the best of intentions was the primary concern of another Christian intellectual of Flannery O'Connor's time, the sociologist Jacques Ellul. Ellul begins his most famous book, *The Technological Society,* with this simple sentence: "No social, human, or spiritual fact is so important as the fact of technique in the modern world" (3). Ellul defines technique in a very specific way, as the *totality of methods rationally arrived at and having absolute efficiency* (for a given stage of development) in *every* field of human activity" (xxv). Ellul believes that although technique as a goal looks good, it inevitably does violence to persons. When all aspects of life are to submit to the goal of greater efficiency, people are viewed abstractly and instrumentally. As Ellul puts it, man "resembles a slug inserted into a slot machine: he starts the operation without participating in it" (135).

For Jacques Ellul and John Paul II even the best contemporary articulations of utilitarian ethics inevitably do violence to people by treating them as slugs in a machine. Peter Singer, for example, preaches an ethic of equal consideration of the rights of humans and of animals, but makes it clear that such consideration applies only to physical harm, not to the basic right to existence. Singer's position allows him to justify abortion and infanticide in cases where a parent's happiness would be compromised by the difficulty associated with, say, bringing up a child with Down syndrome. Abortion and infanticide would be permitted because a fetus or an infant are not yet *persons* in his view.[1] In response to the argument that such actions would eliminate a unique being who would inevitably *become* a human person, Singer responds that he can see no reason to protect the rights of potential people: "There is no rule that says that a potential X has the same value as an X or has all the rights of an X" (158). And if parents want to abort a disabled child in order to have a different one that is not disabled, it is acceptable because fetuses and infants are, in fact, "interchangeable or replaceable" (191). That Singer does not see *all* human beings as "interchangeable or replaceable" does not change the fact that his ethics permit him to see *some* that way when it is expedient to do so. His utilitarian ethics thus boil down to an example of Ellul's reign of technique: if I am permitted to replace an undesirable infant with another one, I see infants as existing primarily for my happiness and for my *use,* not as having value just because they exist. Furthermore, there can be no doubt that the replaceable infant was not asked whether she agrees with the parents about the worth of her life.

Flannery O'Connor, like John Paul II and Jacques Ellul, clearly found such a view abhorrent. In her essay "Introduction to the Memoir of Mary Ann," she describes the desire of the Sisters at Our Lady of Perpetual Help Free Cancer home in Atlanta to write the memoir of a girl they cared for who died from a cancerous facial tumor. The tumor had distorted the child's face and made her life very difficult and short. But the child had a vibrant love of life, causing the Bishop who gave her funeral sermon to remark that the world would ask why Mary Ann should die. O'Connor wrote that since the Bishop was talking to her friends and family, "he could not have been thinking of that world, much farther removed yet everywhere, which would not ask why Mary Ann should die, but why she should be born in the first place."[2]

When the sisters asked O'Connor to introduce their memoir, she was reluctant at first. She agreed with their desire to tell the girl's story, but she cringed at the sentimentality of their approach, as seen in the titles they suggested: "The Crooked Smile," "The Bridegroom Cometh," and "Scarred Angel" (*CW* 1139). But O'Connor did take on the task of writing the introduction when she saw it as a way to illustrate how fiction, especially through the grotesque, can uniquely challenge an instrumental view of human persons. Thus she links her critique to a work of fiction with the same goal, "The Birthmark," by Nathaniel Hawthorne.[3] In that story, Aylmer is a scientist who wants to perfect his beautiful wife by eliminating her only "flaw"—a birthmark—and kills her in the process. O'Connor agreed with Hawthorne that in this kind of human striving the actual woman, Georgiana, becomes ancillary and dispensable to the goal of human perfection as seen abstractly. And O'Connor, like Pope John Paul II and Jacques Ellul, felt she was seeing more and more of this "tenderness that leads to gas chamber" all around her. "The Aylmers whom Hawthorne saw as a menace have multiplied. Busy cutting down human imperfection, they are making headway also on the raw material of good" (*CW* 830).

These three intellectuals agree that to view any individual life primarily instrumentally is to destroy that life as a unique gift. The reign of technique is thus a reign of violence against the "givenness" of life itself. But while John Paul II and Jacques Ellul wrote essays, Flannery O'Connor's response was to offer fiction as the antidote. For her, fiction respects life as gift; it illustrates the complexity of humanity in the scandal of its particularity. It recognizes imperfections in people but chooses them as worthy of aesthetic representation anyway. Humanity seen in the abstract, with eyes closed toward particular people, will always permit the use of human beings for our purposes. But fiction is always about *particular,* concrete persons. And as particular persons, they show themselves to be a bit harder to simply use.

Because of O'Connor's strong convictions, it is not a minor problem for her admirers that her primary response to the violence of technique is the technique of violence.[4] Though she believed creation to be both good and fallen, she more often tried to shock readers into recognition of its fallen aspects than she tried to represent the good. Consequently, it is fair to ask: Is O'Connor's fiction, with its technique of violence, consistent with her critique of the violence of technique?

As I see it, there are three different types of violence that O'Connor was concerned with or could be accused of in some way. First, there is what could be called "God permitted" violence against the characters in most of O'Connor's plots. The Misfit murders a whole family; a bull gores a woman to death; a young prophet is raped by a sexual predator; and so on. Second, there is what could be called the writer's violence against her readers, whereby violence occurs in the effort to get people to pay attention. I am currently calling this O'Connor's "shock and awe" campaign, and it is best typified by her use of the grotesque as an assault on the readers' expectations. Third, there is the possibility of the writer's violence against the truth of the particular individuality and freedom of her characters. This type of violence O'Connor clearly wanted to avoid and used the grotesque in part in an effort to do so. It is doing violence to a story by imposing a theme on it, instead of starting with the characters. In other words, it is viewing characters and fiction instrumentally, as a propaganda of sorts. In O'Connor's view, the sentimental novel is its chief culprit.

It is this third type of violence that links most interestingly to the concerns of Pope John Paul II and Jacques Ellul. Each time I teach my class on Flannery O'Connor and Walker Percy, I have a student or two bristle at what they will call O'Connor's didacticism or dogmatism. Though they agree with her goals, they respond negatively to the ways she bends the characters (such as Rayber, who is as stereotyped as any character) and situations (such as Tarwater's baptism/drowning of Bishop) to her ideological needs. I think the resulting question is a good one: If O'Connor views her characters as tools in service of her vision of the truth, how can she hope that her readers will not think about *people* that way, too?

One of the reasons why this is a difficult question to answer is that it is somewhat unfair. All writers create characters with some purpose in mind; all writers put characters into the situations that they do for a reason. But when a fiction writer uses characters to fight against the idea of using people, she walks quite a tightrope. Although Flannery O'Connor sometimes fell off that tightrope, as her career developed she became increasingly sensitive to it. This movement can be seen in the juxtaposition of two stories at the polar ends of O'Connor's oeuvre: the early and unpublished story "The Crop," which was part of her Iowa MFA thesis, and "Parker's Back," a story she was working on while on her deathbed in 1963.

I

To frame my discussion of these two stories I would like to borrow from James Baldwin's essay "Everybody's Protest Novel," which deals explicitly with the concern to treat characters—and people—properly. Baldwin's main concern is with Harriet Beecher Stowe and Richard Wright. In both these writers Baldwin found that their commitment to a "Cause" too readily overcame their responsibility to treat characters as complex beings. Both writers, therefore, did violence to the truth of human particularity. His remarks are worth quoting in full:

> Let us say, then, that truth, as used here, is meant to imply a devotion to
> the human being, his freedom and fulfillment; freedom which cannot be
> legislated, fulfillment which cannot be charted. This is the prime concern,

the frame of reference; it is not to be confused with a devotion to Humanity which is too easily equated with a devotion to a Cause; and Causes, as we know, are notoriously bloodthirsty. We have, it seems to me, in this most mechanical and interlocking of civilizations, attempted to lop this creature down to the status of a time-saving invention. He is not, after all, merely a member of a Society or a Group or a deplorable conundrum to be explained by Science. He is—and how old-fashioned the words sound!—something more than that, something resolutely indefinable, unpredictable. In over-looking, denying, evading his complexity—which is nothing more than the disquieting complexity of ourselves—we are diminished and we perish; only within this web of ambiguity, paradox, this hunger, danger, darkness, can we find at once ourselves and the power that will free us from ourselves. It is this power of revelation which is the business of the novelist, this journey toward a more vast reality which must take precedence over all other claims. (15)

Flannery O'Connor would agree with this elegant statement in every particular except one. First, she would agree that truth for the novelist means devotion to the particular human being, not devotion to the abstract idea of Humanity. Second, she would agree, along with Ellul, that modernity has tried to "lop this creature down" to the status of a "time-saving invention" that can be explained away by science. Though she might rename Baldwin's "web of ambiguity" that humans inhabit "mystery," she would resonate with Baldwin's argument that it is the revelation of that mystery that is "the business of the novelist." Baldwin's characterization of that journey toward a "more vast reality" she would call, as for Mrs. Shortley in "The Displaced Person," "the tremendous frontiers of her true country," but it is for both writers a journey of spiritual growth. Finally, there is no doubt that her fiction, like Baldwin's, actively resists the sentimental. The paradigmatic example is the scene in which Tarwater drowns Bishop in *The Violent Bear It Away*. In a sentimental scene, O'Connor would have Tarwater, finally seeing the light of his calling, go to baptize Bishop and accidentally drown him. O'Connor's reversal is deliberate: Tarwater accidentally baptizes Bishop while he drowns him. All of the tragic emotion we expect to feel has been sucked out of the scene and replaced by shock and awe.

But where these two writers would profoundly disagree is exactly *how* people—and therefore how characters in the hands of a truthful artist—actually *get* to this other country. Baldwin emphasizes that devotion to the truth is devotion to the human being's freedom and fulfillment; "freedom which cannot be legislated, fulfillment which cannot be charted." Though O'Connor would never say that she is legislating freedom or charting fulfillment, she would insist that created beings have a reality defined in part by their being created, in other words, persons are never *completely* free. Baldwin's devotion to his characters' freedom is, in contradiction to O'Connor's, a recognizably modern American devotion to their *self*-actualization. Personal autonomy is the highest value; fulfillment comes through freedom. But O'Connor's highest value is not autonomy. For her, freedom comes through fulfillment, and fulfillment comes through recognition of one's true state before God, a recognition that must be revealed.

My question as we approach the stories can thus be reworded: Is it violence against the truth for O'Connor to think that she can love her characters, protect their freedom, and still bend events to subject the characters to this kind of revelation?

II

In 1953 O'Connor wrote on an edited version of "The Crop"—a story from her original MFA package—the word "UNPUBLISHABLE." And by her own high standards, it was. It is a didactic story that rails against a didactic writer for her didacticism. But for all its flaws, even this story contains a much more complex parable of O'Connor's deep concern that fiction show love and respect for real human persons.

When the story begins, Miss Willerton, a dilettante who fancies herself a serious writer, is crumbing the kitchen table, a chore she considered to be a "relief" because she got to be apart from others with "time to think and if Miss Willerton were going to write a story, she had to think about it first" (*CW* 732). As she is thinking about her "subject," the real-life personalities in her very own home are in motion all around her—but she ignores them. She retreats to her desk to "think of a subject to write a story about" (*CW* 732). She considers "foreign bakers" because they are "very picturesque" but abandons them when she considers that they are not colorful enough and do not have any "social tension" connected with them. She finally settles on sharecroppers—after all, the poor, she thinks, always do make for a rich social analysis.

For O'Connor, the surest way to get the midwife writing teacher's judgment that the work is stillborn is to begin with a subject worthy of social concern (a Cause, in Baldwin's language) and to create a typical character driven by that theme. To start with a "type" is to know beforehand how they will behave and what they will do, and this guarantees failure. But is Willerton herself only a type? She would certainly be so if O'Connor created her solely to crucify her as an example of what a writer is not supposed to do. Instead, as O'Connor's story develops, Miss Willerton does expand a bit for the reader beyond a stock character. O'Connor has given her an unconscious, instinctual, and, in her case, deeply repressed interest in humanity that has the potential to save her as an artist. As Miss Willerton gives her invented characters Lot Motun and his wife a real physical appearance—"yellow hair, fat ankles, muddy-colored eyes"—her imagination fills in the details right down to their "lumpy grits." And when she does that, the story begins to take off.

Lot Motun and his wife, now "alive," begin to fight. Although Willerton chooses for them a somewhat conventional action, at least she is now seeing the people as people, not as abstractions. She is not writing now at all, only imagining, responding to her own fictional characters as if they were real. The female character does something that Willerton judges to be foolish—which is to pick up a knife and threaten her husband—and so Willerton enters her own story by striking a blow on the woman's head from behind, killing her off and taking her place. The story then proceeds with Miss Willerton—now Willie—herself as the hero.

This move is not without problems. Sarah Gordon argues that Willerton, forty-four and childless, "becomes so much a part of her own plot that it amounts to little more than a very idealized wish fulfillment" (116), and she is certainly correct.[5] Miss Willerton drops herself into a fantasy marriage with Lot Motun. In the short dialogue between them we learn that they care deeply for each other, that Lot is concerned with Willie's having to help with the gathering, and that they are about to lose their crop, but also to have a child. All this is quite conventional, and Lot describes the daughter that they will have leaving him "with two Willies instead of one—that's better than a cow, even" (*CW* 738).

But if we consider the story's title at this juncture—"The Crop"—we are also led to pause and ponder the ties between motherhood, children, the artist, and literature as the crop. The "crop" at the center of this story is ultimately a human crop: a story. It is a story about Willerton having a baby with a man whose description exactly fits that of the country boys at which she would later shudder. Willerton's *instincts* are operating here, which is good, because her *thinking* was getting in the way of her learning anything. In spite of herself and only briefly, she actually inculcates the habit of art.

Much has been written about *habitus* with regard to O'Connor's work. She insisted that fiction "can't be learned only in the head; it has to be learned in the habits. It has to become a way that you habitually look at things (*Mystery* 91–92). This way of looking at things—especially at people—suggests that a writer's attention to her characters resembles a farmer's attention to his crop.[6] And for O'Connor, that attention has a theological dimension. In the gospel of

Mark, Jesus teaches that "so is the kingdom of God, as if a man should cast seed into the earth, and should sleep, and rise, night and day, and the seed should spring, *and grow up whilst he knoweth not.* For the earth of itself bringeth forth fruit, first the blade, then the ear, afterwards the full corn in the ear. And when the fruit is brought forth, immediately he putteth in the sickle, because the harvest is come" (Mark 4:26–29, emphasis mine).

The symbolic weight of "The Crop," therefore, derives from the gathering, the harvesting Miss Willerton *could* do as an artist. For the kingdom of God, a human crop expands and grows only while the sower has his back turned. Here it is also only when Miss Willerton mentally "turns her back" that her story grows to its expansive potential. She does not figure it out on some abstract level first; she only looks in and lets the story take its own form. Even if it is wish fulfillment, it is, at least, an unconscious creation of Willerton's imagination instead of her pseudo-intellectual brain. The action parallels the word become flesh, a living, mysterious, irreducible existence; it is not the word explained by the flesh, or the flesh interpreted by the word.[7] O'Connor bravely and uniquely links Willerton's artistic capabilities to her procreative capabilities and *almost* lets her begin the work.

I do not want to make too much of this connection. But it is essential to note that from the beginning to the end of her career, O'Connor most often chose words like "produce" to describe the act of writing. The writer only partly understands what is going on in the whole, and the rest *grows* around him, in freedom: "the writer doesn't have to understand, only produce. And what makes him produce is not having the experience but contemplating the experience, and contemplating it don't mean understanding it so much as understanding that he doesn't understand it" (*Habit* 180).

In spite of her good instincts, Willerton's problem is that she is a judge, not an artist; a stereotyping reformer, not someone who loves humanity's complexity. She will never be a writer. She goes to the grocery store, resuming her search for significant "subjects" to write about, but finds there is "nothing in it but trifling domestic doings." Miss Willerton has not learned what the true southern woman writer knows, as Patricia Yaeger has demonstrated: that it is precisely the "domestic doings" in her own home that offer the richest place to start. Remember that Miss Willerton's favorite task is crumbing the kitchen table. It is symbolic: committed to tidying up reality, Willerton will never see it for what it is.

For all its flaws—specifically, O'Connor's failure to follow her own convictions and consistently treat Willerton as a person—"The Crop" is thus a window into O'Connor's developing theological concerns about the relationship between artist and hero, self and other. In *Cross Currents* of fall of 1955, O'Connor read and marked the essay "Healing through Meeting: Martin Buber and Psychotherapy," an essay that describes Buber's I-Thou formulation as essential for an ill patient's ultimate recovery. Friedman writes "'Experiencing the other side' means to feel an event from the side of the person one meets as well as from one's own side. It is an inclusiveness which realizes the other person in the actuality of his being, but it is not to be identified with 'empathy' which means transposing oneself into the dynamic structure of the object, hence 'the exclusion of one's own concreteness, the extinguishing of the actual situation in life, the absorption in pure aestheticism of the reality in which one participates'" (297). Friedman's use of the term "aestheticism" here is significant, for it implies that a loss of the I-Thou relationship yields unreality. What has been lost is the other's distinctiveness, and when that is lost, the human is lost. In Buber's terms, the man who lives only in this world of aestheticism "is not a man" (297).

Though the story was written prior to this article, "The Crop" shows that O'Connor was beginning to understand that this I-Thou relationship is central to aesthetic productivity—and to the freedom and fulfillment of the real human beings that she wanted her characters to be. O'Connor underlined the noted section of the following passage in the Friedman article: "Particularly important in this relationship is 'seeing the other' and 'making the other present,' which is not, as we have seen, a matter of 'identification' or 'empathy,' *but of a concrete imagining of the other side which does not at the same time lose sight of one's own*" (301). Beside this passage O'Connor wrote a single word: "fiction."

This description of seeing the other, when applied to the relationship between artist and hero, illustrates what could be called an aesthetics of love. M. M. Bakhtin coined the word "consummation" to describe how the writer enters into the life of the hero and then steps outside in order to lovingly give the character's life a whole form, to give it meaning.[8] Willerton's failure as an artist, then, is much more than a dramatization of the conventional story of art versus life. It is a failure to love. Perhaps the young O'Connor feared her own ability to do so and this tale is a cautionary one, written only to herself. An admonishment to love her characters as people, not as intellectual concepts. An admonishment to love others, not to use them.

III

If O'Connor was afraid of becoming Miss Willerton, "Parker's Back" proves that she certainly did not do so. Having experienced significant illness and suffering, and having grown substantially as a writer and as a Catholic intellectual, at the end of her career O'Connor was fully articulating the grotesque as that place best able to celebrate created humanity in all its mystery. "Parker's Back" is her ultimate realization of the business of the artist to see the face of the divine in the human and to stand over it shouting "LOOK"!

O. E. Parker is a drifter whose search for meaning leads him to get one tattoo after another until his entire body is covered, except for his back. None of his tattoos satisfy him, but in a final effort to appeal to his wife, Sarah Ruth Cates—a fundamentalist interested in little more than nagging Parker and disapproving of everything around her—he gets one more tattoo: the Byzantine Christ. He returns to his wife, thinking that she will finally be pleased with the "looks of God" on his back, but he finds her angrier than ever. She swats him with a broom, kicks him out of the house, and leaves him crying under a tree.

Parker is a good deal like the regular folk that Miss Willerton refused to see as "worthy" of a story being told about them. As "ordinary as a loaf of bread," he simply stumbles through life like all of us, looking for significance. The only rapturous moment in his life occurs when he sees the beauty of a tattooed man at a fair and wants this beauty for himself. He is at once O'Connor's American everyman *and* the one and only Obadiah Elihue Parker, restless, afraid of being stuck, but finding himself married to, and unable to leave, a woman with ice pick eyes who can't even cook. "Parker understood why he had married her—he couldn't have got her any other why—but he couldn't understand why he stayed with her now. She was pregnant and pregnant women were not his favorite kind. Nevertheless, he stayed as if she had him conjured. He was puzzled and ashamed of himself" (*CW* 655).

Parker's tattoos represent his attempt to get others, and now Sarah Ruth, to look at him favorably, to see in him the same arabesque of color he saw on the man at the fair who he thought was beautiful. But when he tries to show her various details of his tattoos, "she would shut her eyes tight and turn her back as well. Except in total darkness, she preferred Parker dressed and with his sleeves rolled down" (*CW* 663).

So Parker pulls out what he thinks will be the trump card and gets a tattoo of Jesus on his back. He does it to please her, to get her to look at him, assuming that she will see God when she sees Parker. When the artist asks Parker if he thinks his wife will now "lay off" him for awhile, Parker responds, "She can't hep herself [. . .] she can't say she don't like the looks of God" (*CW* 670). Parker thinks he's crazy, and the reader knows that with a wife like Sarah Ruth he is crazy to try to appeal to her this way. But his desire to be seen and loved is as human an impulse as there is. When Parker puts Christ's face on his back in an effort to be seen, he proves that he knows instinctively the spiritual truth that many contemporary theologians locate in the Trinity. For example, Ian MacFarland argues that, "with the incarnation Jesus has irrevocably bound his identity to those he has come to save, such that henceforth the divine image can only be discerned in its fullness through a comprehensive act of perception that includes both head and members. It follows that if we want to see the image of god, we need to look at other human beings, not as the source or norm of this image, but as those whose life under the head renders them the ongoing locus of its manifestation" (57). By hinging the story on Parker's instinctive need to be seen by Sarah Ruth, O'Connor answers the question of the human not with an ontological argument, but with a relational one. In other words, the image of Christ on Parker's back does not make him identical with Christ, but illustrates that Christ manifests himself in relationships—both his relationships to his creatures and their relationships with each other.[9] To say that Christ can only be seen fully in others is to offer an ultimate critique of the autonomy of the individual. As Alistair McFayden similarly argues, "Christ is present in a genuine individuality, but by its very definition as an external orientation, this individual conformation is best understood from its relatedness rather than from its isolation [. . .] the presence of Christ is not an indication of an essence but a movement with others towards 'Christ between us'" (60).

The artist's involvement in this process now becomes more clear. Baldwin had argued that the power of revelation is the business of the novelist to "find ourselves and the power that will free us from ourselves"; O'Connor's tattoo artist unwittingly does exactly that. In "Parker's Back" we do not get a pretentious failed artist figure like Willerton or Asbury, but one whose craft—the habit of art—has so eclipsed any "goals" that it leaves room only for the art itself. In unwitting celebration of medieval imitation as the highest form that art can take, the tattoo artist renders the Byzantine Christ in all his glory, leaving the piercing eyes for last. The artist's significance in this story—besides the excellence of his rendering of the Christ—is found in his insistence that Parker look at the tattoo. "The artist took him roughly by the arm and propelled him between the two mirrors. 'Now look,' he said, angry at having his work ignored." Parker does finally look and turns white. "The eyes in the reflected face continued to look at him—still, straight, all-demanding, enclosed in silence" (*CW* 670).

With this move, O'Connor proves that she does not *use* the character of Parker to get a point across any more than the tattoo artist had done so. Instead, the story exists to try to get readers, like Sarah Ruth, to simply look at Parker. It is Parker himself who knows that the stern eyes of Christ are to be obeyed, but that they are also the eyes of an ultimate other, the only other whose gaze can patch Parker's botched life into a meaningful arabesque of colors. When Parker returns home to get Sarah Ruth to look at him, he knocks but she refuses to answer. When Sarah Ruth asks for the fourth time, "Who's there, I ast you?" Parker "bent down and put his mouth near the stuffed keyhole. 'Obadiah,' he whispered and all at once he felt the light pouring through him, turning his spider web soul into a perfect arabesque of colors, a garden of trees and birds and beasts. 'Obadiah Elihue!' he whispered" (*CW* 673).

And it is precisely here where we can see the difference between O'Connor's vision of how a person reaches freedom and fulfillment and James Baldwin's version. Baldwin's characters self-actualize; O'Connor's "other-actualize," or more precisely, "God-actualize." Hans urs von Balthasar puts it this way: the "moment an absolute law of (trinitarian) love irrupts like a lightning bolt from the totality, as from the living God," then everyone must "order themselves to a point that lies outside them, a point that, from this moment on, will be the sole form-giving center" (134). Through the consummating work of the artist, Parker feels the eyes of Christ on him, showing him to be a part of the beauty of creation. He accepts his given name; he moves from the skeletal, everyman initials of O. E. to the fullness of the particularity of Obadiah Elihue. Just as Willerton's story only grew when she turned her back, it is when Parker literally turns his back on the effort to give his own life significance that it gains that significance. Balthasar writes that when God is in the center, "love 'organizes' [man], not the other way around" (135). Parker's freedom comes from his fulfillment, replacing the botched effort he had made to gain fulfillment through his freedom.

Ordinary Parker is thus quite far from Ellul's slug in a machine. He is the possessor now of more dignity, not less; he knows in his wise blood why he is trying to present himself as a gift to Sarah Ruth. Certainly, Sarah Ruth's rejection of him is violent, but it is a rejection that leads Parker to a small share of the sufferings of Christ, which the apostle Paul promises will lead to the sharing of his glory. Crying now like a baby, Parker has never been more whole and, in a way, more free.

Notes

1. For Singer's argument on personhood, see 125–45.
2. *Collected Works,* 830. Future references will be referred to in the text by the abbreviation *CW.*

3. For similar reasons, this story was also a primary selection of President George W. Bush's council on bioethics, led by Leon Kass. It is a part of the anthology they produced entitled *Being Human*.

4. Early criticism, such as that by John Hawkes, asked whether or not O'Connor was on the side of the devil. Joanne McMullen points out that O'Connor tends to use impersonal pronouns in a way that dehumanizes her characters. Many studies, such as Giannone's *Flannery O'Connor and the Mystery of Love* have tried to explain her use of violence as consistent with her aesthetics of love.

5. Gordon also points out that Willerton merely provides herself as a stock femme fatale character who then enters into an archetypal tale with a Garden of Eden plot (105).

6. This idea resonates with Robert Frost's subtle meditation on the dreams of the artist as harvester in "After Apple Picking." "For I have had too much / Of apple-picking: I am overtired / Of the great harvest I myself desired. / There were ten thousand thousand fruit to touch, / Cherish in hand, lift down, and not let fall" (11.27–31).

7. Thus my reading of O'Connor stands in opposition to that of John May, who reads her fiction in light of the "new hermeneutic" of the "word interpreting us." May says that the task of the interpreter is to find the "word of revelation" that is at the center of the stories (20).

8. In "The Artist and Hero in Aesthetic Activity," M. M. Bakhtin more specifically outlines the "dynamically living" relationship between the artist and his hero, a relationship based on the artist's "inside-outsideness." Unlike Friedman, Bakhtin defines the term "aesthetic" by this otherness, by the fact that the author is able to do what the hero cannot: to see the hero's life as a whole: "aesthetic activity proper actually begins at the point when we *return* into ourselves, when we *return* to our own place outside the suffering person, and start to form and consummate the material we derived from projecting ourselves into the other and experiencing him from within himself" (26).

9. McFarland also explains how marriage becomes a special instance of encountering Christ in the other: "The point of the encounter with one's spouse (as with the wider church's encounter with the saints and the poor) is not to abstract from her or his particularity to some generalized norm, but precisely to see in this one person who is most emphatically *not* Christ a being who is nevertheless claimed *by* Christ as someone without whom his own story—and therefore everyone else's story as well—would be incomplete" (120).

Christina Bieber Lake

Works Cited

Bakhtin, M. M. *Art and Answerability: Early Philosophical Essays.* Ed. Michael Holquist and Vadim Liapunov. Trans. Vadim Liapunov, U of Texas P, Slavic Series No. 9. Austin: U of Texas P, 1990.

Baldwin, James. *Notes of a Native Son.* Boston: Beacon, 1984.

Ellul, Jacques. *The Technological Society.* Trans. Jon Wilkinson. New York: Vintage, 1964.

Friedman, Maurice S. "Healing through Meeting: Martin Buber and Psychotherapy." *Cross Currents* 5.4 (Fall 1955): 297–310.

Frost, Robert. *Complete Poems of Robert Frost.* New York: Holt, 1967.

Gianonne, Richard. *Flannery O'Connor and the Mystery of Love.* Urbana: U of Illinois P, 1989.

Gordon, Sarah. "'The Crop': Limitation, Restraint, and Possibility." *Flannery O'Connor: New Perspectives.* Athens: U of Georgia P, 1996. 96–120.

Hawkes, John. "Flannery O'Connor's Devil." *Modern Critical Views: Flannery O'Connor.* Ed. Harold Bloom. New York: Chelsea House, 1986.

John Paul II. *The Theology of the Body: Human Love in the Divine Plan.* Boston: Pauline Books, 1997.

Kass, Leon R., ed. *Being Human: Core Readings in the Humanities.* New York: Norton, 2004.

May, John R. *The Pruning Word: The Parables of Flannery O'Connor.* Notre Dame: U of Notre Dame P, 1976.

McFadyen, Alistair I. *The Call to Personhood: A Christian Theory of the Individual in Social Relationships.* Cambridge: Cambridge UP, 1990.

McFarland, Ian. *The Divine Image: Envisioning the Invisible God.* Minneapolis: Augsburg Fortress, 2005.

McMullen, Joanne Halleran. *Writing Against God: Language as Message in the Literature of Flannery O'Connor.* Macon, GA: Mercer University Press, 1996.

O'Connor, Flannery. *Collected Works.* Ed. Sally Fitzgerald. New York: Library of America, 1988.

———. *The Habit of Being: Letters of Flannery O'Connor.* Ed. Sally Fitzgerald. New York: Farrar, 1988.

———. *Mystery and Manners: Occasional Prose.* Ed. Robert and Sally Fitzgerald. New York: Farrar, 1969.

Singer, Peter. *Writings on an Ethical Life*. New York: Harper, 2000.

von Balthasar, Hans Urs. *Love Alone Is Credible*. Trans. D. C. Schindler. San Francisco: Ignatius, 2004.

Yaeger, Patricia Smith. *Dirt and Desire: Reconstructing Southern Women's Writing, 1930–1990*. Chicago: U of Chicago P, 2000.

"GOD MAY STRIKE YOU THISAWAY": FLANNERY O'CONNOR AND SIMONE WEIL ON AFFLICTION AND JOY

Ralph C. Wood

> I have never been anywhere but sick.
>
> —Flannery O'Connor in a letter
> to Betty Hester, 28 June 1956

> It doesn't finally matter whether we get Faulkner right, for no one's salvation depends on it. But it matters absolutely whether we get O'Connor right.
>
> —John Millis, personal conversation,
> December 1996

There is a persistent misgiving that Flannery O'Connor delighted in death, that she nurtured an incurable malignancy of the imagination, that a fundamental malevolence pervades her fiction, and thus that she reveled in the destruction of bodies if not also souls. Yet the discerning reader will concede that in both her personal life and her literary work few other writers have enabled us to name so clearly the nature of both the violence that wracks our terror-stricken world and the grace that might redirect such violence to nondestructive ends.

Professor William Sessions's forthcoming biography will amply demonstrate that the young Mary Flannery O'Connor had an outsized ego. She did not like for others to cross her. She often conspired with her father against the domineering Regina Cline O'Connor. She had little patience for classmates whose wits were not as keen as hers. Nor could she abide the assurance of her schoolteacher nuns that guardian angels surrounded and protected her. Instead, she often flailed her fists at such ghostly familiars, shadowboxing at such invisible presences, in

This chapter was originally published in *Renascence: Essays on Values in Literature* 59.3 (Spring 2007): 179–94.

the conviction that she needed no such shielding. The young O'Connor was also defiant in her determination *not* to become the southern belle that her mother desired, nor to conform to the conventional female expectations of her male-dominated society. When required to make a dress for a high school sewing class, for example, she brought one of her chickens to school, having first clothed it in the garment she had been told to make.

Even as an adult, O'Connor often chafed at the pusillanimity of small-town existence. Though immensely grateful that her imagination had been chastened by the limits of intimate life in rural Georgia—as it would not if she had lived anonymously in the Deep North—O'Connor often found such provincialism irksome. A good deal of this abiding anger and frustration finds its way into her two most vivid fictional self-portraits: the eponymous Mary Grace of "Revelation" and, still more, in the joy-scorning, name-changing Hulga Hopewell of "Good Country People." O'Connor gives us other fictional versions of herself, of course, especially Sally Virginia Cope in "A Circle in the Fire" and the nameless girl in "A Temple of the Holy Ghost." Yet what remains most remarkable about these renderings of her own persona is the utter effacing of all self-pity. Instead, we find O'Connor exhibiting a steely eyed honesty about these self-absorbed creatures that she could easily have become.

I believe that we make a fundamental misprision of O'Connor's life and work, therefore, by characterizing it as mean in spirit and violent in implication. Only a wooden literalism of the interpretive faculty, a bankruptcy of the imagination, could prompt the counting of dead bodies in her work as if one were counting beans. No one is castrated in her fiction, as is Joe Christmas in the climactic scene of Faulkner's *Light in August*. No one is raped with a corncob, as is Temple Drake in *Sanctuary*. Not a single bed-wetting child is made to spend a subzero Russian night in an outdoor privy, weeping and pleading for mercy from "dear kind God," as in Dostoevsky's *The Brothers Karamazov*. And compared to the fiction of Cormac McCarthy, O'Connor's novels and stories are hardly sanguinary at all. So must it also be observed that almost no one in her work goes to death unwillingly. Only one major and one minor character face their final demise ungraciously—namely, the insufferable Mary Fortune Pitts in "A View of the Woods" and the spiteful June Star in "A Good Man Is Hard to Find." Instead, nearly all of O'Connor's dying characters validate her own witty saying: "A lot of people get killed in my stories, but nobody gets hurt."

O'Connor herself, by contrast, *did* "get hurt." And yet none of her interpreters has sufficiently addressed the violence that was done to *her*. Already as a teenager she was wracked with unaccountable pains in her legs. By the time she was working at Yaddo in 1948, Robert Lowell noticed that she was suffering from unidentifiable aches. Upon her return home from Connecticut at Christmas of 1950, she was deathly ill with lupus. And then she was to spend the last thirteen years of her life dying in Milledgeville. What I find most remarkable about both O'Connor's letters and her fiction is how *little* of her own pain appears there, how seldom she complains about the violence that she herself suffered (as I have sought to show in *Christ-Haunted South* 212–16).

Flannery O'Connor refused to make her illness the central and defining event of her life. In a remarkable testament of faith, she handled her lupus rather as an inconvenient nuisance than as a terrible curse. Yet in the interstices of her letters and interviews, but especially her fiction, there are hints that Flannery O'Connor's personal suffering did require her to ask not one but two of the profoundest questions. This essay will seek to address them both. First, there is the question posed by both Job and the Psalmist: "Why do the wicked prosper? Why does God do such terrible violence to his faithful ones?" Then there is the cosmic question: "How might a proper response to such undeserved suffering offer a potential answer to the unprecedented violence of the late modern world?"

I

O'Connor's wry confession that she spent her mornings writing and her afternoons recovering has led most of us to assume that she was exhausted by the mental exactions of her craft alone. We have supposed that she spent her afternoons "po'ch sittin'" (as she called the splendid southern art of whiling away the time) in order to refresh her depleted imagination. Too little have we acknowledged that she may have mastered her bodily misery only long enough to write for three hours. William Stuntz, a Harvard law professor who suffers from chronic back pain, explains that hope for a cure only worsens his suffering and thus resignation to his torment becomes the only balm and salve. Strangely, he confesses, pain also serves to make his work "more satisfying, even though it's much harder to do. . . . The feeling of accomplishment is indescribably powerful." Physical agony, Stuntz writes, also enables him to live in the present rather than the past or future: "Now, I have to concentrate harder to do anything, so I'm more focused on what I'm doing—not on what it might get me or what I should have done differently. . . . Wanting and regretting take a lot of energy, and I don't have much energy to spare. So I do less of both [wanting and regretting] than in my earlier, healthier life" (Stuntz).

That Flannery O'Connor held out no great hope for the assuaging of her own physical pain was but a part, perhaps even the smallest part, of her suffering. Far more mysterious is her extreme reluctance to seek a miraculous cure for her illness. We know, of course, that she despised Catholic piety of the oleaginous kind. Yet her reluctance to take the baths at Lourdes remains surprising. When she finally relented, she confessed that she prayed more for the healing of her novel-in-progress (*The Violent Bear It Away*) than for the curing of her lupus. She also drolly declared that the *real* miracle of Lourdes is that so little disease is spread via those filthy, germ-laden waters. (Peter De Vries, the lapsed Calvinist novelist, depicts a healthy character who actually *contracts* an illness at Lourdes!) Yet something is at work here deeper by far than O'Connor's tough-minded refusal of all marvel-mongering. She was aware, I am convinced, that never in Christian tradition do believers seek miracles in order to *justify* or *vindicate* their faith: "I believe (and so should others) because I've been healed." Rather and always is the matter the other way around: Christians are *astonished* whenever miracles occur: "I believe no matter what, and this gift of healing is but 'God's importunate bonus.'"[1]

Flannery O'Connor may also have shared Dr. Thomas More's skepticism (in Walker Percy's *Love in the Ruins*) about taking his dying teenaged daughter Samantha to Lourdes. Since Samantha suffers from the same neuroblastoma that afflicts the young girl in *A Memoir of Mary Ann*—the girl who died *without* a miraculous answer to the prayers poured out in her behalf—I suspect that Percy created his character in her image. Tom More confesses, in one of the most riveting scenes in modern fiction, that he feared *not* a denial of a supernatural cure for his dying daughter; on the contrary, he dreaded that she might *indeed* be healed. For then, asks Tom More, what would he do with the rest of his life? How could he continue drinking and fornicating and leading a cynically self-indulgent existence? To receive such a blessing beyond all earthly blessings might be too great a miracle to bear. As a self-confessed "bad Catholic," More speaks darkly of his "delectation of tragedy," his "secret satisfaction" in Samantha's dying. "Is it possible," asks More, "to live without feasting on death" (Percy 374)? Were such miraculous severities, we must ask, too overwhelming even for Flannery O'Connor?

This surely was O'Connor's own question as well. How could she prevent her illness from becoming her oxymoronic poisonous sustenance, making (as George Herbert says) "her purge her food"("Affliction (I)" 51)? That O'Connor was no antimodern made answers all the more difficult. She confessed to having been possessed "of the modern consciousness"—"unhistorical, solitary, and guilty" (*The Habit of Being: The Letters of Flannery O'Connor* 90).[2] There seems little doubt that the chief accomplishment of modernity lies in the triumph of *techné*—the discovery that the world is ruled by both *necessity* and *chance.* Despite all the later qualifications put on the breakthrough insights of Galileo and Newton in the seventeenth century, most of us still believe that (so far as we humans can discern) every natural effect is the product of its antecedent causes, *necessarily* so. Yet these natural occurrences are not morally, much less mercifully, ordered. As Darwin taught us to believe, events in the natural world collide with each other in often unpredictable ways, *chancily* so. O'Connor's lupus was no mystery, therefore, at least scientifically considered. She inherited it from her father. It was the violent result of random variations within the inexorable processes of the natural order, and it could be treated (albeit partially) by medications that controlled (while not curing) the causes that led to such dreadful, even deadly effects.

The victory of *techné* presents a drastic challenge to belief that the world is ruled by logos—that is, the multimillenary conviction that all things are ordered, if not by the just and good God whom Jews and Christians worship, then surely by the governing Reason that Plato and Aristotle honored. This brazen conflict was registered both spiritually and literally in Flannery O'Connor's bones. She was wracked with pains that were more than physical. So sharply did she discern the clash between ancient and modern ideas of nature that she became fascinated with the attempt of the Jesuit paleontologist and mystic, Teilhard de Chardin, to reconcile them. In the end, for reasons I have tried to trace elsewhere, O'Connor believed that Teilhard had failed ("Heterodoxy" 3–29).

II

The more pertinent comparison, I believe, is not with Teilhard but with Simone Weil (1909–1943),[3] the French intellectual who came close to embracing Christianity but who finally refused baptism on the grounds that such religious consolation would spoil the authenticity of her faith. She died at age thirty-four from illnesses that were exacerbated by her prolonged fasts. O'Connor declared that Weil and Edith Stein were "the two 20th century women who interest me most" (*HB* 93). Their deeds, she remarked, "[overshadow] anything they may have written" (*HB* 98). O'Connor admitted that she found Weil "a trifle monstrous, but [with] the kind of monstrosity that interests me" (522). Thus does O'Connor make four times more epistolary references to Weil than to Stein. In the highest of tributes short of calling her a saint, O'Connor described Weil's life as an "almost perfect blending of the Comic and the Terrible" (*HB* 106).[4]

O'Connor leaves her readers to fathom what she means by this cryptic saying. I believe she is using the terms not in a Dantesque but a Kafkaesque sense. By the Terrible, she may refer to the logos-world in which everything is ordered to the will of God, but so obscurely that, given the fallen and finite condition of the world, we are made to walk by terrifying faith rather than comforting sight. By the Comic, she appears to have indicated the natural world as it is ruled by fickle chance and obdurate necessity, making it blithely blind to spiritual matters. For Weil, it is also a world made all the more sinister because it submits so readily to the human machinations and manipulations of *techné*.[5]

Simone Weil's redefined version of the contradiction between *techné* and *logos* became the virtual center of her thought. George Grant quotes her watchword: "As Plato says, an infinite distance separates the good from necessity— the essential contradiction in human life is that man, with a straining after good constituting his very being, is at the same time subject in his entire being, both in mind and in flesh, to a blind force, to a necessity completely indifferent to the good" (248). Weil called the experience of this infinite contradiction between the good and the necessary by the name *malheur,* a word usually translated "affliction" but also connoting "inevitability" and "doom" ("The Love of God" 117). Affliction means for Weil, as it does also for O'Connor, much more than physical suffering alone. *Malheur* is the encounter with all of those inexorable forces, both without and within, that make for oppression and evil, whether they take the form of war or disease, whether of human degradation or natural disaster:

> A blind mechanism, heedless of degrees of spiritual perfection, continually tosses men about and throws some of them at the very foot of the Cross. It rests with them to keep or not to keep their eyes turned toward God through all the jolting. It does not mean that God's providence is lacking. It is in his Providence that God has willed that necessity should be like a blind mechanism.
>
> If the mechanism were not blind there would not be any affliction. Affliction is anonymous before all things; it deprives its victims of their personality and makes them into things. It is indifferent; and it is the coldness of this indifference—a metallic coldness—that freezes all those it touches right to the depths of their souls. They will never find warmth again. They will never believe any more that they are anyone. ("The Love of God" 124–25).

In these strange and provocative sayings, it is difficult not to think of Franz Kafka on the one hand and Flannery O'Connor on the other. No wonder that the anonymous child in "A Temple of the Holy Ghost" would accept martyrdom only if they would "kill her quick." Affliction is not noble like martyrdom, Weil declares, but comic like the Cross. "Christ did not die like a martyr," she writes. "He died like a common criminal, confused with thieves, only a little more ridiculous. For affliction is ridiculous." That this nation's most eminent Christian artist did not hear the choruses of Palestrina as she lay dying but rather "Wooden boxes without topses, They were shoes for Clementine" (*HB* 578), is surely ridiculousness ratcheted to the highest degree. For all their many differences, therefore, Weil and O'Connor are fundamentally agreed that evil serves to thrust us out of an otherwise bestial existence and into the anguishing (though also potentially joyful) contradiction of living in affliction before God.[6] "The extreme affliction which overtakes human beings," writes Weil, "does not create human misery, it merely reveals [human misery]." "Evil," she declares in a staggering paradox, "is the form which God's mercy takes in this world."

In an important letter to Betty Hester, O'Connor makes similarly staggering claims. She seeks to answer the questions of the then-atheistic Hester concerning miracles, which appear to constitute a suspension of material processes and scientific laws. O'Connor suggests, in a passage remarkably redolent of Weil's claims, that we have understood these laws and processes exactly backward. "For me," she explains, "it is the virgin birth, the Incarnation, the resurrection which are the true laws of the flesh and the physical. Death, decay, destruction are the suspension of these laws." O'Connor then offers a drastic affirmation of the body as it is meant to transcend natural necessities, knowing well that her own *corpus* seemed to be at once her burden and her curse—her *malheur:*

> I am always astonished at the emphasis the Church puts on the body. It is not the soul that will rise but the body, glorified. I have always thought that purity was the most mysterious of the virtues, but it occurs to me that it would never have entered human consciousness to conceive of purity if we were not to look forward to a resurrection of the body, which will be flesh and spirit united in peace, in the way they were in Christ. The resurrection of the body seems to be the high point in the law of nature. (*HB* 100)

If "death, decay, and destruction" constitute the suspension of this natural law, then it follows that only by a gigantic act of divine mercy do they exist at all.

A rightful embrace of their "comic" affliction—and thus a rightful affirmation of God's "terrible" mercy—thus become the means of living in accord with the true grain of the universe. No longer do we see ourselves as sufferers understood as passive victims, but sufferers understood as active agents.

The archbishop of Canterbury, Rowan Williams, has discerned this terrifying pattern in O'Connor's fiction. It pushes "toward the limits of what is thinkable and 'acceptable,' let alone edifying," he explains. "She is always taking for granted," he adds, "that God is possible in the most grotesque and empty or cruel situations." Her aim, Williams insists, is to make the natural supernatural, to create "a recognisable world that is also utterly unexpected," a fictional milieu at once familiar and alien. Thus does she create "agents in fiction who embody excess of meaning and whose relations with each other and with the otherness of God are not limited by the visible, though inconceivable without the visible. . . . [T]he infinite cannot be directly apprehended, so we must take appearance seriously . . . enough to read its concealments and stratagems" (Williams). Among its many hidden stratagems is the Cross. As an instrument for shameful death that has been transfigured into the true pattern of life, it makes havoc of ordinary life. Indeed, it discloses the terrible—the terror-striking—character of God himself. "A God who fails to generate desperate hunger and confused and uncompromising passion," writes the archbishop, "is no God at all." O'Connor's grotesque characters are who they are, he notes, because "God is as God is, not an agent within the universe, not a source of specialised religious consolation. If God is real, the person in touch with God is in danger, at any number of levels." To create such hunger and passion, Williams concludes, "is to risk creating in people a longing too painful to bear or a longing that will lead them to take such risks that it seems nakedly cruel to expose them to that hunger in the first place" (Williams).

Unlike both Rowan Williams and Flannery O'Connor, Simone Weil is exceedingly loath to find anything redemptive inherent in *malheur*. Hence her final refusal of baptism and the Eucharist that would have followed from it. Thus did she also express her extreme envy of Christ, since he experienced the ultimate *malheur* of being utterly abandoned by God. Weil may thus have regarded her final refusal of food as a form of crucifixion, a denial of even the most basic worldly sustenance. For O'Connor, by contrast, Christians are meant to imitate rather than replicate Christ. We are his disciples and witnesses, feasting rather than abstaining from his fractured body and streaming blood. Even so, I believe that there remains a deep kinship between O'Connor and Weil—as, for example, when O'Connor declares "Evil is not a problem to be

solved but a mystery to be endured." For it is only by *suffering* the evil, enfold-
ing the *malheur* within ourselves, that we will not turn it outward upon others
in the destructiveness that is the essential characteristic of modernity.[7]

> Extreme affliction, which means physical pain, distress of soul, and so-
> cial degradation, all at the same time, is a nail whose point is applied at the
> very center of the soul, whose head is all necessity spreading throughout
> space and time.
>
> Affliction is a marvel of divine technique. It is a simple and ingenious
> device which introduces into the soul of a finite creature the immensity of
> force, blind, brutal, and cold. The infinite distance separating God from
> the creature is entirely concentrated into one point to pierce the soul in its
> center.[8] ("The Love of God" 134–35)

III

I believe that Flannery O'Connor was thus pierced.[9] Because we have not yet
dealt with this piercing, neither have we penetrated the abysmal depths nor
ascended the sublime heights of her fiction and letters. O'Connor's protagonists consist largely of men and women who refuse such a piercing until the
very end, if only because they could not withstand such affliction if it came
earlier and was less than lethal. This, I contend, is the real violence at the core
of O'Connor's work. As always, she speaks of such terrible things in a jaunty
voice:

> Naw, I don't think life is a tragedy. Tragedy is something that can be
> explained by the professors. Life is the will of God and this cannot be de-
> fined by the professors; for which all thanksgiving. I think it is impossible
> to live and not to grieve but I am always suspicious of my own grief lest
> it be self-pity in sheeps [*sic*] clothing. And the worst thing is to grieve for
> the wrong reason, for the wrong loss. Altogether it is better to pray than to
> grieve; and it is greater to be joyful than to grieve. But it takes more grace
> to be joyful than any but the greatest have. (*Flannery O'Connor: Collected
> Works* 928–29)[10]

To declare that "life is the will of God" is to make the most radical of logocen-
tric claims. It is to offer an unblinkered embrace of the affliction wrought by a
mechanical world whose physical horrors have been worsened by the triumph

of *techné*. As O'Connor declared in one of her letters: "if you believe in the divinity of Christ, you have to cherish the world at that same time that you struggle to endure it." Hence her even more instructive addendum: "This may explain the lack of bitterness in my stories" (*HB* 90). O'Connor presses home this same adamantine truth in her "Introduction" to *A Memoir of Mary Ann*. There she affirms logos-inspired clarity over visceral emotion: "If other ages felt less, they saw more, even though they saw with the blind, prophetical, unsentimental eye of acceptance, which is to say, of faith."

This rarely quoted statement precedes the often controverted claim that "when tenderness is detached from the source of tenderness, its logical outcome is terror. It ends in forced-labor camps and in the fumes of the gas chamber" (*Mystery and Manners* 227). O'Connor does not mean, as many have assumed, that Christ is the only source of unsentimental love, as if humanists were incapable of such love. Rather is Christ the fount of transcendent tenderness because he is also the spring of suffering precisely as Simone Weil defines it. He both embodies and demands the affliction that modernity is bent on denying. Though no Christian herself, Simone Weil nonetheless declared that "the extreme greatness of Christianity lies in the fact that it does not seek a supernatural cure for suffering, but a supernatural use of it." Ours is the Age of Ashes—of the Nazi ovens, of Hiroshima and Nagasaki and Dresden, of al-Qaeda's crumbled World Trade Center towers—all because we have sought to refuse affliction.[11]

Walter M. Miller Jr. makes this case powerfully in *A Canticle for Leibowitz*, an apocalyptic novel about our world after it has already suffered a nuclear holocaust and is seeking to recover its life. There can be no recovery, argues Father Zerchi, so long as we indulge two deadly deviations from the past. The first, he says, is the idea that society alone determines whether an act is right or wrong. The second, he adds, is that pain constitutes the only evil. The real problem, as Zerchi discerns, is how to direct human life to ends which are just rather than expedient, ends which are not humanly devised and managed, ends which enable people to live for a higher good than the avoidance of pain, even agonizing pain. Such life entails affliction—the suffering which, as we have seen, produces pain that is moral and spiritual no less than bodily and physical. The desire to avoid such anguish, Zerchi confesses, makes us seek to create an affliction-free world. Failing to manufacture such a world of ease, our species turns bitter and destructive. The resulting ashes—whether in personal or political holocausts—are the products of what the dying Zerchi calls "the unreasoning fear of suffering. *Metus doloris*. Take it together with its positive equivalent, the craving for worldly security, for Eden, and you might have your 'root of evil.' . . . To minimize suffering and to maximize security were natural and proper ends of society and Caesar. But then they became the only ends, somehow, the only basis of law—a perversion. Inevitably, then, in seeking only them, we found only their opposites: maximum suffering and minimum security" (Miller 330).

Ruby Turpin and Mrs. McIntyre and Mrs. Shortley seek refuge from what they perceive to be suffering. They thus speak of the unwanted souls who are "left over," who are "too many," who ought thus to be ridden off in boxcars to gas ovens or else sent back where they came from, and all for the same reason: Those "extras," as Mrs. McIntyre calls them, threaten to afflict their unafflicted lives. Unlike them, Hulga Hopewell is not a proto-Nazi, but she too nourishes fantasies of annihilation—even if only in her hilariously mistaken dream of seducing and destroying the faith of a faux-naive country Bible salesman. Hulga is an annihilationist because she harbors what Nietzsche called *ressentiment;* she bitterly resents having been pierced at the center of her being. She is afflicted (as we have heard Weil saying) "with physical pain, distress of soul, and social degradation, all at the same time." That in the end Hulga was not slain but made at least to consider embracing her affliction may be one of the most hopeful signs in all of O'Connor's work. It may mean that Hulga has begun to make her way back toward the embrace of her true name: Joy.

IV

All of the other creatures except man, argues Simone Weil, achieve beauty in their utter and necessary docility to God, a docility that she calls "obedience without knowledge" ("The Love of God" 130). Man is not such a docile creature. He alone can know and embrace the mystery that O'Connor described in saying that "Life is the will of God." Man acquires this knowledge, Weil teaches, through acts of attention.[12] These attentive acts, like the moral virtues, must be cultivated. Attention is acquired slowly and habitually. "As one has to learn to read or practice a trade," Weil declares, "so one must learn to feel in all things, first and almost solely, the obedience of the universe to God." "Whoever has finished his apprenticeship," she adds, "recognizes things and events, everywhere and always, as vibrations from the same divine and infinitely sweet word" ("The Love of God" 131).

This sweetness and this beauty are fierce, even rending and piercing. But by no other means than willingly embraced affliction does "the infinite love

51

of God [come] to possess us. He comes at his own time. We have the power to consent to receive him or to refuse" (Weil, "The Love of God" 133). This consent brings joy no less than suffering. Weil describes them as "two equally precious gifts which must be savored to the full, each one in its purity, without trying to mix them." There is a strange quality of force and necessity present even in joy. That the Christ who makes his absolute consent to the will of God in Gethsemane and at Calvary could, in a certain sense, have done no other, is his necessary joy. He dies with a loud shout, as if his joy were forcibly pressed out of him. "In order that our being should one day become wholly sensitive in every part to this obedience that is the substance of matter, in order that a new sense should be formed in us to enable us to hear the universe as the vibration of the word of God, the transforming power of suffering and of joy are equally indispensable" ("The Love of God" 132).

In most cases, O'Connor's characters violently receive the afflicting truth about themselves only *in articulo mortis*. That so many of them find Life only in death has blinded many critics to the joyfulness of rightly embraced affliction—to that deeper and rarer thing that both Weil and O'Connor attest. A better guide in these matters, I believe, is to be found in one of G. K. Chesterton's earliest essays, "A Defence of Farce." There Chesterton makes the surprising claim that, while "black and catastrophic" pain attracts the immature artist, "joy is a far more elusive and elvish matter, since it is our reason for existing, and a very feminine reason; it mingles with every breath we draw and every cup of tea we drink." Precisely because joy is elusive in its strangely invisible ubiquity—being neither pleasure nor delight, not even the fulfillment of transcendent desire, much less any relaxed life of "ease in Zion" (Amos 6:1)—joy requires an extraordinary mode of expression. "And of all the varied forms of the literature of joy," Chesterton concludes, "the form most truly worthy of moral reverence and artistic ambition is the form called 'farce'—or its wilder shape in pantomime" (124–25).

Few critics have noticed the pantomime character of O'Connor's most riveting and revealing scenes. The confrontation of The Misfit and the Grandmother, Manley Pointer's removing of Hulga Hopewell's leg, Bevel Summers's baptizing of Harry Ashfield, Tarwater's drowning of Bishop, the young hoodlums dancing like Daniel in the fiery furnace of Mrs. Cope's burning woods, Hazel Motes performing his awful *ascesis* at the end, Mrs. May whispering into the bull's ear as he buries his horns in her lap, Ruby Turpin trying to shout down God beside her hog pen, Mrs. McIntyre and Mr. Shortley and the two Negroes with eyes frozen in collusion as the tractor crushes Mr. Guizac, the early confrontation of Coleman and Tanner at the sawmill, and especially Nelson and Mr. Head standing before the Sambo Christ—surely these scenes all have the character of pantomime. There is japery here, something slapstick and buffoonish at work, almost a charade quality about them all—as if the deepest things cannot be said but only gestured and mimed. They are comic as Weil sees the Cross as comic. The only thing missing is a horse or cow played by two actors, one as the head and front legs, the other as the tail and back legs. No wonder that O'Connor, when describing Simone Weil's life as "a perfect blending of the Comic and the Terrible," described her own work in terms that are tantamount to farce and pantomime: "everything funny I have written is more terrible than it is funny, or only funny because it is terrible, or only terrible because it is funny" (*HB* 105).

Nowhere do the funny and the terrible come more fully into pantomime expression than in "A Temple of the Holy Ghost." There the little girl who had rather be a martyr than a saint has a dream vision of the hermaphrodite whom her cousins had seen at the fair. She imagines him as a preacher proclaiming the Good News of Affliction as his congregation responds with a steady litany of Amens. What enables this scene to accomplish more than the awakening of a brilliant but proud young girl to her own religious vocation is that the hermaphrodite has borne his affliction in the region that our late modern world regards as the ultimate defining center of human life: his sexuality. Not in spite of such deformity but precisely because of it does this contradictory creature embrace his suffering. Though he has due cause for regarding the cosmos as sheer mechanical necessity and absurd chance, he lives not as a bitter freak of nature but one who has consented to be afflicted by God.

Both Simone Weil and Flannery O'Connor regard such consent as the true means for overcoming the violence that is the terror of our time. To live at the intersection between the creation and its Creator, declares Weil, is to live at the juncture of the arms of the Cross ("The Love of God" 136). The hermaphrodite lives nowhere else. More remarkable still, he leads his fellow worshippers to live there as well: to embrace the inward ferocity of their own affliction so as to produce the lasting joy that might yet prevent another Age of Ashes:

> "God done this to me and I praise him."
> "Amen. Amen."
> "He could make you thisaway."
> "Amen. Amen."
> "But he has not."
> "Amen. Amen."

"Raise yourself up. A temple of the Holy Ghost. You! You are God's temple, don't you know? Don't you know? God's spirit has a dwelling in you, don't you know?

"Amen. Amen."

"If anybody desecrates the temple of God, God will bring him to ruin and if you laugh, He may strike you thisaway. A temple of God is a holy thing. Amen. Amen." (*CW* 246)

Notes

1. The phrase is borrowed from a pivotal scene in Walker Percy's *The Moviegoer*. Having spied a black man entering a white Catholic church on Ash Wednesday—perhaps hoping to be seen as a cultured Negro making his way into the white man's business world—Binx Bolling asks whether the man may have emerged with the Gift he did not seek but was given nonetheless as "God's importunate bonus" (235). The root of the word "miracle" is the Latin *mirari*, "to wonder."

2. All future references to the letters will be indicated *HB*.

3. The only substantial treatment of O'Connor and Weil at the level of their comparative theological visions is to be found in John F. Desmond, "Flannery O'Connor and Simone Weil: A Question of Sympathy" 104–16.

4. If she "were to live long enough and develop as an artist to the proper extent," O'Connor added, "I would like to write a comic novel about [such] a woman [as Weil]—and what is more comic and terrible than the angular intellectual proud woman approaching God inch by inch with ground teeth"? (*HB* 106–7).

5. Dwight Macdonald argues that Hiroshima and Nagasaki and Dresden were horrors actually worse than the Holocaust. For all that was undeniably demonic about it, the Holocaust was perpetrated by humans directly violating others humans—not by sanitized command officers ordering mile-high pilots to drop impersonal bombs on invisible targets.

6. The chief difference, perhaps, is to be found in their opposing ideas of creation and crucifixion. Weil understood creation as an act of divine self-limitation. Because God dwells in complete fullness and perfection of being, all things created (not merely plants and animals but also worlds, even the cosmos itself) can exist only where God is not. Creation thus occurs only where God withdraws himself, where He is deliberately and willfully absent. Evil is thus no deviation or corruption of the good, as in the standard Augustinian account,

but something inherent in the imperfect creation. Weil's attraction to the Albigenses, the heretical medieval sect that sought to live in liberation from bodily necessity, reveals her conviction that the flesh, though created by God, must be transcended.

Such notions completely contradict O'Connor's orthodox Christian emphasis on the utter goodness of creation, especially of the bodily form which God himself assumes in the Incarnation. That Weil died as an anorexic may also exhibit her low regard for the body, though of course bodily deprivations have been central to Christian asceticism. St. Catherine of Genoa died after determining to subsist only on the Eucharist. Even so, Weil's drastic self-deprivation stands in stark contrast to O'Connor's declaration that the Eucharist was the center of human existence, that she fed on it daily whenever possible, and thus that she wanted to make her witness by living rather than dying. "Pray," she requested to a friend in one of her very last letters, "that the lupus don't finish me off too quick."

7. Individuals alone are incapable of such authentic suffering. It will require the church as a redemptive community to absorb such suffering, refusing to return evil for evil, especially in terror and warfare.

8. It may come as a surprise that, in his late novel with a pre-Christian setting, *Till We Have Faces,* C. S. Lewis has his protagonist make similar claims: "the Divine Nature wounds and perhaps destroys us merely by being what it is. We call it the wrath of the gods; as if the great cataract in Phars [a neighboring region] were angry with every fly it sweeps down in its green thunder" (284).

9. O'Connor bristled at any suggestion that she herself might have attained any sort of sanctity: "I haven't suffered to speak of in my life and I don't know any more about the redemption than anybody else does" (*HB* 536). On the other hand, she candidly confessed that "there are some of us who have to pay for our faith every step of the way and who have to work it out dramatically [i.e., in artistic terms] what it would be like without it and if being without it would ultimately be possible or not" (*HB* 349–50).

10. Future references to this work will be indicated *CW.*

11. Roughly 180 million souls were taken by violent means, most of them by their own governments. Wendell Berry points out that we Americans have had our own Holocaust in our destruction of the Native Americans who first occupied this land. He quotes Bernard DeVoto: "The first belt-knife given by a European to an Indian was a portent as great as the cloud that mushroomed over Hiroshima. . . . Instantly the man of 6000 B.C. was bound fast to a way of life that

had developed seven and a half millennia beyond his own. He began to live better and he began to die" (37).

12. "Attention consists of suspending our thought, leaving it detached, empty, and ready to be penetrated by the object; it means holding in our minds, within reach of this thought, but on a lower level and not in contact with it, the diverse knowledge we have acquired which we are forced to make use of. . . . Above all our thought should be empty, waiting, not seeking anything, but ready to perceive in its naked truth the object that is to penetrate it" ("Reflections on the Right Use of School Studies with a View to the Love of God," 111–12).

Works Cited

Berry, Wendell. "The Unsettling of America." *The Art of the Commonplace: The Agrarian Essays of Wendell Berry.* Ed. Norman Wirzba. Washington, DC: Shoemaker & Hoard, 2002.

Chesterton, G. K. "A Defence of Farce." *The Defendant.* London: J. M. Dent and Sons, 1940.

Desmond, John F. "Flannery O'Connor and Simone Weil: A Question of Sympathy." *Logos: A Journal of Catholic Thought and Culture* 8.1 (Winter 2005): 104–16.

Grant, George. "Introduction to Simone Weil." *The George Grant Reader.* Ed. William Christian and Sheila Grant. Toronto: U of Toronto P, 1998.

Herbert, George. "Affliction (I)." In *The Poems of George Herbert.* London: Oxford Press, 1961.

Lewis, C. S. *Till We Have Faces.* Grand Rapids: Eerdmans, 1966.

Miller, Walter M. *A Canticle for Leibowitz.* New York: Bantam, 1997.

O'Connor, Flannery. *Flannery O'Connor: Collected Works.* Ed. Sally Fitzgerald. New York: Library of America, 1988.

———. *The Habit of Being: The Letters of Flannery O'Connor.* Ed. Sally Fitzgerald. New York: Farrar, 1979.

———. *Mystery and Manners: Occasional Prose.* Ed. Sally Fitzgerald. New York: Farrar, 1969.

Percy, Walker. *Love in the Ruins.* New York: Farrar, 1971.

———. *The Moviegoer.* New York: Farrar, 1967.

Stuntz, William J. "Suffering's Strange Lessons." *New Republic,* Sept. 11 and 18, 2006: 8–9.

Weil, Simone. "The Love of God and Affliction." *Waiting for God.* Trans. Emma Craufurd. New York: Harper, 1973.

———. "Reflections on the Right Use of School Studies with a View to the Love of God." *Waiting for God.* New York: Harper Torchbooks, 1973.

Williams, Rowan. "Grace, Necessity and Imagination: Catholic Philosophy and the Twentieth Century Artist." The Clark Lectures. "Lecture 1: Modernism and the Scholastic Revival." Trinity College, Cambridge University, 10 Feb. 2005. http://www.archbishopofcanterbury.org/sermons_speeches/050120a.html.

Wood, Ralph C. *Flannery O'Connor and the Christ-Haunted South.* Grand Rapids: Eerdmans, 2004.

———. "The Heterodoxy of Flannery O'Connor's Book Reviews." *Flannery O'Connor Bulletin* 5 (Autumn 1976): 3–29.

EATING THE BREAD OF LIFE: MUTED VIOLENCE IN *THE VIOLENT BEAR IT AWAY*

J. Ramsey Michaels

Flannery O'Connor, in letters to Ted Spivey less than a year apart, described *The Violent Bear It Away* before it appeared as a novel "built around a baptism," and after it appeared as "a very minor hymn to the Eucharist" (*HB* 341, 387). The first comment echoes an earlier letter to Elizabeth Bishop and has often served as a key to the interpretation of the book (*CW* 1092). The latter comment has received less critical attention, understandably in light of Tarwater's calling to baptize Bishop, and the violent nature of that baptism. Bishop's drowning by baptism (or baptism by drowning) has placed its stamp on the book's interpretation, accenting the "violence" of which the title speaks. Baptism, to be sure, is the more "violent" sacrament, at least in its New Testament origins. The Apostle Paul wrote of being baptized into Jesus' death, viewing it metaphorically as a kind of burial (Rom. 6:3–4). To Peter it was, if not a drowning, at least a narrow escape from drowning, in waters that evoked for him the memory of Noah's flood (1 Pet. 3:20–21). John the Baptist foresaw a coming baptism "in Holy Spirit and fire" (Matt. 3:11). Jesus himself saw a second "baptism" in his future, one that would bring fire on the earth (Luke 12:49–50), and challenged his disciples to share in it (Mark 10:38–39).

The Eucharist, despite its association with Jesus' death, has less violent connotations for O'Connor. Her controlling metaphor of "eating the bread of life" evokes the imagery of the feeding of the five thousand, not the formal institution of the Eucharist at the last supper. This is in keeping with the New Testament, where Jesus, as if anticipating the Eucharist, "takes" the loaves and fishes and "breaks" them before giving them out to the gathered crowd (Mark 6:41). Even more explicitly, the Gospel of John appends to the feeding narrative a discourse of Jesus in which he speaks of himself as "the bread of life" (John 6:35, 47), claiming, "If anyone eats of this bread he will live forever" (6:51a). O'Connor, had she chosen, could have made "eating the bread of life" into a violent image, like that of baptism, for Jesus added immediately, "and the bread that I will give is my flesh for the life of the world" (John 6:51b), and continued, "Unless you eat the flesh of the Son of man and drink his blood, you do not have life in yourselves. He who eats my flesh and drinks my blood has eternal life and I will raise him up at the last day" (John 6:53–54). Gretlund and Westarp (x–xi), citing "the widely broadcast story of prearranged cannibalism, where a man in Germany recently agreed to be killed and eaten by another man and was," offer the comment that O'Connor "would perhaps have created a story about the Eucharist out of that material. After all, Jesus's followers asked disgustedly, 'How can this man give us his flesh to eat?' (John 6:52)." Significantly, that is precisely what O'Connor does *not* do in *The Violent Bear It Away.* On the contrary, her image of "eating the bread of life" is the one major nonviolent image in the book, muting to some degree the violence of the baptismal drowning of Bishop, the rape of Tarwater, and the burning of Powderhead.

From the beginning, Tarwater resists his great uncle's prophetic legacy, not because of the old man's tumultuous visions of "wheels of light and strange beasts with giant wings of fire and four heads turned to the four points of the universe." To these he would have been willing to say, "Here I am, Lord, ready!" What repels him are those "other times, when there was no fire in his uncle's eye and he spoke only of the sweat and stink of the cross, of being born again to die, and of spending eternity eating the bread of life" (*CW* 334). The thought of "eating the bread of life" is not so much violent, in Tarwater's eyes, as demeaning, something to be ashamed of, and yes, boring. "Had the bush flamed for Moses," he wonders,

> the sun stood still for Joshua, the lions turned aside before Daniel only to prophesy the bread of life? Jesus? He felt a terrible disappointment in that conclusion, a dread that it was true. The old man said that as soon as he died, he would hasten to the banks of the Lake of Galilee to eat the loaves and fishes that the Lord had multiplied. "Forever?" the horrified boy asked. "Forever," the old man said. (*CW* 342)

Tarwater fears the materiality of such a vision, the sheer physical hunger it summons within him. He shuns such a "threatened intimacy of creation" (*CW* 343).[1] When the call comes, "he wished it to be a voice from out of a clear and empty sky, the trumpet of the Lord God Almighty, untouched by any fleshly hand or breath. He expected to see wheels of fire in the eyes of unearthly beasts. He had expected this to happen as soon as his great-uncle died" (*CW* 343).

No such thing happens when old Mason dies. Yet there is a call of sorts, a much more modest one: to baptize Bishop, the deformed and retarded child of

Rayber the schoolteacher. That is what Tarwater resists, but the moment he lays eyes on Bishop, he knows that resistance is futile: "He did not look into the eyes of any fiery beast or see a burning bush. He only knew, with a certainty sunk in despair, that he was expected to baptize the child he saw and begin the life his great-uncle had prepared him for. He knew that he was called to be a prophet and that the ways of his prophecy would not be remarkable" (*CW* 388–89). Tarwater's perception that "the ways of his prophecy would not be remarkable" is telling. It is easy to assume that he is not a reliable observer at this point. Christina Bieber Lake probably speaks for many readers in commenting that "it is only through Tarwater's eyes that the ways of prophecy are 'unremarkable'" (158). Yet everything else that Tarwater perceives turns out to be true. Already, less than halfway through the novel, there is an inevitability to everything else that happens. He *will* baptize Bishop. He *will* be a prophet. He *will* eat the bread of life. And the "ways of his prophecy" *will not* be remarkable.

O'Connor's own comment in a 1959 letter to Betty Hester bears this out. "Now about Tarwater's future," she writes, "He must of course not live to realize his mission, but die to realize it. The children of God I daresay will despatch [*sic*] him pretty quick. Nor am I saying that he has a great mission or that God's solution for the problems of our particular world are prophets like Tarwater. Tarwater's mission might only be to baptize a few more idiots. The prophets in the Bible are only the great ones but there is doubtless unwritten sacred history like uncanonized saints" (*CW* 1101). If Tarwater must die to realize his mission, his mission can only be understood as "eating the bread of life," not simply baptizing Bishop. If he is a prophet, he is one of those minor prophets, or "uncanonized saints." O'Connor, in her "Note to the Second Edition" of *Wise Blood*, famously refers to Hazel Motes as a Christian "in spite of himself" (*malgré lui*). When she wrote that in 1962, *The Violent Bear It Away* was already in print, and it is just as true of Tarwater as of Hazel. The temptation is to qualify it, as Richard Giannone has done, by calling Tarwater a "prophet *malgré lui*" (147) rather than simply a "Christian" (in Hazel's case a martyr). Yet to O'Connor the distinction is a fairly narrow one. If, as she predicts, "the children of God will despatch him pretty quick," he too is a martyr, and a real one, not a martyr by his own hand. Her use of the phrase "children of God" can only be understood ironically. Possibly she has in mind the thought that ancient Israel persecuted and killed its own prophets, implying an analogy between Israel and nominal Christianity, be it Catholic or Protestant. In any event, Francis Tarwater is one who "suffers violence," and thereby lays hold of the Kingdom of God and the "bread of life."

All of which brings us to O'Connor's flagship text in the Gospel of Matthew: "From the days of John the Baptist until now the kingdom of heaven suffereth violence and the violent bear it away" (Matt. 11:12). In the same 1959 letter to Betty Hester she reflected on her celebrated title. "The violent are not natural," she wrote, "St. Thomas's gloss on this verse is that the violent [whom] Christ is here talking about represent those ascetics who strain against mere nature" (*CW* 1101). Again, *Wise Blood* comes to mind, where Mrs. Flood asks Hazel Motes, "What do you do these things for? It's not natural" (*CW* 126). "Not natural," but "not remarkable" either. Like Hazel, Tarwater is not so much in the process of becoming a great biblical prophet as simply in the process of becoming a true Catholic. It is true that in a letter to William Sessions in 1960 she characterized old Mason as "a prophet, not a church member,"[2] yet she quickly added, "As a prophet, he has to be a natural Catholic" (*HB* 407). To O'Connor, a "natural" Catholic is "unnatural" by any other standards, be they Protestant or merely secular. It involves far more than being a "church member," whether Catholic or Protestant. "Church member," in fact, sounds a lot like the dreaded "children of God"! In a second letter to Sessions, O'Connor explained further: "There is one very dominant Protestant trait which old Tarwater exhibits. When the Protestant hears what he supposes to be the voice of the Lord, he follows it regardless of whether it runs counter to his church's teaching. . . . his being a Protestant allows him to follow the voice he hears which speaks a truth held by Catholics" (*HB* 410).

In short, what Tarwater is going through in this novel is more like a conversion than a calling. Like Hazel Motes, or any believer, he is called first to eternal life. Whatever else he is called to is secondary to that. He will be found at the end, just as he found his great-uncle Mason, simply one of a multitude, "eating the bread of life." He will indeed be a prophet, but only in the sense that all genuine believers are both prophets (in that they speak for God on occasion) and martyrs. The very word "martyr" comes from a Greek verb meaning to "testify" or "bear witness." Strictly speaking, the so-called martyrs were not martyrs because they were put to death; they were put to death because they were *already* "martyrs" in the proper sense of the word. In the book of Revelation, for example, believers (or "the saints"), prophets, and martyrs are scarcely distinguishable.[3] Tarwater turns out to be all three, not a solitary prophet in the great biblical tradition but, like his great-uncle, part of a redeemed community.

Tarwater's worst fears, all that goes through his mind at the sight of Bishop, play out in the remainder of the novel. Above all, he wants a sign that, contrary to those fears, his prophetic career will be "remarkable," like Moses or Joshua or Daniel, not "unremarkable," as he knows in the end it will be. His "friend," the stranger at his side, nourishes that demand: "What you want is a sign, a real sign, suitable to a prophet" (*CW* 430). Readers of the New Testament may remember Paul's words to the Corinthians, "For the Jews ask for signs and the Greeks seek wisdom, but we proclaim Christ crucified, to the Jews a stumbling-block and to the Greeks foolishness, but to those who are called, whether Jews or Greeks, Christ the power of God and the wisdom of God" (1 Cor. 1:22–24). If Rayber is the rationalistic "Greek" extolling wisdom, Tarwater is more tempted by the perspective of "the Jews" and their fondness for visible signs. His "friend" knows this and suggests that "he demand an unmistakable sign, not a pang of hunger or a reflection of himself in a store window, but an unmistakable sign, clear and suitable" (*CW* 431). Nothing of the kind is forthcoming, at least nothing Tarwater is prepared to recognize. The signs given are more subtle: the nagging hunger above all, the sun shining on Bishop's head as he stands in a shallow pool in the city park (*CW* 421), and the "little lake" by the Cherokee lodge, "glass-like, still. . . . so unused that it might only the moment before have been set down by four strapping angels for him to baptize the child in" (*CW* 434).[4] None of these qualify as the kind of "sign" he wants, yet when the time for action comes, Tarwater cannot help himself. The baptismal words come out, even as he drowns Bishop in the glassy lake (see *CW* 458).

Here, if anywhere, the violence is real, not muted. Yet as we have seen, a "violent" baptism is quite in keeping with the imagery of baptism in the New Testament. This literal violence is sacred violence, for by it Bishop is redeemed. While Susan Srigley seems not to recognize it as redemptive in itself, she does so by introducing a distinction that Mason Tarwater himself would probably not have made. "Old Tarwater does not see Bishop as damned and in need of this rite to save him," she writes, "—in fact, he sees him as already saved from Rayber because his limited rational capabilities protect him from Rayber's rationalistic view of the world. The rite is the recognition and proclamation of Bishop's spiritual worth and dignity before and by God" (112). But that judgment is more applicable to young Harry Ashfield in "The River," who hears the healer say, "You'll count" (*CW* 165), than to Bishop, and attributes to the old man (not to mention O'Connor) a sophistication he does not possess. It should not be forgotten that Harry's real redemption is his drowning, not his baptism by the healer.

The baptismal drowning of Bishop is not the last act of literal violence in the book. Its sequel, a homosexual rape, casts Tarwater in the role of victim, not perpetrator, at the hands of the now embodied stranger with the panama hat and lavender eyes (*CW* 468–73). The incident gives the lie once and for all to Tarwater's repeated insistence that "I can act," prompted ironically enough by the invisible stranger himself, who whispers, "No finaler act than this. . . . In dealing with the dead you have to act. There's no mere word sufficient to say NO" (*CW* 462). It also brings us back to the text in Matthew, "the kingdom of heaven suffereth violence and the violent bear it away" (Matt. 11:12). Biblical scholars have long debated whether the first clause in Greek is passive or middle voice. Does the kingdom of heaven "suffer violence," or does it "exercise violence" as it breaks into a sinful world? The Douay version is probably right in opting for the former, and O'Connor faithfully follows the text she knows. Tarwater literally "suffers violence" here, as he will later at the hands of "the children of God" in the course of his mission. The more difficult question centers on the second clause, which gave the work its title: "and the violent bear it away." Who are "the violent," and is their "violence" a good or a bad thing? Is the second clause parallel to the first, so that "the violent" are those attacking the kingdom and trying to destroy it? Or are they the redeemed, who out of hunger for "the bread of life" eagerly seize the kingdom and make it their own?[5] O'Connor's letters, as we have seen, leave little doubt that to her "the violent" are in fact the redeemed and that "violence" is by no means necessarily a bad thing. Significantly, the only character in the novel who worries about "violence" is Rayber, who is himself "divided in two—a violent and a rational self" (*CW* 417)[6]—and who denounces the old man's "foolish violence" and counsels young Tarwater to "avoid extremes," because "they are for violent people." Both times he chokes on his own words (*CW* 377, 420). By contrast, "violence" to O'Connor is (or can be) sacred violence, for it is the fate of the redeemed, those whose number Tarwater is about to join, "who would wander in the world, strangers from that violent country where the silence is never broken except to shout the truth" (*CW* 478).[7]

What is this sacred company? Who are these "minor prophets" from a "violent country," called to break the silence by shouting the truth? They are no abstraction, but are well represented within the novel itself, and not just by old Mason, or Lucette Carmody, the child preacher whose sermon exposes Rayber as "a dead man Jesus hasn't raised" (*CW* 415). Call them prophets, or angels, or just call them reliable narrative voices. Whoever they are they speak for O'Connor, and to that extent for God. One is the "tall and Indianlike" black woman with Buford Munson who had seen old Tarwater for two nights in a dream, "unrested" (*CW* 357). Another is the hard-boiled doctor who delivered Bishop at birth and told Rayber, "You should be grateful that his health is good

. . . I've seen them born blind as well, some without arms and legs, and one with a heart outside." When Rayber replies (echoing Ivan Karamazov), "How can I be grateful . . . when one—just one—is born with a heart outside?" the doctor tells him, "You'd better try" (*CW* 416).[8] Later, a woman at the Cherokee Lodge warns Tarwater, "Mind how you talk to one of them there, you boy!" and looks at him fiercely "as if he had profaned the holy," yet marvels when he ties Bishop's shoes, and finally says, "Whatever devil's work you mean to do, don't do it here" (*CW* 426–27). Hers too is a prophetic voice, as is that of the "black-eyed woman with a granite face" at the filling station. "There was all knowledge in her stony face," we are told "and the fold of her arms indicated a judgment fixed from the foundations of time. Huge wings might have been folded behind her without seeming strange." Whether woman or angel, she tells Tarwater that what he did "shames the dead" and "scorns the Resurrection and the Life," and Tarwater hurls an undisclosed obscenity at her that leaves him troubled and unsatisfied (*CW* 467–68).

Finally, there is Buford Munson himself, who had known the old man "very well indeed" and who tells the drunken Tarwater, "He was deep in this life, he was deep in Jesus' misery" (*CW* 357, 360).[9] Buford comes for whiskey but stays to bury old Mason, and at the end is able to say, "It's owing to me he's resting here. I buried him while you were laid out drunk. It's owing to me his corn has been plowed. It's owing to me the sign of his Saviour is over his head." With this, O'Connor tells us in Buford's own words what she announced at great length in the novel's celebrated opening sentence. Now, as Buford rides off on his mule, "The boy remained standing there, his eyes still reflecting the field the Negro had crossed" (*CW* 477). While it is tempting to linger on the possible word play in the word "crossed," the text focuses relentlessly on Tarwater and his destiny. Now at last he sees, simultaneously, the vision he has long feared, of the feeding of the multitude and what it would mean to "eat the bread of life," and with it the vision he always sought, of "the fire that had encircled Daniel, that had raised Elijah from the earth, that had spoken to Moses and would in the instant speak to him." He knows that he cannot have one without the other, and "after a moment, without looking back he moved across the far field *and off the way Buford had gone*" (*CW* 478, italics added). The unremarkable "ways of his prophecy" will be the ways of old Mason for sure, but also, and more immediately, the ways of Buford Munson. As Richard Giannone puts it, "From Buford's selflessness there flows an outpouring of spirit that spreads into a eucharistic vision at the end of the novel" (121). But not all interpreters see Buford as the role model. While giving Buford his due, Frederick Asals, for example, sees Buford and Tarwater very differently: "Unlike *Wise Blood, The Violent Bear It Away* does have a representative of enduring Christian community, but it is Buford Munson, the Negro who finally gives the old man his proper burial, not the vehemently divided boy himself. Tarwater is, to borrow the language of his great-uncle, 'more than a Christian, a prophet'"(195).[10] Yet the "vehemently divided boy" in the end embraces, *malgré lui,* the shared legacy of old Mason Tarwater and Buford Munson—eating the bread of life. Nowhere that I know of in O'Connor's writings is a black man—a real man, not an Artificial one—so unmistakably a model for redemption.

In the end, the realization of Tarwater's calling is not the prophetic ministry to the sleeping "children of God" in the "dark city." Quite deliberately, O'Connor leaves that story untold. It is rather the vision of a multitude, a vision which Tarwater not only sees but in which he participates, of a hungry old man "lowering himself to the ground. . . . his face turned toward the basket, impatiently following its progress toward him" that he might eat the bread of life (*CW* 477–78). To that extent, the violence in *The Violent Bear It Away* is, at the very least, muted violence, and at most the kind of sacred violence of which O'Connor approves. Four days before *The Violent Bear It Away* was published, she wrote to Andrew Lytle, "I keep seeing Elias in that cave, waiting to hear the voice of the Lord in the thunder and lightning and wind, and only hearing it finally in the gentle breeze, and I feel I'll have to be able to do that sooner or later, or anyway keep trying" (*CW* 1121). My contention is that in this novel she has already begun to do just that.

What are we to say of the violence in O'Connor's writings, even (or perhaps especially) her "muted" or "sacred" violence? I suspect that even (or especially?) readers with a high tolerance for violent literature and film are uncomfortable with O'Connor for the same reason they are uncomfortable with violence in the Bible—not because of the violence per se, but because of its religious dimension. So it is with Walter Tilman's mother in "Why Do the Heathen Rage?": "Then it came to her, with an unpleasant jolt, that the General with the sword in his mouth, marching to do violence, was Jesus" (*CW* 800). Violence in O'Connor—and in the Bible—is a problem for some, not because it is gratuitous but because it is not. It has a definite purpose, and if the purpose is judged to be in any way religious, that creates a difficulty for some. But in a world that O'Connor called "territory held largely by the devil" (*MM* 118), any abrupt invasion or visitation of the good can be just as grotesque and terrifying as an onslaught of evil, and human nature by itself is ill equipped to tell the difference. Or, as Joyce Carol Oates observed, O'Connor "sees man as dualistic: torn between the conventional polarities of God and the devil, but further confused because the choice must be made in human terms, and the divine might share superficial similarities with the diabolical. Indeed, it is difficult for the average reader at times to distinguish between the two in her fiction" (150). Charles Williams makes a similar point in dialog form in his 1949 novel, *Descent into Hell,* where Mr. Stanhope fastens on Miss Fox's offhand use of the phrase "terribly good":

> "Nature's so terribly good. Don't you think so, Mr. Stanhope?"
>
> "That Nature is terribly good? Yes, Miss Fox. You do mean 'terribly'?"
>
> "Why certainly," Miss Fox said. "Terribly—dreadfully—very."
>
> "Yes," Stanhope said again. "Very. Only—you must forgive me; it comes from doing so much writing, but when I say 'terribly' I think I mean 'full of terror.' A dreadful goodness."
>
> "I don't see how goodness can be dreadful," Miss Fox said, with a shade of resentment in her voice. "If things are good they're not terrifying, are they?"
>
> "It was you who said 'terribly,'" Stanhope reminded her with a smile, "I only agreed."
>
> "And if things are terrifying," Pauline put in . . ."can they be good?"
>
> He looked down at her. "Yes, surely," he said, with more energy. "Are our tremors to measure the Omnipotence?" (11–12).

Doubtless Mr. Stanhope would have considered Flannery O'Connor a "terribly good" writer, and *The Violent Bear It Away* a "terribly good" novel. In O'Connor's own words in the preface to *A Memoir of Mary Ann*, "good is another matter. Few have stared at that long enough to accept the fact that its face too is grotesque, that in us the good is something under construction. The modes of evil usually receive worthy expression. The modes of good have to be satisfied with a cliché or a smoothing down that will soften their real look" (*CW* 830).

To end on a lighthearted (and distinctly nonviolent) note, O'Connor wrote to Maryat Lee in 1959 while working on *The Violent Bear It Away*: "Dear Gargantua, Anybody else would just bake a loaf of bread but old Maryat she bakes corn bread, banana bread, nut bread and I-talian bread. Who eats it? If I lived near you I would beg my bread at your back door" (*CW* 1112). Whether in O'Connor or in the Bible, "bread" is a classic metaphor for life, and Christian scholars have long debated whether "our daily bread" in the Lord's Prayer is our food for each day in this life or the Bread of the age to come. Buford Munson knew that old Mason was "deep in this life"—no less than in the life to come—and Tarwater's hunger was physical no less than spiritual. They both speak for O'Connor herself, who knew that flesh and spirit are both real, and that they are inseparable.

Notes

1. This fear is strikingly similar to what is said about Rayber, for whom almost any object in the physical world could awaken "the horrifying love" he felt for his son Bishop (*CW* 401).

2. The words simply echo old Mason himself, who told Tarwater, "I brought you out here to raise you a Christian, and more than a Christian, a prophet" (*CW* 338).

3. See Rev. 16:6, "they have poured out the blood of saints and of prophets"; 17:6, "the blood of the saints and the blood of the witnesses [that is, 'martyrs'] of Jesus"; 19:10, "For the witness [Greek, *martyria*] of Jesus is the spirit of prophecy."

4. The "glass-like" lake evokes not so much the Jordan River, John the Baptist, and Elisha (Giannone 139) as the book of Revelation: "And before the throne *a sea of glass,* like crystal, and in the midst of the throne and around the throne *four living creatures* full of eyes in front and behind" (Rev. 4:6, italics added); see also Rev. 15:2: "like a sea of glass mixed with fire"—a sea the victorious martyrs have crossed.

5. The Greek verb is a very strong verb, as is the Latin verb from which the Douay version was translated. "Seize" or "snatch" is a more accurate translation.

6. The reader is compelled to ask: Which self is good and which is bad?

7. The text continues, "He felt it building from the blood of Abel to his own, rising and engulfing him." The whole passage evokes the letter to the Hebrews, chapter 11, particularly in reference to "strangers from that violent country" (Heb. 11:13–16) who would "wander in the world" (11:38), and especially "the blood of Abel" (11:4, 12:24).

8. In an earlier draft, Rayber has a "recurring dream" in which not a doctor but "a large blonde nurse" would "draw herself up, with mountainous white wings rising high over her head, fierce and ugly as an archangel," saying much the same thing that the doctor says in the published version, and Rayber responds similarly (O'Connor Special Collection, File 180a; see Driggers and Dunn, 96).

9. Buford's reference to "misery" is appropriate, from O'Connor's perspective, on the lips of a black man, for blacks, she thought, knew what "misery" was and were fond of the word. The lawn statue in "The Artificial Nigger" has a "chipped eye and the angle he was cocked at gave him a wild look of misery" (*CW* 229), and in a 1954 letter to Sally Fitzgerald she wrote, "As the niggers say, I have the misery" (*CW* 928).

10. For the quotation, see note 2.

Works Cited

Asals, Frederick. *Flannery O'Connor: The Imagination of Extremity.* Athens: U of Georgia P, 1982.

Driggers, S. G., and R. J. Dunn. *The Manuscripts of Flannery O'Connor at Georgia College.* Athens: U. of Georgia P, 1989.

Giannone, Richard. *Flannery O'Connor and the Mystery of Love.* 2d ed. New York: Fordham UP, 1999.

Gretlund, Jan Nordby, and Karl-Heinz Westarp. *Flannery O'Connor's Radical Reality.* Columbia: U of South Carolina P, 2006.

Lake, Christina Bieber. *The Incarnational Art of Flannery O'Connor.* Macon, GA: Mercer UP, 2005.

Oates, Joyce Carol. *New Heaven, New Earth: The Visionary Experience in Literature.* New York: Vanguard, 1974.

O'Connor, Flannery. *Collected Works.* New York: Library of America, 1988.

———. *The Habit of Being.* New York: Farrar, 1979.

———. *Mystery and Manners.* New York: Farrar, 1969.

Srigley, Susan. *Flannery O'Connor's Sacramental Art.* Notre Dame, IN: U of Notre Dame P, 2004.

Williams, Charles. *Descent into Hell.* New York: Pellegrini & Cudahy, 1949.

TOWARD A CONSISTENT ETHIC OF LIFE IN O'CONNOR'S "A STROKE OF GOOD FORTUNE"

Linda Naranjo-Huebl

Thomas Haddox, in his article on urban community in "A Stroke of Good Fortune," refers to the story as one of the most "unloved" of Flannery O'Connor's works, but the extremely diverse interpretations of the story by critics suggests its significance—if not its beloved status (4). These perspectives cover an impressive range of issues and approaches; they variously read the protagonist Ruby Hill as tragically flawed in her rejection of life, proud and selfish, comic and ridiculous in her naïveté and misery at the discovery of her pregnancy, horrified at the materiality of her identity, overcome by the psychodynamics of the early mother-infant relationship, or sympathetic in her very real fear of the costs to women of reproduction and in her betrayal by her husband.[1]

Interpretations of the story that pass harsh judgment on Ruby Hill for rejecting her pregnancy, encouraged by O'Connor's own characterization of the theme of the story as "the rejection of life at the source" (*HB* 85), recognize the strong life ethic that is characteristic of O'Connor's fiction, but they tend to minimize the story's details about the very real experience of Ruby's mother and the equally real fear it instills in Ruby. Readings that sympathize with Ruby in her authentic and understandable fears and her choice not to parent—or not to define her personhood only in terms of motherhood—provide a necessary feminist perspective that appropriately extends concern to Ruby herself, but they do not deal adequately with the story's obvious endorsement of life over death as it applies to Ruby's pregnancy. Thomas Haddox offers impressive insight concerning the story's privileging of community over an atomizing individuality, exemplified in the various neighbors' participation in the diverse urban community contrasted to Ruby's desire to escape such connection by fleeing to the suburbs, and Ralph Wood indirectly supports his reading in his broader discussion of O'Connor's privileging of a communal ethos over one based on individual rights. While insightful, their criticism does not address the very real situation of many women in urban, suburban, and rural communities in which the self, according to prevailing definitions of motherhood in patriarchal culture, is entirely sacrificed to, rather than complemented by, the life of the child. I argue that while such varied readings may seem mutually exclusive, when the textual evidence for these disparate interpretations is brought into dialogue and added to a more historically feminist and inclusive idea of motherhood and childbirth, O'Connor's story begins to offer a critique of limited and polarized visions of womanhood and motherhood. The story thus can be read not as an outdated or patriarchal characterization of women but rather as an embracing of mutually life-affirming alternatives for both women and children—a truly consistent life ethic compatible with O'Connor's Christianity.

Louise Westling's and Margaret Bauer's sympathetic, feminist interpretations of Ruby Hill provide necessary perspectives missing from previous readings of the story but that admittedly stand in opposition to O'Connor's Christianity. Westling notes the story's protest against "sentimentalized stereotypes of motherhood" by presenting Ruby's very real fear of the physical cost of reproduction and her realization she has been betrayed by her husband (516). Bauer sympathizes with Ruby for the same reasons, taking critics to task for finding fault with her while refusing to acknowledge her husband's treachery; and Bauer also aptly criticizes those readings of the text that would reinscribe woman's identity only in terms of motherhood—a well-founded criticism considering O'Connor's own position (41–46). Interestingly, both Westling and Bauer suggest that to get at these feminist readings of the text, one must subordinate O'Connor's Christian perspective. Bauer notes,

> Reading "A Stroke of Good Fortune" . . . from a *feminist rather than Christian* perspective allows for the recognition of Bill Hill's betrayal of his wife's trust, which, I would argue, is vital to an objective reading of this story, for such a recognition illuminates the story's feminist concerns and thereby renders Ruby a more sympathetic character than she has heretofore been perceived. (41, emphasis added)

Westling similarly comments,

> the reader *must do some violence to the religious theme* in order to assess the sexual problem, denying the rightness of the author's intended solution. This problem is particularly troubling in [O'Connor's] handling of women. Her mind fastened intensely on painful experiences women endure, but her conscious effort was to ignore this whole area of experience and concentrate

on what she felt to be wider, universal human problems. (521, emphasis added)

Christian feminists who eschew violence, perhaps even to literary themes, certainly find Bauer's and Westling's assertions challenging. A fuller reading of the story becomes possible by considering the consistent life ethic characteristic of O'Connor's Christianity, a reading that refuses to value the life of Ruby's child over Ruby herself and that likewise refuses to subordinate the life of Ruby's child to Ruby's very real concerns. As Ralph Wood points out, "the treatment of the utterly helpless and vulnerable was, for Flannery O'Connor as for all Christians, the index of a church's or a culture's moral life. This was not a matter of her mere opinion but of her deepest conviction, and here she stood with the central Christian tradition" (240). This tradition is rooted in the concept of the sanctity of all human life, an absolutely egalitarian life ethic that uses as its barometer the treatment of those who lack the power to demand and/or seize full recognition of their personhood and right to life. Historically children and women have been included among the disempowered, and to favor the rights of children over women, or vice versa, is clearly inconsistent with an orthodox Christian ethos and, I would add, a violation of the founding principles of feminism as it has been articulated over the last two centuries. Surely the oppression of any group of people strikes at the very foundation of a feminism based upon the equality of all humans.

Feminist activists in the Catholic peace movement in the early 1970s articulated the concept of a consistent life ethic and called attention to those social injustices responsible for oppression in general. The statement of the Catholic Peace Fellowship in response to the 1973 *Roe v. Wade* decision, signed by Dorothy Day, Eileen Egan, and others, outlines "life issues" characterized by society's failure to recognize the equal humanity of all people:

> For many years we have urged upon our spiritual leaders the interrelatedness of the life issues, war, capital punishment, abortion, euthanasia and economic exploitation. We welcome the energetic leadership our bishops are giving in the abortion controversy and we are proud to join our voices with theirs. At the same time we must point out that, ultimately, the sincerity of our words and theirs on any of these issues will be measured by our readiness to recognize and deal with the underlying social problems which turn many people to these deadly alternatives, to condemn all forms of social and economic injustice and to work for their elimination and the

establishment of a social order in which all may find it easier to be "fully human."

Elizabeth McAlister, pacifist activist in the Catholic peace movement, called for an "and" instead of an "or" definition of humanity that probably would have resonated with O'Connor. In a letter written from prison, while serving time for a protest at Griffiss Air Force base in 1983, McAlister writes in response to an advertisement in the *New York Times* taken out by Catholics for a Free Choice:

> Years ago, many of you taught me about Christ. I learned with you how he grasped the wondrous profundity of the human. He resolved conflicts and reconciled differences, placing an "and" where most of us insist on an "or." Confronted with a narrow image labeled "reality" (an image that was, in fact, inhuman or antihuman), he simply enlarged the frame, insisted on, included, all the variety and verve that is our glory—slave and free, woman and man, gentile and Jew. (253)

Christians are compelled, McAlister argues, to "welcome and cherish the human in all its likely and unlikely guises and disguises, to protect our endangered human family from all that seeks to destroy it" (253). McAlister and fellow activists privilege what Eilenn Egan and later Joseph Cardinal Bernardin called the "seamless garment of life," a consistent life ethic upon which many Catholic social justice efforts today are based.[2] Of that ethic, Cardinal Bernardin explains, "it is very necessary for preserving a systemic vision that individuals and groups who seek to witness to life at one point of the spectrum of life not be seen as insensitive to or even opposed to other moral claims on the overall spectrum of life" (Sec. I, para. 11). This ethic places the views of activists like Day, Egan, and McAlister within a consistent nonviolent feminist context, a different voice in the debates around women's reproductive issues.

Reproductive issues play an important role in "A Stroke of Good Fortune," for, as Sarah Gordon has noted, the story comes out of drafts of *Wise Blood*, in which Ruby Hill (as Hazel Motes's sister) contemplates abortion (Gordon 104), and we see in the critical response to Ruby's horror over her pregnancy many ties to the abortion debate. Discourse surrounding women's reproductive issues has generally been polarized over the last forty years, characterized by a tendency to pit the interests of the woman against those of the fetus,[3] and the critical discourse on Ruby Hill and the child in her womb is similarly polarized:

critics either deal harshly with Ruby's self-centeredness and her rejection of her pregnancy, thus privileging the life of her in utero child, or sympathize with her in her betrayal by her husband and her right to control her body, privileging the life of the woman. In larger culture, those espousing a pro-life position focus primarily on the right to life of the fetus, citing the vulnerability of these in utero members of the human family. To the extent that they narrowly focus on the fetus and not the mother, they tend to ignore those social injustices and inequitable gender relationships that fuel women's oppression and that can lead to crisis pregnancies and ultimately abortion. They often fail to speak out against the injustices faced by pregnant and parenting women, including lack of adequate pre- and postnatal care and education, affordable childcare, child support, protection from abuse and assault, and equitable policies surrounding childbirth and childcare in the workplace and in schools. Feminist abortion rights advocates respond by drawing attention to these injustices and further assert that female agency requires that a woman have control over her own body. Furthermore, they see women's full equality as possible only if the life of the in utero child is subordinated to the woman's interests.[4] Other feminists, however, "refuse to choose" between the interests of women and children, and instead point to the structuring of the debate as evidence of continued dysfunction and gender inequities in our society.[5] They echo nineteenth-century feminist Mattie Brinkerhoff, who said that "when a man steals to satisfy hunger, we may safely conclude that there is something wrong in society—so when a woman destroys the life of her unborn child, it is an evidence that either by education or circumstances she has been greatly wronged" (63). These feminists point to those social and cultural forces that offer few life-affirming alternatives for both women and children and also to those societal constructions of selfhood that privilege rigid individuation rather than an identity in relationship and community.[6]

Certainly when viewing the polarized debate over reproduction issues through the lens of O'Connor's Christianity, it should be clear that something is profoundly wrong when the interests of women and children are perceived as mutually exclusive, when the life ethic upon which human value is based is inconsistent. In line with these observations, any reading of "A Stroke of Good Fortune" that favors the interests of the new life in Ruby Hill's womb over Ruby Hill herself suggests such an inconsistency. Judging by critical responses, many readers of "A Stroke of Good Fortune" incorrectly assume that to sympathize with Ruby Hill's fear of pregnancy is to ignore her shortcomings, and that to recognize her failed perspective requires that we ignore the very real crisis that pregnancy may represent to many women in a male-dominated culture that idealizes motherhood and narrowly defines women within its terms. This assertion, of course, raises the question of how the story presents Ruby Hill and her desire to avoid pregnancy (as well as readers' responses to the story), and the criticism evinces quite diverse interpretations, as Margaret Bauer has documented.

Details of the narrative, specifically those dealing with the life of Ruby's mother and Ruby's childhood experiences with the medical profession, show that Ruby's horrified response to her pregnancy is more than a selfish reaction, a unilateral rejection of motherhood, or a dread of the "inconvenience" of a child: it results from her experience of women's lives. Louise Westling aptly notes that the story serves as a "vivid protest against sentimental stereotypes of motherhood, by presenting Ruby's horrified sense of the physical cost of reproduction and her awful realization that she has been tricked into paying it" (516). Ruby's horror stems from witnessing her mother's experience, and while readings of Ruby Hill are disparate, there seems to be consensus on interpretations of Ruby's mother—by those who take notice of her. As Bauer notes, we are given "no reason to doubt the accuracy of her assessment of her mother's life" (43). Ruby's fear of motherhood is not based merely on the negative impact it will have on her upward mobility, and it is more complex than a simple rejection of life in favor of her material interests. Ruby's distress results from accurate perceptions of her mother's experience and women's experience in general. She describes her mother's premature aging, or the "death-in-life" her motherhood represented: "All those children were what did her mother in—eight of them: two born dead, one died the first year, one crushed under a mowing machine. Her mother had got deader with every one of them" (97). The loss of so many of one's offspring is tragic but not unrealistic in poor rural farming communities of the period. Further, the passage suggests it was the *deaths* of her children, more than their births or their lives, that "did her mother in." Four of Ruby's seven siblings died tragically; arguably Ruby fears the *death* of children at least as much as their birth. Wanting to avoid the possible loss that attachment to a child represents would not suggest a devaluation of the child but, rather, an understanding of the power of the relationship and one's vulnerability within it. Certainly, if children are viewed as a burden, then losing a few of them could be perceived as lessening that burden; but in mentioning the deaths of so many children, the narrative suggests that Ruby's motivation is not merely selfishness but rather a fear of loss.

Ruby's fear of loss can also be seen in her interpersonal relationships, particularly in her protective and maternal attitude toward Rufus. Critics have carefully delineated Ruby's association of Rufus with the child she carries, noting that she refers to him several times as a "baby" and that Laverne labels him the "enfant."

They point to her disgust with Rufus stemming from his refusal to leave behind his "hick" ways, even after his military travels, and they correlate it with her disgust for the child she carries (Di Renzo 103–4; Kahane 245–46). Ruby further blames Rufus for the slow death of her mother: "She saw him waiting out nowhere before he was born, just waiting, waiting to make his mother, only thirty-four, [Ruby's age] into an old woman" (97). While Ruby is clearly unjust and hypercritical toward Rufus, it is the type of criticism a frustrated mother has for the child who does not live up to her hopes and expectations, as misguided as they may be, but who nevertheless is sincerely concerned for that child. While Ruby expresses her disgust that Rufus chooses collard greens for his "special" meal, she is still going to prepare them for him. And the occasion of the meal—his return from the war—marks her relief over his safe return. She is alarmed by Laverne's sexual interest in her brother, her response like that of a mother reluctant to view her child as grown up. We are all vulnerable in our valued relationships, and a fear of loss, founded on a history such as that of Ruby's family, seems predictable. She, not surprisingly, attempts to protect herself from such loss by fleeing the community that offers her an identity only in (tragic) motherhood and instead seeking refuge in suburbia and the material comfort her culture tells her it represents, however ill-founded those assumptions may be.[7]

Loss, of course, is the story of life, but a consistent life ethic finds unacceptable those losses caused by social injustices arising from the valuation of some lives over others. Indeed, if a culture's moral life can be measured by how it treats its most vulnerable members, as Ralph Wood argues is characteristic of the Christian tradition O'Connor participated in (450), the tragic deaths of Ruby's siblings signify a profound moral failing in society. In her poverty, Ruby's mother lacked pre- and postnatal care, and this poverty likewise dictated the need for young children to work around dangerous agricultural equipment. While it is not uncharacteristic of O'Connor to present childbirth as horrific, to show life as emerging from the grotesque, as Anthony Di Renzo illustrates (68), the agony of Ruby's mother's labor also calls attention to the lack of reproductive health care among the poor. Her mother's screams, which last over the period of a twenty-mile walk, four film features, and all night upon Ruby's return, suggest the dangers of childbirth when there is no medical support or skilled midwives, no prenatal care and education, no health advocates or pain management techniques and medicines. Social justice efforts by both progressive Christians and feminists have long targeted such injustices.

O'Connor also suggests that medical intervention, as it existed in Ruby's era (and now, as many feminist health care reformers would point out), was not always much better.[8] Ruby compares her sisters' experience to her mother's: "And there her two sisters were, both married four years with four children apiece. She didn't see how they stood it, always going to the doctor to be jabbed at with instruments" (97). O'Connor undoubtedly knew much about intrusive medical procedures, as did many feminists who in the 1970s effected reform in obstetric practices. Ruby fears the type of childbirth her mother suffered through, but she also fears doctors. When she has difficulty climbing the stairs, she thinks, "No, I'm not going to no doctor, she said. No. No. She was not. They would have to carry her there knocked out before she would go. She had done all right doctoring herself all these years—no bad sick spells, no teeth out, no children, all that by herself" (98). When Ruby tells Laverne that she is sick, Laverne, who has guessed Ruby is pregnant, suggests she see a doctor, and Ruby refuses. She describes her one trip to the doctor for treatment of a boil: "They carried me once when I was ten . . . but I got away. Three of them holding me didn't do any good" (104). Ruby treats the boil herself after consulting a local black woman. Clearly Ruby's own childhood experiences have given her good reason to fear childbirth as she witnessed it.

The reference to Ruby consulting a local black woman for treatment of her boil may be an allusion to the efficient lay midwifery that was sustained among poor communities in the South as an alternative to inadequate or inaccessible institutionalized health care. These skilled midwives held quite alternative views from their more "official" counterparts in the medical profession and from those, like Ruby Hill, who tended to see the needs of mother and children as oppositional. Debra Anne Susie interviewed some of these lay midwives from poor, dispossessed southern communities—primarily African Americans, Native Americans, Latina, and white Appalachian women—who provided a number of health services for women and children in a manner considered progressive today. Their treatment included an equal regard for the lives of both mother and child. In the case of unwanted pregnancy, Susie explains that none of the women she interviewed "accepted the notion of illegitimate children: 'They's all children to me,' was a commonly shared sentiment. So when the topic of abortion came up, the answer was easy: 'No.' Yet their conviction was not so much a moralistic principle as an affirmation of life as positive and legitimate, as they knew it from their intimate familiarity with birth" (30). Many of them crossed racial and class barriers, notes Susie, to "lend support to those choosing to go ahead with an unwanted birth . . . to not only deliver the child but raise it, black or white, and then turn it over to the mother" if she later changed her mind (30). If O'Connor knew of such lay midwives, her reference to the black woman Ruby mentions suggests that she was aware of more holistic alternatives surrounding women's healthcare.

We are reminded by Sarah Gordon and others, however, that O'Connor did not have the advantage of the insights of "second wave" feminism. In her study of dualism in O'Connor's fiction, most notable in "her treatment of women and male-female relationships," Gordon attributes O'Connor's adoption of male models of spiritual development at least in part to the fact that she lacked the insights of the women's movement of the 1970s, specifically its critique of dualism as it relates to the female body (96). Second wave feminism, however, was similarly lacking in that it had lost the perspective of earlier feminists and the views of women like the lay midwives of the South who embraced nonviolent alternatives to crisis pregnancies and identified and denounced the societal factors that lead women to seek abortion. These women understood that the state of women's reproductive health was symptomatic of woman's continued oppression arising from inequitable legal, civil, and cultural gender relations.

O'Connor at some level recognized some of these inequities, as seen most clearly in the story's ironic presentation of the young Hartley Gilfeet revealing the daunting burden of the single mother and the lack of societal support to aid in her plight. As Clair Katz Kahane notes, young Hartley Gilfeet symbolizes the life that Ruby is supposedly rejecting, and one can undoubtedly see fetal imagery in his name and birth imagery in his appearance on the stairs at the end of the story. He represents the "stroke of good fortune" that Ruby had instead hoped was her move to the suburbs. But even readers who do not sympathize with Ruby recognize the irony of associating Hartley with good luck: there is little "fortune" to be found in Mrs. Gilfeet's single motherhood, despite her repeated claims that Hartley is her "Little Mister Good Fortune" (98). Mrs. Gilfeet has been widowed by a man who left his family with no financial provision, and she parents her son in a culture that provides minimal support to single mothers. She has little control over Hartley, who seems already to understand his male prerogative, emphasized by his ownership of at least three toy pistols. In the last scene, he comes charging up the stairs "with two pistols leveled," upsets the entire building with his racket, refuses to listen to his mother's scolding, and almost knocks Ruby over (107). Even Ruby sees how Mrs. Hartley routinely projects her frustrations: "all she did was scream at him and tell people how smart he was"—that is, she alternately yells at her son and denies her anger by emphasizing his intelligence and reiterating the story of her good fortune (107). Single mothers are expected to feel blessed by the mere existence of their children, as if their love is all that is needed to raise them, and our society has never instituted adequate support systems for single mothers to successfully raise those children. Furthermore, the inequality in gender relationships results in even married mothers bearing the primary responsibilities of childrearing. There is no romanticization of motherhood here.

Another social factor implicated in the story is the inequality in interpersonal relationships characteristic of patriarchal cultures. Clearly Ruby and Bill Hill's relationship lacks mutuality and is characterized by domination and subordination: they will move to the suburbs only when Bill Hill is ready to do so. In struggling up the stairs, Ruby realizes that only *his* experience, not hers, will motivate him: "As soon as Bill Hill fell down these steps once, maybe they would move" (99). Ruby clearly accepts her husband's authority over her and defers to his opinions. When Bill Hill tells her that it only took him three minutes, compared to her five, to realize Rufus was "good for absolutely nothing," she thinks, "it was mortifying to let that kind of a husband see you had that kind of a brother" (96). Even her perception of her own body comes from her husband: "She was warm and fat and beautiful and not too fat because Bill Hill liked her that way" (99). When she climbs the four flights of twenty-eight steps, representing her four months of pregnancy, she sits down on Hartley's toy pistol; and, as Margaret Bauer has observed, these "nine inches of treacherous tin" signify Bill's masculine treachery, his violation of Ruby's trust.[9] When Laverne later reveals Ruby's pregnancy to her, Ruby is truly shocked: "Not me! . . . Bill Hill takes care of that. Bill Hill takes care of that! Bill Hill's been taking care of that for five years! That ain't going to happen to me!" (104). Clearly, Bill Hill not only controls their living arrangements, he also is in charge of Ruby's reproductive system. Earlier in the narrative, Ruby takes the credit for remaining childless—"She would have had five children right now if she hadn't been careful" (98)—but here we see that Bill Hill has had complete control all along.

Ruby's rejection of pregnancy certainly contradicts the Catholic doctrinal concept of sex as primarily for procreation, but O'Connor is too skilled a writer to merely "punish" Ruby by making her pregnant. O'Connor's view of sexuality was undoubtedly more nuanced, as Sarah Gordon suggests, placing emphasis on its "sacramental value." Gordon characterizes O'Connor's view as revealed in her writing: "in a society in which the sexual relationship is denied its sacramental value, sexual pleasure is sought for its own sake, and abortion is therefore a popular option" (104). But even the church recognizes that pregnancy is not always desired or expedient. The church's endorsement of natural family planning evinces its acknowledgment of the toll or danger to the mother's life that pregnancy can sometimes represent; indeed, it must if its positions are founded on a consistent life ethic. Ironically, natural family planning, more than any other form of birth control, is predicated on egalitarian relationship. The responsibility falls equally to both the man and the woman to be aware of the woman's reproductive cycle and to agree when to avoid intercourse. Ruby and her husband clearly have no such egalitarian relationship—he is the head of their household. Ruby's reproductive life is in his hands despite the heavier burden she bears in childbearing. Indeed, she seems most naive in having placed her trust in him. Even today, the consequences of failed contraception fall much more heavily on women, as do the responsibilities of childbearing and child rearing. We are a long way from egalitarian sexual relationships.

The gender inequities apparent in Ruby's relationship with her husband are paralleled by inequitable standards applied by many readers to Ruby and Bill Hill. Those who view Ruby as exercising her prerogatives over the life of her child fail to likewise note how her interests have been eclipsed by Bill Hill, who has violated the trust of his wife and is, in fact, happy with himself. This historic double standard, in which the woman bears more guilt than her male partner, plays out among critics who judge Ruby but not her husband. As Bauer appropriately asks, "what makes [Ruby's] refusal to fulfill [Bill Hill's] desire any more reprehensible than his betrayal of her? If both are guilty of insensitivity to their spouse's desires, . . . why is she the only one of the two who receives so many readers' scorn?" (Bauer 48).

In a culture that has historically defined women by their relationship to men and in terms of motherhood (certainly at a peak in the 1950s), women who resist those definitions find their interests unjustly at odds with those of their children. Ruby fears her potential offspring and perceives him or her as a threat in the same way she sees her brother Rufus as having laid in wait to sabotage her mother: "It was as if it were out nowhere in nothing, out nowhere, resting and waiting, with plenty of time" (107). The child is presented as an enemy, like the cancer she fears when she feels a pain in her stomach: "It was a pain like a piece of something pushing something else. She had felt it before, a few days ago. It was the one that frightened her most. She had thought the word *cancer* once and dropped it instantly because no horror like that was coming to her because it couldn't" (101). Nineteenth- and twentieth-century feminists battled against just such a perception of pregnancy (and woman's biology in general) as a weakness or illness requiring a cure and recognized such characterizations as symptomatic of women's oppression. Society's tendency to pathologize woman's biology or to define her only in biological terms has caused some women facing an unwanted, crisis pregnancy to view the fetus as a type of cancer and abortion as a cure for the disease of pregnancy, an association encouraged in the discourse of some abortion apologists. Ruby's fear of her in utero child is an ironic reversal of the fear of the devouring mother, but her fear is real, nevertheless. She feels *her* face "drawn puckered: two born dead one died the first year and one run under like a dried yellow apple no she was only thirty-four years old, she was old" (106). Her failure to recognize her pregnancy does not result merely from her self-absorption and ignorance, as some critics have claimed (Di Renzo 70), but from an unconsciously constructed psychological defense not uncommon in women when faced with a crisis pregnancy.

In acknowledging these feminist perspectives premised on a consistent life ethic, I am not asserting that O'Connor shared (or would share) these insights, only that her narrative reflects the tension of an inconsistent life ethic characteristic of her culture. In fact, O'Connor had mixed views of progressive social activists and pacifists in the Catholic Worker Movement, such as Dorothy Day (Gordon 236–37), in whose footsteps pro-life feminists such as Elizabeth McAlister follow.[10] Nevertheless, implicit in her story are the societal forces that would make a woman's pregnancy catastrophic. In general, I concur with those feminist critics like Louise Westling who find troubling some of O'Connor's "handling of women" (521). In her study of O'Connor's daughters and mothers, Westling observes, "her mind fastened intensely on painful experiences women endure, but her conscious effort was to ignore this whole area of experience and concentrate on what she felt to be wider, universal human problems" (521). But because O'Connor presents a realistic world to her reader, free of romanticized notions of womanhood, she provides those details and distortions that Westling claims "express a passionate but inadvertent protest against the lot of woman-kind. Flannery O'Connor can make these women live because she is one of them" (511). O'Connor's own observation on writers' intentionality seems fitting in light of feminist perspectives and is ironic in its use of the male pronoun: "If a writer is any good, what he makes will have its sources in a realm much larger than that which his conscious mind can encompass and will always be a greater surprise to him than it can ever be to his reader" (*MM* 83).

O'Connor characteristically raises the questions and lets the reader sift through possible meanings. But in a world where mothers view their children as agents of their death, things are terribly askew. By bringing into dialogue the diverse interpretations of O'Connor's story within the parameters of a consistent life ethic characteristic of O'Connor's Christianity, one can see how the story implicitly offers a critique of limited and polarized visions of womanhood and (to the extent that they are inextricable in patriarchal culture) motherhood, and critiques those social, cultural, and interpersonal forces that set the interests of women against those of children. The story reveals the lack of a vision of motherhood that is not tragic or devouring for the child and/or the mother, and the related absence of a model of relationship that is not hierarchical, in which one person's life is not subordinated to the other. By viewing relationship, identity, motherhood, marriage, and sexuality in the story through the lens of a consistent life ethic characteristic of the progressive Christian tradition, we can see what is missing, not only in the story but in culture in general. Louise Westling believes that "if Flannery O'Connor had lived long enough for the feminist movement to arouse her awareness of society's injustices to women and of her own repressed rage, surely she would have confronted these problems consciously in her stories as she did those of race" (Westling 522). I would agree, with a caveat. If she had lived long enough to be influenced by second wave feminism, it would not have had to "do violence" to her religious themes (Westling 521): it could have been entirely consistent with her Christianity.

Notes

1. Margaret Bauer provides an excellent summary and bibliography of Ruby's critics. Clair Katz Kahane presents a psychoanalytic reading of the story. Bauer and Louise Westling offer countercriticisms of prevailing readings from a feminist perspective, and Sarah Gordon offers a feminist reading of O'Connor's tendency toward dualism in her treatment of the female body with a brief mention of "A Stroke of Good Fortune."

2. Cardinal Bernardin's ideas build on those of the Catholic Peace Fellowship and were articulated in 1983 as a specific response to the threats of euthanasia, nuclear proliferation and modern warfare, capital punishment, and abortion. He identified the "political and psychological linkage among the life issues—from war to welfare concerns" (sec. II). He helped form the Seamless Garment Network, an international coalition of individuals and organizations promoting peace, justice, and life, and opposing all forms of violence, including capital punishment, war, poverty, euthanasia, abortion, and military proliferation. This organization continues today within a broader-than-Catholic scope as Consistent Life (http://www.consistentlife.org).

3. See Mary Krane Derr, "Pro-Every Life; Pro-Nonviolent Choice," and Rachel MacNair.

4. Very few pro-choice theorists today deny the life of the fetus, although many refuse to extend "personhood" to in utero life. Instead, they claim a woman's right to make life-or-death decisions. See Derr et al., *ProLife Feminism: Yesterday and Today*, 2nd ed. 188–90, 372.

5. See Kennedy; Derr et al.; Sweet; and MacNair. "Refuse to Choose" is the slogan of Feminists for Life, a U.S. grassroots organization dedicated to fighting the systemic injustices and inequalities that lead to the perceived need for abortion (http://www.feministsforlife.org).

6. Ralph Wood, in his discussion of the rejection of nihilism in O'Connor's fiction, discusses the move in Western culture from a communitarian ethos (including a religious one) to one based on individual rights. He cites the privacy argument of *Roe v. Wade* as exemplary of this move, and while I agree with his general analysis (and believe O'Connor would concur), he suggests that abortion typically occurs within a paradigm in which the woman is looking out only for her own interests or that she uses her body "according to the sole criteria of pleasure and efficiency" (Wood 239). The majority of women who seek an abortion are motivated by a litany of external social and interpersonal pressures and lack of support. Those who suggest that most women get abortions for reasons of "convenience" fail to privilege the very real gender inequalities in society (see Mary Krane Derr, "Pregnancy Is No Mere Inconvenience, Abortion Is No Solution," *ProLife Feminism,* 1st ed.). Interestingly, some pro-choice feminists, such as Catharine MacKinnon, have similarly critiqued the privacy argument of *Roe v. Wade* without abandoning their pro-choice views (see Derr et al., *ProLife Feminism,* 2nd ed., 189). Concerning psychological concepts of identity formation, feminist and relational psychologists often use such terms as *self-in-relation, identity-in-relation,* and *relational self* to signify the concept of a coherent, stable sense of self defined within relationship, in contrast to the view that the "self" is entirely individuated from others.

7. See Thomas Haddox for a historicization of the development and perceptions of suburbia as they relate to the story.

8. Health care reform is integral to feminist movements. Western feminists' advocacy for women's health care has its roots in midwifery and lay practices and was promoted in the writings of feminists such as Mary Wollstonecraft, with her call for attention to women's health; nineteenth-century activists such as Elizabeth Cady Stanton, Sarah Norton, Charlotte Denman Lozier, and Alice Bunker Stockham; physicians like Elizabeth Blackwell, who fought for women's admittance to the medical profession; social reformers like Jane Adams, Francis Willard, and Julia Lathrop and their promotion of governmental health care reform; those feminists who labored long for safe and effective birth control; and the women's health collectives of the 1970s (see Derr et al., *ProLife Feminism,* 2nd ed., pt. 1; Carol S. Weisman; and Sheryl B. Ruzek and Julie Becker).

9. Charles W. Mayer first pointed out how the revisions made from the earlier versions of the story show the change in Bill Hill's role from incidental to primary agent behind Ruby's pregnancy (the perpetrator of the "joke").

10. On O'Connor's view of Day, see Sarah Gordon (236–37). For Day's views and experience with abortion and crisis pregnancy, see Paul Elie (34–39, 48); "Dorothy Day" in Derr, et al., *ProLife Feminism: Yesterday and Today,* 2nd ed. (173–79); and Dorothy Day. For an extended comparison of the lives of Day and O'Connor (along with Thomas Merton and Walker Percy), see Paul Elie.

Works Cited

Bauer, Margaret. "The Betrayal of Ruby Hill and Hulga Hopewell: Recognizing Feminists Concerns in 'A Stroke of Good Fortune' and 'Good Country People.'" *"On the Subject of the Feminist Business": Re-Reading Flannery O'Connor.* Ed. Teresa Caruso. New York: Peter Lang, 2004. 40–63.

Bernardin, Joseph Cardinal. "A Consistent Ethic of Life: Continuing the Dialogue." William Wade Lecture Series, St. Louis U, 11 Mar. 1984. http://www.priests forlife.org/magisterium/bernardinwade.html.

Brinkerhoff, Mattie H. "Woman and Motherhood." *ProLife Feminism: Yesterday and Today.* 2nd ed. Ed. Mary Krane Derr et al. Kansas City, MO: Feminism & Nonviolence Studies Assoc., 2005. 62–63.

Day, Dorothy, Eileen Egan, Hermene Evans, Joseph Evans, Thomas C. Cornell, James H. Forest, and Gordon C. Zahn. The Catholic Peace Fellowship Statement on Abortion. 28 June 1974. Qtd. in *Houston Catholic Worker,* Sept.–Oct. 2004. http://www.cjd.org/paper/cathpeac.html.

Derr, Mary Krane. "Pregnancy Is No Mere Inconvenience, Abortion Is No Solution." *ProLife Feminism: Yesterday and Today.* 1st ed. Ed. Mary Krane Derr et al. New York: Sulzburger & Graham, 1995. 251–56.

———. "Pro-Every Life; Pro-Nonviolent Choice." *ProLife Feminism: Yesterday and Today.* 2nd ed. Ed. Mary Krane Derr et al. Kansas City, MO: Feminism & Nonviolence Studies Assoc., 2005. 371–83.

Derr, Mary Krane, Rachel MacNair, and Linda Naranjo-Huebl, eds. *ProLife Feminism: Yesterday and Today.* 2nd ed. Kansas City, MO: Feminism & Nonviolence Studies Assoc., 2005.

Di Renzo, Anthony. *American Gargoyles: Flannery O'Connor and the Medieval Grotesque.* Carbondale: Southern Illinois UP, 1995.

Elie, Paul. *The Life You Save May Be Your Own: An American Pilgrimage.* New York: Farrar, 2003.

Gordon, Sarah. *Flannery O'Connor: The Obedient Imagination.* Athens: Georgia UP, 2000.

Haddox, Thomas F. "The City Reconsidered: Problems and Possibilities of Urban Community in 'A Stroke of Good Fortune' and 'The Artificial Nigger.'" *Flannery O'Connor Review* 3 (2005): 4–18.

Kahane, Claire Katz. "The Maternal Legacy: The Grotesque Tradition in Flannery O'Connor's Female Gothic." *The Female Gothic.* Ed. Juliann E. Fleenor. Montreal: Eden Press, 1983. 242–56.

Kennedy, Angela, ed. *Swimming Against the Tide: Feminist Dissent on the Abortion Issue.* Dublin: Open Air/Four Courts Press, 1997.

MacNair, Rachel. *Achieving Peace in the Abortion War.* 2000. http://www.fnsa.org/apaw.

Mayer, Charles M. "The Comic Spirit in 'A Stroke of Good Fortune.'" *Studies in Short Fiction* 16 (1979): 70–74.

O'Connor, Flannery. *The Complete Stories.* New York: Farrar, 1971.

———. *Mystery and Manners: Occasional Prose.* Ed. Sally and Robert Fitzgerald. New York: Farrar, 1957.

Ruzek, Sheryl B., and Julie Becker. "The Women's Health Movement in the United States: From Grass Roots Activism to Professional Agendas." *Journal of the American Medical Women's Association* 54 (1999): 4–8.

Susie, Debra Anne. *In the Way of Our Grandmothers: A Cultural View of Twentieth Century Midwifery in Florida.* Athens: Georgia UP, 1988.

Sweet, Gail Grenier. *Pro-Life Feminism: Different Voices.* Toronto: Life Cycle Books, 1985.

Weinstein, Philip M. "'Coming Unalone': Gesture and Gestation in Faulkner and O'Connor." *Faulkner, His Contemporaries, and His Posterity.* Ed. Waldemar Zacharasiewicz. Tubingen: Francke, 1993. 262–75.

Weisman, Carol S. *Women's Health Care: Activist Traditions and Institutional Change.* Baltimore: John Hopkins UP, 1998.

Westling, Louise. "Flannery O'Connor's Mothers and Daughters." *Twentieth-Century Literature* 24 (1978): 510–22.

Wood, Ralph C. *Flannery O'Connor and the Christ-Haunted South.* Grand Rapids: Eerdmans, 2004.

Part Two

CONNECTING O'CONNOR'S VIOLENCE

GORY STORIES: O'CONNOR AND AMERICAN HORROR

Jon Lance Bacon

A few weeks after the publication of *A Good Man Is Hard to Find,* Flannery O'Connor complained that reviewers were describing her narratives as "horror stories" (*HB* 90). Considering all the morbid images they encountered, the reviewers could hardly be blamed for doing so. As *The New Yorker* observed, a "macabre air" hangs over the collection (93). *A Good Man* features scenes of violent death, characters with "a corpse-like composure" (*CW* 318) and "a skeleton's appearance of seeing everything" (*CW* 167), and eerie settings like "the graveyard where the Judge lay grinning under his desecrated monument" (*CW* 315). What's more, *A Good Man* typifies O'Connor's work in general: images of the macabre can be found throughout her fiction, from *Wise Blood* to "Judgment Day." O'Connor insisted that she wrote "Christian realism," as opposed to "horror stories," but the truth is, she made extensive, strategic use of motifs from the horror genre.

Some of these go back to Edgar Allan Poe, who had, she confessed, influenced her more than any other writer. This influence, which she said she "would rather not think about" (*HB* 98–99), is most evident in *Wise Blood*. Mrs. Flood refers to "The Black Cat," for instance, when she chastises Hazel for behaving like someone in "one of them gory stories," doing something anachronistic like "walling up cats" (*CW* 127). Elsewhere in the novel, O'Connor employs the motif of premature burial to which Poe returned obsessively. On the train to Taulkinham, Hazel dreams that his upper berth is a coffin—his mother's coffin—and its lid is closing down on him (*CW* 14). Later, in his car, he dreams that "he was not dead but only buried" (*CW* 91).

Hollywood, as well as Poe, provided O'Connor with classic horror motifs. Both her novels, for example, allude to iconic figures from horror films of the 1930s and 1940s. The figure of the vampire makes a brief yet prominent appearance in *The Violent Bear It Away,* in the guise of the sexual predator who picks up Tarwater: after molesting the boy, the man looks "as if he had refreshed himself on blood" (*CW* 472). In *Wise Blood,* Hazel dreams that his mother is a vampire, flying out of her coffin "like a huge bat" (*CW* 14). With its frequent references to picture shows, *Wise Blood* is especially rich in horror movie icons. "The Eye," the villain of the B-movie that frightens Enoch Emery (*CW* 79), recalls the figure of the mad scientist in films such as 1940's *Dr. Cyclops.*[1] Gonga, "Giant Jungle Monarch" (*CW* 100), recalls King Kong. There's even a mummy, of sorts—the "new jesus," preserved by some mysterious Middle Eastern process.

Like the girl in "The Comforts of Home" who lets out "a loud tormented-sounding laugh in imitation of a movie monster" (*CW* 587), O'Connor was clearly familiar with the conventions of Hollywood horror. More surprisingly, her narratives share a striking number of elements with a new horror medium, which came into being just as she was starting her literary career. This medium was the horror comic—a publishing sensation, a flashpoint of nationwide controversy, and, as David Hajdu maintains, a crucial factor in the evolution of postwar popular culture.[2]

Introduced by comic book publishers in the late 1940s, horror titles exploded in popularity after 1950, when EC (short for Entertaining Comics) launched *Tales from the Crypt, The Vault of Horror,* and *The Haunt of Fear.*[3] Spurred by their success, the industry would produce about 150 horror titles by 1952—nearly 30 percent of all comics being published, at a time when average monthly circulation was approaching 70 million copies (Benton 51, 159). As David J. Skal points out, horror comics had a larger audience than *Reader's Digest* or *The Saturday Evening Post* (230). If we could examine the comic books that June Star and John Wesley are reading on their fatal car ride in "A Good Man Is Hard to Find" (*CW* 139), we would surely see some horror titles. By 1953, the year "A Good Man" was first published, the horror craze was near its peak.

In many of their stories, comic books recycled traditional horror motifs. There were vampires, mad scientists, apes run amok, and mummies. There were storylines adapted, or stolen, from Poe. The first story in the first issue of *The Haunt of Fear* was a variation on "The Black Cat," set in 1950; in a later issue, a story called "Thump Fun!" showed a murderer reading aloud from "The Tell-Tale Heart."[4] Poe's influence on the comics was also evident in the countless tales of premature burial. One of these, "Terror Train," involves a nightmare that neatly parallels Hazel's dream aboard the train: a female passenger, sleeping in an upper berth, dreams that she is trapped in a coffin. (Unfortunately, as soon as she awakens, her husband has her committed to a mental institution.)[5]

Even as they recycled the old forms, the horror comics of the early 1950s developed their own, radically new conventions. Foremost among these was

HE GASPED, DROPPING THE AXE. HE PULLED THE BOOK FROM THE SHELF, GIGGLING...

THE TELL-TALE HEART. OF COURSE! I REMEMBER!

Acknowledging Poe's influence. Graham Ingels, "Thump Fun!" *Haunt of Fear,* July–August 1953, 6. Copyright © William M. Gaines, Agent, Inc. Reprinted with permission.

the graphic depiction of physical violence, death, and decay. Essentially, horror comics translated the verbal gore of Poe into a visual medium. Artists competed to show the lengths to which the human body could be damaged, disfigured, debased. Mutilation was a common occurrence, with detailed images of limbs cut off and organs cut out. People were always being decapitated, their heads sometimes ending up as bowling balls.[6]

Often, an entire body would be dissected, as in a notorious 1953 story from *The Haunt of Fear.* "Foul Play!" shows a baseball team avenging the murder of a star player, first dismembering the killer, then playing a night game with his body parts. His intestines mark the base lines; his lungs and liver, the bases; his heart, home plate. His head, naturally, serves as a baseball.[7] The story was so incredibly tasteless that Fredric Wertham reproduced a panel as a key exhibit in *Seduction of the Innocent,* his 1954 attack on comic books.

In the horror comics, the forms of physical violence weren't just brutal; they were increasingly bizarre. If you weren't careful, you could be crushed by an elephant or flattened by a steamroller. You could be devoured by ants or piranhas, a huge tapeworm or a giant spider. You could drown in a vat of cheese, dive into a swimming pool of acid, or drink something that dissolved your bones, turning you into a human jellyfish. You could be cut in half by an oversized mousetrap, or into thin slices by industrial machinery.[8]

Wertham's key exhibit. Jack Davis, "Foul Play!" *Haunt of Fear,* May–June 1953, 7. Copyright © William M. Gaines, Agent, Inc. Reprinted with permission.

To anyone who has read O'Connor, an aesthetic that combines maimed bodies and bizarre violence should sound awfully familiar. Her work abounds with images of physical mutilation, both literal and metaphorical. "The Eye," the B-movie villain in *Wise Blood,* steals body parts from unsuspecting victims. "You would wake up in the morning," O'Connor writes, "and find a slit in your chest or head or stomach and something you couldn't do without would be gone" (*CW* 79). In "The Life You Save May Be Your Own," Tom T. Shiftlet is missing half an arm; in "Good Country People," Joy-Hulga had a leg "blasted off" when she was a child (*CW* 267). When Tarwater was a baby, O'Connor writes in *The Violent Bear It Away,* he had the face of a martyr whose "limbs are being sawed off" (*CW* 442).

In "The Displaced Person," Mrs. Shortley envisions the complete disintegration and confusion of the human form: "'The children of wicked nations will be butchered,' she said in a loud voice. 'Legs where arms should be, foot to face, ear in the palm of hand'" (*CW* 301). Though couched in biblical language, the vision bears an uncanny resemblance to one of the ghastliest images in horror comics, an image from 1953 of a man dismembered and badly reassembled:

SIDNEY, OR WHAT WAS *ONCE* SIDNEY BUT IS NOW NOTHING MORE THAN A *CON-FUSED REORGANIZATION* OF *SIDNEY'S DISMEMBERED BODY,* STANDS BEFORE HIM . . . THE *UPSIDE-DOWN HEAD HANGING* FROM THE *LEFT HIP,* SOBBING . . . THE *LEFT LEG,* SEWN TO THE *LEFT SHOULDER,* CROOKED AWKWARDLY AROUND A MAKESHIFT CRUTCH . . . THE *RIGHT LEG* SWAYING FROM THE *RIGHT SHOULDER*

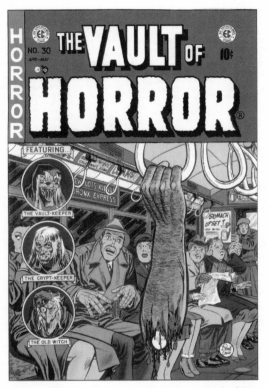

The rest of Mr. Shiftlet's arm? Johnny Craig, *Vault of Horror,* April–May 1953. Copyright © William M. Gaines, Agent, Inc. Reprinted with permission.

. . . THE *LEFT ARM*, ERUPTING FROM THE *NECK*, GESTICULATING . . . AND THE *RIGHT ARM* SUPPORTING THE ENTIRE GRISLY SIGHT . . . [9]

When it comes to violent imagery, O'Connor can be just as outlandish as the horror comics. Indeed, almost every moment of violence in her fiction has a parallel in a comic book story. The freakish death of Mrs. May, gored by a bull in "Greenleaf," has its counterpart in a 1951 cover story from *The Haunt of Fear*—the aptly named "Bum Steer!"[10] In this instance, O'Connor is actually more explicit than the comic book. While the bull in "Bum Steer!" kills its victims out-of-frame, O'Connor, if you'll pardon the expression, gives us the gory details: "One of his horns sank until it pierced her heart and the other curved around her side and held her in an unbreakable grip" (*CW* 523).

The complete confusion of the human form. Graham Ingels, "Horror We? How's Bayou?" *Haunt of Fear*, January–February 1953, 8. Copyright © William M. Gaines, Agent, Inc. Reprinted with permission.

A pivotal moment of violence in *Wise Blood* has parallels in any number of comic book stories. When Hazel blinds himself, his act mirrors a widespread image in the comics, an image that Wertham dubbed "the injury-to-the-eye motif."[11] Examples of this ranged from the purely sadistic—a man blinded by hot irons—to the downright insane—a pair of eyeballs used as golf balls.[12] Hazel's blinding may allude to the myth of Oedipus, as dramatized by Sophocles (*HB* 68), but a phrase like "the mess he had made in his eye sockets" (*CW* 120) would fit perfectly in the text of a horror comic tale.

In addition to violent content, O'Connor shares a key structural element with horror comics: the "shock" ending. In the typical horror story, the writer and the artist save the most gruesome image for the last page, when everyday reality is shattered. Sometimes, a seemingly ordinary person goes mad and commits a grisly murder. More frequently, the supernatural invades the natural world, as a dead man comes back to life. Either way, normalcy proves to be an illusion. As Mrs. Flood would say, what happens in "them gory stories" is "not normal" (*CW* 127).

THE NEXT MORNING, WHEN THE TOURNMENT STARTED, THE JUDGES FOUND AMY ON THE FIRST GREEN OF THE GOLF COURSE, HER HAIR STRINGY, HER FACE PALE, GLEEFULLY PRACTIC- ING HER PUTTING...

AMY WAS USING ROBERT'S EYEBALLS...

A sample of the injury-to-the-eye motif. Jack Kamen, "How Green Was My Alley," *Tales from the Crypt,* June–July 1953, 6. Copyright © William M. Gaines, Agent, Inc. Reprinted with permission.

O'Connor, of course, felt obliged to make her vision "apparent by shock." A Christian writing for secular readers, she said, "may well be forced to take ever more violent means to get his vision across to this hostile audience" (*CW* 805–6). Her statement helps explain the endings to her stories, so many of which involve ordinary people doing startling things: a little boy, only ten years old, hangs himself; an elderly man kills his favorite grandchild, smashing her head on a rock; a Bible salesman steals a woman's leg.[13] And, obviously, O'Connor's endings concern the invasion of the natural world by the supernatural—a moment of grace that she suggests with her own version of the injury-to-the-eye motif, her repeated description of eyes burned clean or "shocked clean" (*CW* 379, 572).

The question, at this point, is why there should be all these similarities between O'Connor's fiction and a visual medium aimed primarily at young people. Given her interest in popular culture, O'Connor must have been aware of horror comics. She could hardly have missed the nationwide outcry over comic book violence; since 1948, critics blaming the comics for juvenile delinquency had been featured in national magazines, including *Time, Collier's,* and *The Saturday Review of Literature* (Hajdu 97, 100, 113). In December 1948, when O'Connor was working at Yaddo in Saratoga Springs, New York, she could have heard that Catholic schools were burning comic books in Binghamton and Auburn (Hajdu 119–27). Back in Milledgeville, she would have seen horror comics on display at the local newsstand or drugstore. She was certainly familiar with the comic book ads that offered prizes to get children to sell seeds—as Norton does in "The Lame Shall Enter First."

Even so, I doubt that O'Connor was poring over the latest issue of *Witches Tales* or *Black Cat Mystery,* looking for story ideas. I would argue, instead, that she was responding to the same nightmares, the same real-life horrors, as the creators of comic books: the atomic bomb and the Nazi death camp. Skal links horror comics with these "radical new forms of mechanized death," suggesting that the comics gave indirect expression to American anxieties over annihilation (229–30).[14] The traumas inflicted on the human body in the comics pointed to the physical violence that millions had suffered—or still could suffer—and signaled a pervasive psychic trauma.

A few stories in the horror comics dealt directly with the effects of atomic radiation on the human form. In school, American children heard they could "duck and cover" to survive a nuclear attack unscathed. Horror comics told them the truth, or at least a surreal version of it. A 1952 story from *Mystery Tales* showed what nuclear warfare could really do to their bodies: in a city that suffers a "RED-LAUNCHED SURPRISE ATTACK," the main character instantly becomes "A GROTESQUE THING WITH BLISTERED FLESH FALLING AWAY FROM CHARRED BONES."[15] Other stories suggested that even the survivors would see their bodies disfigured. "Day of Doom," from a 1954 issue of *Weird Terror,* shows giant mutants with various deformities: one has a bald, skull-like head, complete

Atomic anxiety in the comics. Ed Winiarski, "The Traitor!" *Mystery Tales,* December 1952, 4. Copyright © 2008 Marvel Characters, Inc. Used with permission.

Bodies deformed by radiation. Bill Discount, "Day of Doom," *Weird Terror,* May 1954, 7. Copyright © 1954 Allen Hardy Associates, Inc. Reprinted with permission.

with dark eye sockets, while another has two heads. (Curiously, the survivors all have washboard abs, like comic book superheroes.) "UNDER RADIOACTIVITY," says one of the mutants, "STRANGE THINGS HAPPENED TO US PHYSICALLY."[16]

Like most other forms of popular culture in the 1950s, horror comics avoided the subject of the Holocaust. Still, evidence suggests that their editors and publishers—many of whom were Jewish—had been keenly affected. In

A real-life nightmare. Wallace Wood, "Desert Fox!"*Frontline Combat,* November–December 1951, 5. Copyright © William M. Gaines, Agent, Inc. Reprinted with permission.

the case of EC, the evidence can be found in non-horror titles like *Frontline Combat* and *Impact*. A story about Erwin Rommel, published in a 1951 issue of *Frontline Combat,* keeps switching between scenes of his military prowess and scenes of Nazi atrocities:

> MEANWHILE, IN THE GERMAN CONCENTRATION CAMPS, CORPSES PILED UP LIKE SO MUCH GARBAGE! *MIND YOU! THESE WERE PEOPLE! TAKE A CLOSE LOOK AT THIS PILE OF PEOPLE!*[17]

The first issue of *Impact,* an EC suspense title, devoted an entire story to the Holocaust. The viewpoint character in "Master Race" is the former commandant of Bergen-Belsen, now hiding in Manhattan in 1955. Encountering a former prisoner on the subway, he flashes back to his days in the camp:

> DO YOU REMEMBER, CARL? DO YOU REMEMBER THE AWFUL SMELL OF THE GAS CHAMBERS THAT HOURLY ANNIHILATED HUNDREDS AND HUNDREDS OF YOUR COUNTRYMEN? . . .
> DO YOU REMEMBER THE STINKING ODOR OF HUMAN FLESH BURNING IN THE OVENS . . . MEN'S . . . WOMEN'S . . . CHILDREN'S . . . PEOPLE YOU ONCE KNEW AND TALKED TO AND DRANK BEER WITH? . . . [18]

As such monstrosities shaped the sensibility of the comics, so they made a deep, lasting impression on O'Connor at the very beginning of her literary career. She was only twenty in the spring of 1945, when, like most Americans,

Flashing back to the Holocaust. Bernie Krigstein, "Master Race," *Impact,* March–April 1955, 4. Copyright © William M. Gaines, Agent, Inc. Reprinted with permission.

she first learned about the Nazi death camps; in the late summer, shortly before entering the Writers' Workshop at the State University of Iowa, she learned about Hiroshima and Nagasaki. In one of her lectures, nearly two decades later, O'Connor stated flatly that her writing had been informed by the bombing of Japan. "So far as I am concerned as a novelist," she said, "a bomb on Hiroshima affects my judgment of life in rural Georgia . . ." (*MM* 134). Privately, O'Connor suggested that the A-bomb and the Holocaust not only affected her judgment, but also invaded her subconscious. In a 1961 letter, she wrote that "I dream of radiated bulls and peacocks and swans" (*HB* 449). In a 1963 letter, she observed that "I've always been haunted by the boxcars" (*HB* 539).

The image of the boxcar appears in one of her last stories, "Revelation," when Mrs. Turpin dreams that all the classes of people are "crammed in together in a box car, being ridden off to be put in a gas oven" (*CW* 636). The memory of the ovens in the death camps underlies O'Connor's various references to people burning—including the stranger's remark in *The Violent Bear It Away* about people who "get burned up . . . one way or another" (*CW* 352) and the movie poster in *Wise Blood* showing "a monster stuffing a young woman into an incinerator" (*CW* 78).

The most significant reference to the Holocaust appears in "The Displaced Person." Mrs. Shortley's vision of jumbled body parts has its source in film footage of a German concentration camp:

> Mrs. Shortley recalled a newsreel she had seen once of a small room piled high with bodies of dead naked people all in a heap, their arms and legs tangled together, a head thrust in here, a head there, a foot, a knee, a part that should have been covered up sticking out, a hand raised clutching nothing. (*CW* 287)

O'Connor was undoubtedly recalling a newsreel that she herself had seen in 1945—a newsreel she identifies as the March of Time, produced by Time, Inc. "Before you could realize that it was real and take it into your head," she writes, "the picture changed and a hollow-sounding voice was saying, 'Time marches on!'" (*CW* 287). In this passage, O'Connor conveys a sense of the magnitude, the incomprehensibility, of the Holocaust. How, exactly, could you "take it into your head" and make sense of it? The newsreel provided the images but not the means by which to understand them.

O'Connor would not have seen a newsreel of the Japanese who were killed or maimed by the atomic bombs, as the U.S. government kept such footage from the public.[19] A year after the bombings, however, she and other Americans could learn about the physical effects of nuclear war by reading John Hersey's *Hiroshima*. First published in *The New Yorker* in August 1946, *Hiroshima* contained harrowing descriptions of the dead and mutilated, such as the woman whose skin came off her hand "in huge, glove-like pieces" (60). The most horrific description was that of a group of soldiers: "Their mouths were mere swollen, pus-covered wounds, which they could not bear to stretch enough to admit the spout of the teapot." They must have looked directly toward the blast, Hersey speculated, since "their faces were wholly burned, their eyesockets were hollow, the fluid from their melted eyes had run down their cheeks" (68). One can scarcely imagine a grimmer example of the injury-to-the-eye motif.[20]

With images like this entering the national consciousness, the old icons of the horror genre didn't seem all that scary anymore. As Dwight Macdonald wrote in September 1945, the atomic bomb was far more terrifying: "How human, intimate, friendly by comparison are ghosts, witches, spells, werewolves and poltergeists!" (265). By the end of the decade, Hollywood was spoofing Dracula, Frankenstein's monster, and the Wolfman—having them cavort with Abbott and Costello. King Kong had been domesticated, reduced, and renamed as Mighty Joe Young, the lovable, often comical ape that inspired Lonnie the baboon in *Wise Blood* (*CW* 79). At the same time, the movie studios had yet to provide any new horrors for postwar audiences. The first of the atomic-age monsters—all those giants awakened by nuclear testing—would not appear until 1953, when *The Beast from 20,000 Fathoms* wreaked havoc on New York City.

To fill this void in the horror genre, the horror comics relied on one figure more than any other: the zombie. Hardly an issue appeared without a story about a corpse returning to life and walking the earth again. The zombie was especially popular as a subject for cover art—a key factor in newsstand sales. *The Vault of Horror*, for instance, featured the living dead on more than a third of its covers.

The living dead, of course, were not entirely new. They had appeared in a handful of films before 1950, such as *White Zombie* from 1932 and *I Walked with a Zombie* from 1943. But the zombies in horror comics differed in significant ways from their cinematic predecessors. In the movies, a voodoo priest or some kind of scientist would revive the dead, usually to do his bidding. In the comics, zombies were autonomous, uncontrollable. With a few exceptions, they rose on their own, for reasons of their own.[21] Occasionally, they came back for love—to rescue a wife in peril or to reunite with a grieving girlfriend.[22] In the vast majority of cases, though, they came back for revenge—to kill their killers. And unlike their Hollywood counterparts, who resembled sleepwalkers

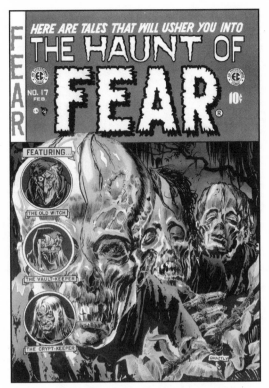

The new breed of zombie. Graham Ingels, *Haunt of Fear,* January–February 1953. Copyright © William M. Gaines, Agent, Inc. Reprinted with permission.

more than corpses, the comic book zombies *looked* dead. They bore the marks of whatever violence they had suffered—like a meat cleaver to the forehead—and their flesh was quite obviously rotting away, revealing the bones below. The text would reinforce the disgusting visuals, noting the sickening stench of decay, the presence of maggots, and the chunks of skin that fell off as the figure stumbled forward. A description from 1951 is typical:

THE CLOTHING HUNG IN SHREDS FROM ITS MAGGOT-COVERED LIMBS! RALPH
CLAWED AT ITS FACE AND PIECES OF DEAD, FOUL-SMELLING FLESH CAME OFF
IN HIS HANDS . . . [23]

Here, now, was something truly horrific—something commensurate, in the popular imagination, with piles of bodies or men with melted eyes.

Being courted by a corpse. Graham Ingels, "Reunion!" *Vault of Horror,* June–July 1951, 7. Copyright © William M. Gaines, Agent, Inc. Reprinted with permission.

Though more restrained in her descriptions, O'Connor used elements of the zombie motif as reimagined by the comics. With a skull whose outline is "plain and insistent" under his skin (*CW* 3)—and a pair of empty eye sockets, following his blinding—Hazel could easily pass for the new breed of zombie. At one point, in fact, he specifically enacts the role of the zombie driven by love. When he sits on the porch with Mrs. Flood, anyone walking by "would think she was being courted by a corpse" (*CW* 122). In "Judgment Day," on the other hand, O'Connor alludes to the vengeful zombie. During a fight, Tanner's eyes are trained on his daughter "like the eyes of an angry corpse" (*CW* 678).

As she does with Hazel and Tanner, O'Connor describes other characters as if they existed, like zombies, somewhere between life and death. Mr. Shortley, with his "corpse-like composure," seems more dead than alive. Folding his arms on his "bony chest," he actually pretends to be a corpse. "I'm a dead man," he says concisely (*CW* 297). The late Judge, meanwhile, seems alive and alert. Mrs. McIntyre has "a superstitious fear of annoying the Judge in his grave," O'Connor writes. "Of her three husbands, the Judge was the one most present to her although he was the only one she had buried" (*CW* 309). Similarly, the dead old man in *The Violent Bear It Away* remains eerily present to his great-nephew. Sitting across the table from the corpse, Tarwater feels "as if he were in

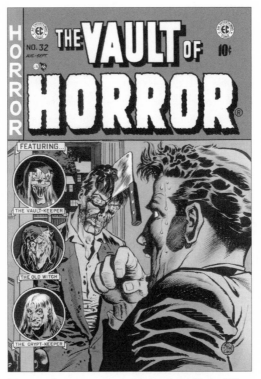

The eyes of an angry corpse. Johnny Craig, *Vault of Horror,* August–September 1953. Copyright © William M. Gaines, Agent, Inc. Reprinted with permission.

the presence of a new personality." Until he buries the body, Tarwater believes, the old man won't be "thoroughly dead" (*CW* 336).

Escaping the grave, as a zombie would, is a fantasy shared by Tanner and Hazel. Tanner dreams about thrusting open the lid of his coffin and springing up (*CW* 691–92). Hazel remembers seeing his grandfather in a coffin and thinking, "he ain't going to let them shut it on him; when the time comes, his elbow is going to shoot into the crack" (*CW* 9). He remembers his mother in her coffin, looking "as if she were going to spring up and shove the lid back" (*CW* 14).

Escaping the grave remains a fantasy, of course. O'Connor writes of Hazel's grandfather: "When it was time to bury him, they shut the top of his box down and he didn't make a move" (*CW* 10). The same holds true for Hazel's mother, his brothers, and his father: the coffin lid shuts on all of them. Their failure to rise from the dead is the driving force in *Wise Blood,* starting Hazel on the path to atheism. For Hazel, faith hinges on the resurrection of the body. In this respect, he is very much like The Misfit, who reduces all human action to the question of whether Jesus raised the dead:

> If He did what He said, then it's nothing for you to do but thow away everything and follow Him, and if He didn't, then it's nothing for you to do but enjoy the few minutes you got left the best way you can—by killing somebody or burning down his house or doing some other meanness to him. (*CW* 152)

O'Connor, too, viewed humanity in the light of bodily resurrection. "I am always astonished at the emphasis the Church puts on the body," she wrote in a 1955 letter. "It is not the soul she says that will rise but the body, glorified" (*HB* 100). In another letter, later that year, she affirmed her belief "that our resurrected bodies will be intact as to personality, that is, intact with all the contradictions beautiful to you . . ." (*HB* 124).

On this point, she and the horror comics parted company. In the comics, the bodies that rose were anything but glorified. Their features gone, their skin in tatters, the dead were no longer recognizable as their former selves. They were stripped of their personalities, their unique identities. And it wasn't Jesus raising the dead. It was simply the desire for revenge, for brutal retribution, in the absence of divine justice. Victory over the grave meant one more round of violence, an eye for an eye—not redemption. In effect, the living dead represented a parody of Christian resurrection.

For all their emphasis on the supernatural, horror comics were not exactly congenial to religion. The stories of postmortem revenge displayed a straightforward morality—the killer always got his comeuppance—but other stories depicted a world of moral chaos. In this world, the innocent suffered just as much as the guilty—and, often, just as horribly. People could perish for satisfying a need as basic as hunger: in one story, a man looking for a midnight snack ends up with a tap in his jugular vein at a restaurant catering to vampires; in another, two castaways on a desert island discover that the fruit they've been eating, the only food they've been able to find, will rot their skin and eventually dissolve their bodies.[24] To paraphrase The Misfit, it's hard to make the characters' actions fit their punishment (*CW* 151).

A story from *The Haunt of Fear*, published in 1953, takes this disjunction to an absurd, Kafkaesque extreme. A loving husband and father, arriving at his office as usual, is drugged and abducted by a mad scientist, who transplants his

FOR A LONG MOMENT, GLORIA STARES AT YOU... STARES INTO YOUR BEADY EYES! A FLICKER OF RECOGNITION SEEMS TO BRIGHTEN HER PALE AND DRAWN FACE! BUT SUDDENLY, IT IS GONE! SHE TURNS AWAY! YOU CLUTCH THE BARS OF YOUR CAGE, DRAW YOUR BLACK LIPS BACK REVEALING YOUR CRUEL YELLOWED FANGS, AND YOU SHRIEK...

GEEEAAAAAAGGH!

IT IS A SHRIEK OF UTTER RESIGNATION, PHILIP STOKER! A SHRIEK OF SURRENDER! THE BODY HAS WON! YOU ARE A GORILLA...

Another Enoch Emery. George Evans, "Gorilla My Dreams!" *Haunt of Fear,* January–February 1953, 7. Copyright © William M. Gaines, Agent, Inc. Reprinted with permission.

brain into the body of a gorilla. He escapes, but everyone assumes he was killed by the animal. He winds up in a circus cage, with his children screaming at him, "*WE HATE YOU!*" "*HATE YOU! HATE YOU!*" Finally, like Enoch Emery in *Wise Blood,* the man loses himself forever in the figure of an ape: "THE BODY HAS WON! YOU ARE A GORILLA . . ."[25] At the point where the classic horror films would restore order—destroying Dracula or Frankenstein's creature—the comic book simply abandons the man to his meaningless fate.

A dark nihilism runs through the horror comics, negating any kind of transcendent moral value. Love and loyalty, bravery and self-sacrifice—all come to nothing. A woman trying desperately to save her brother becomes his victim when she finds out he craves human flesh. A woman intent on proving that her neighbor chopped up his wife—her best friend—discovers that her husband has the same plans for her. A man gives his life to help his brother capture the vampire who killed their father, only to realize that his brother *is* the vampire.[26] As stories like these illustrate, the bonds of family have no more meaning than anything else.

Indeed, the horror comics were most clearly nihilistic in their portrayal of the American family. While mainstream popular culture idealized the nuclear family, horror comics featured cheating wives, abusive husbands, and even some

A typical family meal. Johnny Craig, "Sink-Hole!" *Vault of Horror*, April–May 1951, 5. Copyright © William M. Gaines, Agent, Inc. Reprinted with permission.

homicidal children. People married under false pretenses—for money, for cheap labor, or, as a vampire tells his shocked wife on their wedding night, for a blood supply.[27] Motivated by greed or hatred, family members seemed willing to kill each other at the drop of a hat. In *Seduction of the Innocent,* Wertham complained that the comics lacked images of "ordinary home life," like "a normal family sitting down at a meal" (236). More often than not, a family meal would end with the wife using a skillet to kill her husband.[28] Symbols of domesticity would frequently be associated with savage violence. In a 1953 story from *The Haunt of Fear,* a woman chops her husband into pieces, which she cooks on his outdoor barbecue grill—that status symbol of postwar suburbia.[29] Ultimately, the home became a slaughterhouse; the body, nothing more than meat.

Horror comics died out after 1954, thanks largely to Wertham, but their influence on American popular culture would prove enormous in the decades to follow, as their readers came of age and started creating their own works of horror. George A. Romero, for instance, has credited the EC horror line as an inspiration for *Night of the Living Dead,* released in 1968. The key elements are all there in his landmark film: relentless zombies, explicit violence, disfigured and mutilated bodies. The film, like the comics, is darkly nihilistic; love and courage and family ties count for nothing, and the human body loses any sacred significance. According to a doctor interviewed on television, the zombies are

The body as meat. Jack Davis, "Garden Party!" *Haunt of Fear,* January–February 1953, 7. Copyright © William M. Gaines, Agent, Inc. Reprinted with permission.

"just dead flesh." Driven by hunger—not revenge—the dead eat the living. Once again, the body is nothing but meat.

The nihilism of the comics was not surprising, considering the religious and moral implications of Auschwitz and Dachau, Hiroshima and Nagasaki. With the six million bodies it left behind, the Holocaust raised serious, perhaps overwhelming doubts about a just and loving God. "After Auschwitz," wrote theologian Richard L. Rubenstein, "many Jews did not need Nietzsche to tell them that the old God of Jewish patriarchal monotheism was dead beyond all hope of resurrection" (227). For many leading Catholics, the U.S. bombings of Japan seemed to negate everything that Christians believed.[30] In September 1945, the editor of *The Catholic World* attacked the bombings as "the most powerful blow ever delivered against Christian civilization. . . ." James Martin Gillis blamed moral relativism, or what he called "ethical anarchy," for the willingness to drop the A-bomb: "If that kind of 'ethics' prevails, our Christian civilization will dissolve in a gas like the bodies of the 100,000 or 300,000 victims of the first atomic bombing. Nothing remains but nihilism" (278–79).

A decade later, O'Connor would use similar language, referring to nihilism as "the gas you breathe" in the modern world. As a Catholic, O'Connor felt compelled to fight nihilism, calling this fight a "necessity" (*HB* 97). She was just as subversive as the creators of horror comics—just as violent in her imagery, sardonic in her humor, and critical in her treatment of the American family—but her aim was revelation rather than revulsion. "With the serious writer," she maintained, "violence is never an end in itself. It is the extreme situation that best reveals what we are essentially . . ." (*MM* 113). This faith in an essential nature shaped her response to the horrors of the Holocaust and the atom bomb. For O'Connor, even a deformed body carried sacred significance. "A Temple of the Holy Ghost" makes this point by having the freak proclaim, "God done this to me and I praise Him" (*CW* 207).

Nevertheless, O'Connor recognized the reasons her contemporaries had for "believing in nothing," as Manley Pointer would say (*CW* 283). Defending the sacredness of the body, in her introduction to *A Memoir of Mary Ann,* she recalled "the fumes of the gas chamber." While rejecting "the massacre of the innocents" as a reason to reject Christ's divinity (*CW* 830–31), she couldn't ignore the mass deaths of recent history—the real-world atrocities behind the comic book variety. By incorporating the zombie and other horror motifs, by adapting the "large and startling figures" of the horror genre (*CW* 806), she gave the devil his due.

Notes

1. The fact that "Cyclops" refers to a creature with one eye suggests that O'Connor had this film specifically in mind.

2. Hajdu argues that comic books were instrumental in creating "the postwar sensibility" that is commonly attributed to rock and roll: a "raucous and cynical" sensibility, "inured to violence and absorbed with sex, skeptical of authority, and frozen in young adulthood . . ." (7).

3. For its first three issues, *Tales from the Crypt* was called *The Crypt of Terror.*

4. Comic books rarely gave story credits to individual writers. The editor of a particular comic would often write the copy, as Al Feldstein did for the three horror titles published by EC. That being the case, my notes identify the artists (including Feldstein) who illustrated the stories. In this instance, see Johnny Craig, "The Wall," *Haunt of Fear,* May–June 1950, and Graham Ingels, "Thump Fun!" *Haunt of Fear,* July–Aug. 1953. Each story has separate page numbers.

5. Al Feldstein, "Terror Train," *Vault of Horror,* Apr.–May 1950.

6. See Jack Kamen, "How Green Was My Alley," *Tales from the Crypt,* June–July 1953, as well as the cover art for *Mysterious Adventures,* Aug. 1953 (cited in Benton 160).

7. Jack Davis, "Foul Play!" *Haunt of Fear,* May–June 1953.

8. Graham Ingels, "Squash . . . Anyone?" *Tales from the Crypt,* Oct.–Nov. 1952; Jack Davis, "Graft in Concrete," *Vault of Horror,* Aug.–Sept. 1952; Bernie Krigstein, "Numbskull," *Haunt of Fear,* Nov.–Dec. 1954; Bernie Krigstein, "The Bath," *Tales from the Crypt,* June–July 1954; Graham Ingels, "Dying to Lose Weight!" *Vault of Horror,* Apr.–May 1951; George Evans, "Roped In!" *Tales from the Crypt,* Oct.–Nov. 1952; Hy Rosen, "The Tarantula!" *Adventures into Terror,* Jan. 1953; Jack Davis, "Cheese, That's Horrible!" *Haunt of Fear,* Mar.–Apr. 1951; "The Murder Pool," *Strange Fantasy,* Aug.–Sept. 1954; Jack Davis, "The Jellyfish!" *Vault of Horror,* June–July 1951; and Jack Davis, "The Chips Are Down!" *Vault of Horror,* Dec. 1952–Jan. 1953. (Thanks to Angie Meyer for helping me locate some of these titles.)

9. Graham Ingels, "Horror We? How's Bayou?" *Haunt of Fear,* Jan.–Feb. 1953.

10. Jack Davis, "Bum Steer!" *Haunt of Fear,* Nov.–Dec. 1951.

11. Wertham illustrated this motif with a panel showing a man about to jab a hypodermic needle into a woman's eyeball. Wertham didn't identify the original story, which was actually a cautionary tale against drug abuse. See Jack Cole, "Murder, Morphine, and Me," *True Crime Comics,* May 1947.

12. Wallace Wood, "Horror in the Freak Tent!" *Haunt of Fear,* Jan.–Feb. 1951, and Jack Kamen, "How Green Was My Alley," *Tales from the Crypt,* June–July 1953.

13. Despite the humorous context, the last image is definitely horror related, resembling a 1953 cover that shows a monster stealing both legs from its victim. See Sol Brodsky, *Uncanny Tales,* Nov. 1953. For a comprehensive guide to *Uncanny Tales* and other titles published by Atlas, see the *Atlas Tales* website.

14. In a 1980 *Heavy Metal* interview, Stephen King made the same connection between horror comics, the Holocaust, and the bombings of Hiroshima and Nagasaki (Michlig).

15. Ed Winiarski, "The Traitor!" *Mystery Tales,* Dec. 1952, 4. For a particularly gruesome expression of radiation anxiety, see the June 1954 issue of *Black Cat Mystery.* The cover art by Lee Elias shows a man's face and hands decomposing from exposure to radium.

16. Bill Discount, "Day of Doom," *Weird Terror,* May 1954, 7.

17. The text is by Harvey Kurtzman; the art, by Wallace Wood. See "Desert Fox!" *Frontline Combat,* Nov.–Dec. 1951, 5.

18. The text is by Al Feldstein; the art, by Bernie Krigstein. See "Master Race," *Impact,* Mar.–Apr. 1955, 4.

19. For details about the suppression of film shot in Hiroshima and Nagasaki, see Mitchell.

20. Over a decade later, the connection between the atomic bomb and empty eye sockets would find its way into American movies. *The Amazing Colossal Man* and its sequel, *War of the Colossal Beast,* featured a soldier who ventures too close to a nuclear test, grows to a height of sixty feet, and goes on a rampage before losing an eye to a bazooka blast.

21. Some stories showed Haitian natives using voodoo to reanimate the dead. See Johnny Craig, "Voodoo Death!" *Tales from the Crypt,* Apr.–May 1951, and Johnny Craig, "Till Death . . . ," *Vault of Horror,* Dec. 1952–Jan. 1953.

22. Al Feldstein, "The Thing from the Grave!" *Tales from the Crypt,* Feb.–Mar. 1951, and Graham Ingels, "Reunion!" *Vault of Horror,* June–July 1951.

23. Wallace Wood, "Scared to Death!" *Tales from the Crypt,* June–July 1951, 7.

24. Joe Orlando, "Midnight Mess!" *Tales from the Crypt,* Apr.–May 1953, and Joe Orlando, "Forbidden Fruit," *Haunt of Fear,* Sept.–Oct. 1951. For more on the mixture of "rigid moralism" and "outright nihilism" in the horror comics, see Skal 231–32.

25. George Evans, "Gorilla My Dreams!" *Haunt of Fear,* Jan.–Feb. 1953.

26. Jack Kamen, "The Tunnel of Terror!" *Haunt of Fear,* Nov.–Dec. 1950; George Evans, "Curiosity Killed . . . ," *Tales from the Crypt,* June–July 1953; and Graham Ingels, "Sucker Bait!" *Haunt of Fear,* May–June 1953.

27. Reed Crandall, "Bloody Sure," *Haunt of Fear,* July–Aug. 1953.

28. Johnny Craig, "Sink-Hole!" *Vault of Horror,* Apr.–May 1951.

29. Jack Davis, "Garden Party!" *Haunt of Fear,* Jan.–Feb. 1953.

30. According to Boyer, Catholic leaders were among the most vehement critics of the bombings (245).

Works Cited

Adventures into Terror. New York: Atlas, Jan. 1953.

The Amazing Colossal Man. Dir. Bert I. Gordon. American International, 1957.

Atlas Tales. http://www.atlastales.com/.

The Beast from 20,000 Fathoms. Dir. Eugene Lourie. Warner Brothers, 1953.

Benton, Mike. *The Comic Book in America: An Illustrated History.* Dallas: Taylor, 1989.

Bird, Kai, and Lawrence Lifschultz, eds. *Hiroshima's Shadow: Writings on the Denial of History and the Smithsonian Controversy.* Stony Creek: Pamphleteer's, 1998.

Black Cat Mystery. New York: Harvey, June 1954.

Boyer, Paul. "'Victory for What?'—The Voice of the Minority." Bird and Lifschultz 239–52.

"Briefly Noted." Rev. of *A Good Man Is Hard to Find,* by Flannery O'Connor. *New Yorker,* 18 June 1955, 93.

Bud Abbott and Lou Costello Meet Frankenstein. Dir. Charles Barton. Universal-International, 1948.

Dr. Cyclops. Dir. Ernest B. Schoedsack. Paramount, 1940.

Duck and Cover. Dir. Anthony Rizzo. Archer, 1951.

Frontline Combat. New York: EC, Nov.–Dec. 1951.

Gillis, James Martin. "Nothing but Nihilism." Bird and Lifschultz 278–80.

Hajdu, David. *The Ten-Cent Plague: The Great Comic-Book Scare and How It Changed America.* New York: Farrar, 2008.

Haunt of Fear Annual. 6 vols. West Plains, MO: Gemstone, 1994–99.

Hersey, John. *Hiroshima.* New York: Knopf, 1946.

I Walked with a Zombie. Dir. Jacques Tourneur. RKO, 1943.

Impact. New York: EC, Mar.–Apr. 1955.

King Kong. Dir. Merian C. Cooper and Ernest B. Schoedsack. RKO, 1933.

Macdonald, Dwight. "The Decline to Barbarism." Bird and Lifschultz 263–68.

Michlig, John. "Gasp! William Gaines and the Legend of EC Comics." *John Michlig's Pop Culture Gill Net.* 2008. http://www.fullyarticulated.com/EC.html.

Mighty Joe Young. Dir. Ernest B. Schoedsack. RKO, 1949.

Mitchell, Greg. "Hiroshima Film Cover-up Exposed." *Global Security Institute,* 6 Aug. 2005. http://www.gsinstitute.org/archives/000288.shtml.

Mystery Tales. New York: Atlas, Dec. 1952.

Night of the Living Dead. Dir. George A. Romero. Walter Reade, 1968.

O'Connor, Flannery. *Collected Works.* New York: Library of America, 1988.

———. *The Habit of Being.* Ed. Sally Fitzgerald. New York: Farrar, 1979.

———. *Mystery and Manners.* Ed. Sally Fitzgerald and Robert Fitzgerald. New York: Farrar, 1969.

Poe, Edgar Allan. "The Black Cat." 1843. *The Unabridged Edgar Allan Poe.* Ed. Tam Mossman. Philadelphia: Running, 1983. 837–45.

Romero, George A. Interview. *Tales from the Crypt: From Comic Books to Television!* Dir. Chip Selby. CS Films, 2004.

Rubenstein, Richard L. *After Auschwitz: Radical Theology and Contemporary Judaism.* Indianapolis: Bobbs, 1966.

Skal, David J. *The Monster Show: A Cultural History of Horror.* New York: Penguin, 1994.

Strange Fantasy. New York: Ajax-Farrell, Aug.–Sept. 1954.

Tales from the Crypt Annual. 6 vols. West Plains, MO: Gemstone, 1994–99.

True Crime Comics. New York: Magazine Village, May 1947.

Uncanny Tales, New York: Atlas, Nov. 1953.

Vault of Horror Annual. 6 vols. West Plains, MO: Gemstone, 1994–99.

War of the Colossal Beast. Dir. Bert I. Gordon. American International, 1958.

Weird Terror. New York: Allen Hardy, May 1954.

Wertham, Fredric. *Seduction of the Innocent.* New York: Rinehart, 1954.

White Zombie. Dir. Victor Halperin. United Artists, 1932.

ALL THE DEAD BODIES: O'CONNOR AND NOIR

William Brevda

> Whoever would kill most thoroughly, *laughs*.
>
> —Nietzsche, *Thus Spoke Zarathustra*

In her prepared remarks before reading from her notorious psycho-killer story "A Good Man Is Hard to Find," Flannery O'Connor warned her audience to "be on the lookout for such things as the action of grace in the Grandmother's soul, and not for the dead bodies" (*MM* 113). Perhaps O'Connor worried that people would associate her fiction with the school of dead bodies known as noir. After all, every time she read from "A Good Man Is Hard to Find," O'Connor found herself in the extreme situation of a Jim Thompson novel: the good Catholic writer reveals "the killer inside me."

In exploring the relationship between Flannery O'Connor and noir writers, we can presume that despite the dead bodies, these writers all shed "wise blood." I am particularly interested in the affinities between O'Connor and two crime novelists who shared her style of violent comedy and black humor: James Ross and Jim Thompson. O'Connor admired Ross's 1940 country noir novel *They Don't Dance Much* (*HB* 8) and probably learned a few things about how "the Comic and the Terrible . . . may be opposite sides of the same coin" from reading it (*HB* 105). I don't know if O'Connor ever read Jim Thompson, but in some ways they were opposite sides of the same coin, much like O'Connor and her own terrible Misfit. If both writers had a "penchant for writing about freaks," then, as O'Connor says, "it is because we are still able to recognize one" (*MM* 44). Although O'Connor's comedy issues from religious belief and Thompson's from disbelief, both writers depict their freaks against a "conception of the whole man" that is "theological" (*MM* 44).

O'Connor met James Ross at Yaddo and was so taken by his novel that she recommended him to her agent, Elizabeth McKee, in a 28 January 1949 letter: "James Ross, a writer who is here, is looking for an agent. He wrote a very fine book called, *They Don't Dance Much*. It didn't sell much. If you are interested in him, I daresay he would be glad to hear from you" (*HB* 8). O'Connor was probably one of the few people to have read *They Don't Dance Much* before it was reprinted in the Lost American Fiction series thirty-five years after its original publication.

Tony Hilfer describes *They Don't Dance Much* as "a type of crime novel where the setting is effectually a kind of Hell" (46). Narrated in a dead-pan voice by Jack MacDonald, who has lost his land for not paying taxes, the central character in Jack's story is a rogue named Smut Milligan. Smut operates a combination filling station and general store where liquor is sold and gambling goes on just outside the city limits of Corinth. When Jack stops by for a pint, Smut offers him a job in the roadhouse he plans to open. The roadhouse will include a dance hall with a nickelodeon, a back room for gambling, a filling station, and six tourist cabins that can be rented by the hour. To advertise the opening of the roadhouse, Smut puts up a big sign over the highway that reads:

BIG FORMAL OPENING, OCT. 28

RIVER BEND ROADHOUSE

DINE AND DANCE

FRESH PIT BARBECUE

· CHICKEN DINNERS

EVERYBODY WELCOME. (57)

Smut Milligan's roadhouse foreshadows O'Connor's conception of The Tower in "A Good Man Is Hard to Find" as a "filling station and dance hall set in a clearing outside of Timothy" where the ill-fated family stops for barbecue (*CS* 120). Like Ross, O'Connor typographically reproduces the sign that the enterprising Red Sammy Butts puts up along the highway: "TRY RED SAMMY'S FAMOUS BARBECUE. NONE LIKE FAMOUS RED SAMMY'S! RED SAM! THE FAT BOY WITH THE HAPPY LAUGH! A VETERAN! RED SAMMY'S YOUR MAN!" (*CS* 121).

Like Smut's roadhouse, The Tower contains a space for dancing and a nickelodeon. I doubt there were many joints like this that O'Connor spent time in outside of the one in Ross's novel. O'Connor might also have modeled the roadhouse in "A View of the Woods" on Smut Milligan's River Bend Roadhouse. In this story, old Mr. Fortune sells his property with a view of the woods to Tilman, who runs "a combination country store, filling station, scrap-metal dump, used-car lot and dance hall" (*CS* 345). Tilman has set up highway signs, the final one reading "'Here it is, Friends, TILMAN's! in dazzling red letters'" (*CS* 345). The dance hall is divided into "Colored and White" sections, "each with its private nickelodeon," and Tilman, like Smut, sells barbecue sandwiches (*CS* 345).

Jack's descriptions of what the clientele play on the nickelodeon at Smut's roadhouse are a rich source of the kind of ironic humor that O'Connor would have appreciated and remembered. Baxter Yance likes to get drunk listening to "Nearer My God to Thee." When Jack tells Smut that people thinks it's strange to hear a hymn on a nickelodeon, Smut replies that "if the customer didn't like 'Nearer My God to Thee' they could go to hell" (185). When Old Man Joshua gets drunk, he likes to listen to Billie Holiday's "Strange Fruit." Sometimes he even cries. "It was just when he was pretty full that he was like that," explains Jack. "When he was sober he'd as soon lynch a nigger as to blow his nose" (185).

Smut employs a roadhouse gallery of grotesques that anticipate O'Connor but without the allegorical implications. There's Catfish Wall, who makes the liquor at his still, and the bartender Badeye Honeycutt, who has a glass eye that he sometimes puts in his pocket. One customer, Old Man Joshua Lingerfelt, has a wooden leg. Smut Milligan himself shares some of the characteristics of The Misfit. As tough as he is, Smut is anything but stupid. On one occasion, he compares the local corrupt politician who covets his roadhouse to "King Ahab wanting a vineyard that belonged to a one-horse farmer named Naboth. In the long run Naboth got the works and Ahab got the vineyard" (100). When Jack says, "I didn't know you were acquainted with the Bible," Smut replies: "Old Lady Milligan used to read me a chapter every night, just before she whaled the tar out of me" (100). Smut even has a few principles: "I don't rent cabins to pimps and their whores," he explains. "If I'd made any money off whores, I couldn't hold up my head in hell" (273).

Like The Misfit, Smut Milligan is a man of incongruities. With a note coming due at the bank that he can't meet, Smut decides he will rob Bert Ford, who is rumored to have buried thirty thousand dollars on his property. The scene of the robbery is terrible in its violence and shocking in a novel that is also quite funny. When Bert denies he has buried money, Smut beats and tortures him. "What you got against me?" Bert asks. "I ain't got a thing in the world against you, but I want your money," Smut replies (113). "The smell of him burning made me a little sick," says Jack, in his flat sardonic voice. "I reckon that was what fixed Bert too" (113). Later in the novel, after Smut frames Dick Pittman for the crime, Jack asks, "What have you got against Dick?" and Smut repeats the same chilling line: "I ain't got a thing in the world against him. He's a dope, but I like him. I just rather it would be him than me" (234).

A good man is hard to find in Ross's better-him-than-me world. Everyone is corrupt. By the end of the novel, Smut Milligan has been murdered, and the most hypocritical and undeserving characters have inherited the earth, or Corinth's microcosmic corner of it.

The novel's most dreadful character is the undertaker, Leroy Smathers. Smathers and the other members of his Snopes-like family run the Smathers Furniture & Undertaking Company and the Smathers Finance Company. "I dreaded him worse than anybody else in Corinth," says Jack of Leroy Smathers: "He could take a fellow that had been cut all to pieces in a knife fight, or had his head busted open in a bad wreck, or had a stick of dynamite explode under him, and make him look better dead than he'd ever looked living. When he wasn't working on dead folks Leroy was the bill collector" (7).

Jack's existential dread of the undertaker is the only strong feeling that shows through his otherwise zero-at-the-bone narrative voice. O'Connor took stock of how James Ross combines the sickness unto death and gallows humor to create a literary style that can be likened to a sick joke. Her own Misfit, a former undertaker, takes pleasure in this kind of humor. When the grandmother offers to give him all the money she has for not shooting her, The Misfit replies: "Lady, . . . there never was a body that gave the undertaker a tip" (*CS* 132). The Misfit drives "a big black hearse-like automobile," a sick joke of a car (*CS* 126). Ross's novel ends with images of the Smathers' hearse and the burial of Smut Milligan that no mourners attend. "I reckon it was sort of private too," someone says. "It was private beyond the shadow of a doubt," thinks Jack (296). O'Connor's story ends with the slaughter of the grandmother and her family. "*[T]hrow* her where you *thrown* the others," says The Misfit, turning his signature line that Jesus "*thrown* everything off balance," into a throwaway one-liner (*CS* 133, 132, my emphasis). To complete the sick joke, the grandmother's murderer and undertaker turns into her minister when he replies to Bobby Lee with what amounts to a eulogy that also underlines the meaning of O'Connor's noir parable. As Ross's Jack Macdonald might sum up, when he wasn't killing folks The Misfit was the spiritual bill collector.

That O'Connor admired "Ross's rather dreadful book," as Tony Hilfer describes it, tells us a lot about her own noir sense of humor.[1] "Ross was studying the void," writes George V. Higgins in the afterword of the reissued *They Don't Dance Much* (301). As Hilfer observes, even the title *They Don't Dance Much* "is about what isn't there" (48). O'Connor was also studying the void when she wrote "A Good Man Is Hard to Find," and she also created a title that "is about what isn't there." Of course, there are differences between the Lazarus jokes in Ross's novel and the one in O'Connor's story about a killer's obsession with the story of Lazarus. The Misfit suffers from a form of despair that Kierkegaard called the "sickness unto death," a phrase he derived from the story of Lazarus in the gospel of John (11:4). The Misfit agonizes over not having been *there* when Jesus raised the dead, so he would know if it were true, repeating the word "there" five times. O'Connor agrees with Kierkegaard that when it comes to faith, there's no there there.

Whether or not Ross's anagogical setting is hell, his world is beyond redemption. A good man is *impossible* to find in *They Don't Dance Much*, and The Misfit's former motto, "No pleasure but meanness," best describes the novel's black humor (132). Whereas a good man or woman remains possible to find in O'Connor's sickness-unto-death joke if there's "somebody there to shoot her every minute of her life" (*CS* 133). Ross depicts a "setting in which the reader beholds nothing that is not there and the nothing that is" (Hilfer 47). O'Connor depicts a setting in which the reader beholds something that is not there and the something that is: grace.

As has often been noted, The Misfit sounds like an existentialist in some of his speeches (Asals 5). When O'Connor complained about a correspondent being "full up to her ears of the Existentialists" (*HB* 202), she was really describing the situation of any intellectual who had ears during the 1950s. However, the writers of noir tended to be atheist existentialists, whereas O'Connor was drawn to the religious existentialists. The Misfit identifies himself as one of those who "has to know why it is" (*CS* 129). The answer the secular existentialists gave to the question of "why?" was "why not?" and their answer explains why The Misfit kills. If God is dead, why not? One imagines O'Connor's shock of recognition when she read in *Fear and Trembling* that "only he who draws the knife gets Isaac" (38). "What they leave out of Abraham's history is dread," complains Kierkegaard (*Fear* 39), but O'Connor never left the dread out of her own histories of faith.

Noir is fear without the trembling. In Jim Thompson's *The Killer Inside Me* (1952), published the same year as *Wise Blood*, the narrator Lou Ford has a condition he calls "*the sickness.*" The words have been "italicized for those who read with their finger," quips R. V. Cassill, who disparages "*the sickness*" as "the dismal vocabulary of the paperback medium" (234). Maybe so, but it also the dismal vocabulary of Flannery O'Connor and Kierkegaard. Both Lou Ford and The Misfit suffer from that killer inside us all: the "sickness unto death." O'Connor agrees with Kierkegaard that only faith in God "cures" *the sickness.* What Thompson believes is more questionable. True, his narrators seem to have returned from the dead, like Lazarus, to tell their sick tales. But the killer joker inside Thompson seems more like a nihilist or a Nietzschean than the killer jester inside O'Connor, who is clearly a Christian.

Thompson was one of the noir masters of the cosmic joke at the center of things. His twist was to make the joke actually funny in a twisted sort of way. Thus he had a precursor in James Ross. O'Connor was also a master of the cosmic joke at the center of things, but it was the laughter of God rather than the laughter of the void that she listened to and wrote about. Yet O'Connor could be Thompson when she says that "everything funny I have written is more terrible than it is funny, or only funny because it is terrible, or only terrible because it is funny," and Thompson could be O'Connor when Deputy Lou Ford says: "Polite, intelligent: guys like that are my meat" (*HB* 105; *Killer* 4). Both writers bait their readers by creating a kind of story that, when paraphrased, seems as if it were "simply a low joke" (*MM* 99).

In *The Killer Inside Me,* Lou Ford pretends to be a "dull good natured guy," but it's just an act (92). Having discovered that "striking at people" by playing "a corny bore" is "almost as good as the other, the real way," Ford bores people to death with platitudes and clichés (4, 5). "I began needling people in that dead-pan way—needling them as a substitute for something else," says Ford (13). The "something else" is what Ford calls "*the sickness,*" which he sublimates by laughing at people when he isn't killing them (11). Ford's mask conceals his satanic intelligence and despair. His "good country people" persona resembles that of O'Connor's satanic Bible salesman Manley Pointer. Like their own characters, Thompson and O'Connor don a "Country Bumpkinish" (*HB* 406) mask and then begin "needling people in that dead-pan way" (*Killer* 13). Both writers use blasphemy as a weapon.

Laughter is an important concept for Jim Thompson and Flannery O'Connor, as it is for Nietzsche. Lou Ford tries to hold off the *sickness* by laughing at the world through his mask of irony. The laughter of Lou Ford and Nick Corey contains mockery, misery, and defiance. Like O'Connor's Misfit, Lou Ford has a split personality. "All I can do is wait until I split," he tells one of his victims. "Right down the middle" (119). This split can be heard in Ford's laughter at the end of the novel. Similarly, the grandmother in O'Connor's story hears the sound of The Misfit splitting right down the middle when his voice seems "about to crack" and she makes her gesture that triggers his response that leaves her lying in a puddle of wise guy blood (*CS* 132).

The violent comedies of Jim Thompson and Flannery O'Connor call to mind Nietzsche's aphorism that "Not by wrath does one kill but by laughter" (*Thus* 153). In *Thus Spoke Zarathustra,* Nietzsche's fictional prophet asks: "Who among you can laugh and be elevated at the same time?" (153). Certainly, Flannery O'Connor is one of the select few who could do both at the same time. O'Connor shares Nietzsche's sense of humor, his interest in prophets, and his talent for mockery. Of course, Nietzsche was mocking Christianity and O'Connor was mocking its mockers.

In *Thus Spoke Zarathustra,* the prophet calls upon his followers to "kill the spirit of gravity" (153). Having overcome "the great nausea," Zarathustra has learned to laugh (381). In one passage of dead-pan needling, Zarathustra rhetorically asks: "What has so far been the greatest sin here on earth? Was it not the word of him who said, 'Woe unto those who laugh here'?"(405) (an allusion to the sermon on the mount; see Luke 6:25). Striking at Christians this way is even better than the other, the real way. "Whoever would kill most thoroughly, *laughs*" (427). Thus spoke Zarathustra.

In opposition to Nietzsche, O'Connor's laughter is sanctioned by the Bible. In the Old Testament psalm that begins "Why do the heathen rage," a line O'Connor borrows for an unfinished novel title, the Psalmist goes on to say: "He that sitteth in the heavens shall laugh: the Lord shall have them in derision" (Ps. 2:1, 4). This pattern of the wicked laughing at the good and of God having the last laugh continues in the New Testament, where Jesus becomes the derided scapegoat: "And they laughed him to scorn" (Matt. 2:24, Mark 5:40, Luke 8:53). In response, Jesus issues his "Woe unto you that laugh now!" warning that Nietzsche derided (Luke 6:25). "Blessed are ye that weep now; for ye shall laugh," says Jesus (6:21).

In the name of the last laugh, O'Connor writes her violent comedies. She becomes a scourge of God, a hit man to enforce divine irony. She holds her own in a shootout with Nietzsche and Jim Thompson because she practices their philosophy that "Whoever would kill most thoroughly, laughs" (Nietzsche 427). In "A Good Man Is Hard to Find," after The Misfit blows the grandmother literally to kingdom come, O'Connor describes her lying "in a puddle of blood with her legs crossed under her like a child's and her face smiling up at the cloudless sky" (*CS* 132). The wisdom in this blood isn't hard to find. O'Connor alludes to the same scripture that Nietzsche had mocked: "whosoever shall not receive the Kingdom of God as a little child, he shall not enter therein" (Mark 10:15). But there is nothing childish about this joke at the expense of a harmless old bad Christian. It even wipes the smile off the face of The Misfit, who concludes that there's no pleasure even in meanness. One of O'Connor's sources for The Misfit is said to have been a fugitive outlaw whom the newspapers described as "a self-styled maniac who laughed weirdly" (qtd. in Tate 69). If this description fits Lou Ford better than The Misfit, it also fits the unsuspecting reader's image of the kind of author who would write "A Good Man Is Hard to Find."

The blurb on the cover of *The Killer Inside Me* describes it as the story of a "criminally warped mind," and so might "A Good Man Is Hard To Find" appear to be. Both works would be more accurately described as the story of a spiritually warped mind. The despair of Lou Ford and The Misfit is a sickness of the spirit. The Misfit personifies O'Connor's view that "there is no suffering greater than what is caused by the doubts of those who want to believe" (*HB* 353). Lou Ford suffers a similar torment.

This despair turns into defiance when Lou Ford and Thompson's Nick Corey in *Pop 1280* (1964) become devilish jokers who repeat the trick that life's played on people by killing them. It's a "hell of a trick" that they laugh themselves sick over. They confirm Kierkegaard's point that "the devil's despair is the most intense despair" and that his despair is "absolute defiance" (*Sickness* 175). Since their "mission to further God's injustice" doubles the irony, Ford and Corey also confirm Dante scholar F. De Sanctis's point that "the devil is irony incarnate"(Hilfer 147; qtd. in Sinclair 344 and Hilfer 140).

Similarly, O'Connor's despairingly defiant Misfit reckons that life has played a hell of a trick on people, and it becomes his "mission" to repeat it. Because The Misfit is unable to believe in God's justice, though he wants to, he has chosen to become the agent of His injustice. That is to say, he has chosen to become the devil, irony incarnate.

As such, he is also the grandmother's conscience. As De Sanctis observes: "the devil is, in the poetic sense, the man himself, his conscience answering his sophistries with a great guffaw, countering his syllogism with another and making game of him" (qtd. in Sinclair 344). O'Connor associates The Misfit with the grandmother's conscience in the first paragraph of the story: "I wouldn't take my children in any direction with a criminal like that aloose in it. I couldn't answer to my conscience if I did" (*CS* 117). In the poetic sense, it is no "ACCIDENT" that she meets The Misfit and he makes a game of her sophistries (*CS* 125, 126). It is justice. In O'Connor's divine comedy, a good devil is easy to find.

In Jim Thompson's *The Getaway* (1958), the fugitives escape to a criminal refuge run by an "uncrowned king" known as El Rey (167). In the anagogical sense, El Rey is the devil. He and the subjects of his kingdom "delight in irony, in symbolism; in constantly holding a mirror up to you so that you must see yourself as you are, and as they see you" (176). O'Connor's own fugitive holds such a mirror up to the grandmother. When people curse El Rey, as they might The Misfit, "they call him the devil, and accuse him of thinking he is God" (170). El Rey responds to these charges with a devilish paradox: "But is there a difference, senor? Where the difference between punishment and reward when one gets only what he asks for?" (170). A similar irony informs The Misfit's statement that the grandmother "would of been a good woman if it had been somebody there to shoot her every minute of her life" (*CS* 133). The grandmother and The Misfit only get what they ask for.

Kierkegaard defines irony as "infinite absolute negation" (*Concept* 261). He observes, however, that the ironic mentality and the pious mentality share the view that "existence has no reality" (257). They agree that "all is vanity" (257). But irony "does not destroy the vanity"; it reinforces it (257). Irony "makes what is lunatic even more lunatic"; it would resolve things "not into a higher unity but into a higher lunacy," an "infinite nothing" (257, 26). There are other subtle differences between devilish irony and devout piety. The pious mentality makes no exception of its own person in the general vanity. In irony, however, the "more vain everything becomes," the more "free" the subject becomes (258). "And while everything is in the process of becoming vanity, the ironic subject does not become vain in his own eyes" (258). From Kierkegaard's perspective, The Misfit would be an ironist while he lives by the rule of "'No pleasure but meanness'" (*CS* 132). But in the story's final sentence, when he says "'It's no real pleasure in life,'" he switches to the devout mentality and begins to show signs of "the prophet he was meant to become" (*CS* 133; *MM* 113).

Kierkegaard also points to subtle similarities and differences between the ironist and the prophet that bear on Flannery O'Connor's characters and on her own character:

> In one sense the ironist is certainly prophetic, because he is continually pointing to something impending, but what it is he does not know. He is prophetic, but his position and situation are the reverse of the prophet's. The prophet walks arm and arm with his age, and from this position he glimpses what is coming. . . . The ironist, however, has stepped out of line with his age, has turned around and faced it. That which is coming is hidden from him, lies behind his back, but the actuality he so antagonistically confronts is what he must destroy; upon this he focuses his burning gaze. (261)

Lou Ford, Nick Corey, El Rey, and The Misfit are ironists. They have turned around to confront their age. With their burning gaze and guns, they attempt to destroy it. Their irony is an "infinite absolute negativity" (*Concept* 261).

Is Flannery O'Connor herself irony incarnate? With her comic inversions, reverse prophets, and "backwards to Bethlehem" (*WB* 219) plots, she certainly uses a lot of irony in her fiction. But since O'Connor wanted to incarnate the Word of God, I would call her a prophet in Kierkegaard's sense of the term. That which is to be established lies before her. Unlike the ironist, she knows what is coming, and she negates in the name of this higher actuality that she believes is really there. Her irony does not seek a negative freedom that excludes the subject from the vanity of the world.

The difference between Flannery O'Connor and Jim Thompson and James Ross is that O'Connor has made the leap of faith from irony to prophecy. In the world of noir, "*It's always lightest just before the dark*" (*Killer* 214). In the world of Flannery O'Connor, it's always darkest just before "the pinpoint of light" (*WB* 232). This is why O'Connor wants her readers to "be on the lookout for such things as the action of grace in the Grandmother's soul, and not for the dead bodies" (*MM* 113). O'Connor believes in the "dark night of the soul" that St. John of the Cross defines as "an inflowing of God into the soul, which purges it from its ignorances and imperfections" (100). These failings are what cause the anguished soul to see darkness instead of the Divine light and to feel that God has forsaken it. "It's almost impossible to write about supernatural Grace in fiction," says O'Connor. "We almost have to approach it negatively" (*HB* 144). O'Connor echoes Kierkegaard's point that "the highest principles of thinking can be demonstrated only negatively" (*Concluding* 455). Although this negativity involves indirection, it is not the "infinite absolute negation" of irony (*Concept* 261). It is the infinite absolute leap of faith.

Readers of O'Connor learn to be "on the lookout" for Kierkegaard's "leap" that turns negatives into positives: darkness is light, despair is sin, suffering is purgation, the end is the beginning (*MM* 113). A "SINsational" writer, O'Connor does share with the writers of noir a preoccupation with angst, the sickness unto death, the killer inside me (*WB* 60). But the ironist-freaks of Thompson and Ross remain suffering doubters "within the sphere of infinite resignation" and the prophet-freaks of Flannery O'Connor find the cure for their sickness in "the paradoxical movement of faith" (*Fear and Trembling* 62). O'Connor would deepen faith. Thompson just deepens the irony. The structure of his novels incorporates "the ironic infinite elasticity" that Kierkegaard describes: "the secret trap-door through which one suddenly plunges down . . . into irony's infinite nothing" (*Concept* 26). Thompson's fiction illustrates the mortal danger of irony. O'Connor's fiction illustrates the "mortal danger of lying out on 70,000 fathoms of water, and only there finding God" (Kierkegaard, *Concluding* 232).

The masters of noir laugh themselves sick inside. O'Connor laughs herself well. By all accounts, her parables of grace under pressure reflected her own. In one letter, she describes an old lady who saw her on crutches: "she fixed me with a moist gleaming eye and said in a loud voice, 'Bless you, darling!' I felt exactly like The Misfit and I gave her a weakly lethal look" (*HB* 117). Nietzsche writes that "at any master who lacks the grace to laugh at himself—I laugh" (epigraph, *Gay Science*). He would have appreciated O'Connor's lethal humor. "I have a one-legged friend and I asked her what they said to John at the gate," continues

O'Connor in that letter about the old lady: "She said she reckoned they said, 'The lame shall enter first.' This may be because the lame will be able to knock everybody else aside with their crutches" (*HB* 117). The violently funny bear it away.

Notes

1. The sick joke motif is everywhere in O'Connor's fiction: from Joy-Hulga's "great joke" in "Good Country People" (*CS* 283), to Rufus Johnson's joke on Sheppard in "The Lame Shall Enter First," to the joke on the intellectual enthusiasts of Nietzsche and Colin Wilson's *The Outsider* in "The Partridge Festival," to the drowning/baptism jokes in "The River" and *The Violent Bear It Away* on people for whom "everything was a joke" (*CS* 167). In *Wise Blood,* Onnie Jay Holy says of the Holy Church of Christ without Christ: "'You don't have to believe nothing you don't understand and approve of. If you don't understand it, it ain't true, and that's all there is to it. No jokers in the deck, friends'" (152).

Works Cited

Asals, Frederick. Introduction. *Women Writers: Texts and Contexts.* Ed. Frederick Asals. New Brunswick: Rutgers UP, 1993. 3–25.

Cassill, R. V. "*The Killer Inside Me:* Fear, Purgation, and the Sophoclean Light." *Tough Guy Writers of the Thirties.* Ed. David Maddon. Carbondale: Southern Illinois UP, 1968. 230–38.

Higgins, George V. Afterword. *They Don't Dance Much.* By James Ross. Carbondale: Southern Illinois UP, 1975. 297–302.

Hilfer, Tony. *The Crime Novel: A Deviant Genre.* Austin: Texas UP, 1990.

John of the Cross. *Dark Night of the Soul.* Trans. E. Allison Peers. New York: Doubleday, 1990.

Kierkegaard, Søren. *The Concept of Irony.* Ed. and Trans. Howard V. Hong and Edna H. Hong. Princeton: Princeton UP, 1989.

———. *Concluding Unscientific Postscript to Philosophical Fragments.* Ed. and Trans. Howard V. Hong and Edna H. Hong. Princeton: Princeton UP, 1992.

———. *Fear and Trembling.* Ed. and Trans. Walter Lowrie. Princeton: Princeton UP, 1941.

———. *The Sickness unto Death.* Trans. Walter Lowrie. *Fear and Trembling and The Sickness unto Death.* Princeton: Princeton UP, 1974.

Nietzsche, Friedrich. *The Gay Science.* Trans. Walter Kaufmann. New York: Vintage, 1974.

———. *Thus Spoke Zarathustra: The Portable Nietzsche.* Trans. and Ed. Walter Kaufmann. New York: Penguin, 1982. 103–439.

O'Connor, Flannery. *The Complete Stories.* New York: Farrar, 1990.

———. *The Habit of Being.* Ed. Sally Fitzgerald. New York: Vintage, 1980.

———. *Mystery and Manners.* Ed. Sally and Robert Fitzgerald. New York: Farrar, 1969.

———. *Wise Blood.* 1952. New York: Farrar, Straus and Giroux, 1991.

Ross, James. *They Don't Dance Much.* 1940. Carbondale: Southern Illinois UP, 1975.

Sinclair, John, ed. and trans. *Dante's Inferno.* New York: Oxford UP, 1972.

Tate, J. O. "A Good Source Is Not So Hard to Find." *Flannery O'Connor, "A Good Man Is Hard to Find,"* ed. Frederick Asals. *Women Writers: Texts and Contexts.* New Brunswick: Rutgers UP, 1993. 67–71.

Thompson, Jim. *The Getaway.* 1958. Berkeley: Black Lizard, 1984.

———. *The Killer Inside Me.* 1952. New York: Vintage, 1991.

———. *Pop. 1280.* 1964. Berkeley: Black Lizard, 1984.

HOW THE SYMBOL MEANS: DEFERRAL VS. CONFRONTATION IN *THE SOUND AND THE FURY* AND "THE ARTIFICIAL NIGGER"

John D. Sykes Jr.

Flannery O'Connor was in a peculiar position in regard to literary modernism, as I have argued elsewhere. On the one hand, she was an heir and proponent of prose techniques developed by writers such as Gustave Flaubert, Henry James (especially as commented upon by Percy Lubbock in *The Craft of Fiction*), and James Joyce. The presuppositions of this poetics were impressed upon her from the time of her first serious writing instruction at the Iowa Writers' Workshop, some of it under the tutelage of New Critical theorists, as Sarah Fodor has detailed. Once O'Connor left graduate school and began sending her work to Caroline Gordon, the established writer gave her constant advice along modernist lines, and was in matters of style her modernist conscience. Sally Fitzgerald does not exaggerate when she calls these exchanges O'Connor's "master class." Both O'Connor's correspondence and her essays show her dedication to such ideals as "show, don't tell" and her close attention to point of view. But because of her sense of Christian vocation, she sometimes chafed under modernist rules. In one letter, having briefly explained Gordon's devotion to Jamesian technique to her friend Betty Hester, O'Connor confessed her frustration with its rigors: "Point of view runs me nuts," she declared (*HB* 157). Modernism is strongly antididactic. O'Connor had a message. Her problem might be stated in this form: How do I convey Christian truth without stating it? An important part of her solution to this problem had to do with her use of symbol, and the degree to which her use of symbol is a departure from modernism becomes apparent when one compares her work to Faulkner's.

A caveat is in order here. When I say O'Connor sought to convey Christian truth as a part of her vocation as a Catholic writer, I do not mean to suggest she was a preacher looking for sermon illustrations. She does not set out to write example stories—Aesop's fables for the faithful—and she certainly has no truck with promoting sentimental piety. No Little Evas or Uncle Toms here. Indeed, even the phrase "conveying Christian truth" is misleading insofar as it suggests O'Connor has a list of doctrines she must somehow inject into her readers' minds. But as her eloquent statements in the essays collected in *Mystery and Manners* make clear, she believed that Christian doctrine accurately disclosed the nature of God and God's dealings with creation, and she thought that belief inevitably shaped how she saw the world and what she found in it. More specifically, what she expected to see when she looked honestly at the world through her fiction was God's activity, no matter how disguised and even repugnant it might be. She wrote Betty Hester that "the moral basis of Poetry is the accurate naming of the things of God" (*CW* 980). Rather than Christian dogma's imposing blinders, O'Connor believed that "dogma is an instrument for penetrating reality" (*MM* 178). And here we come to a crucial point about symbol. It is an epistemological point.

For O'Connor, an effective symbol has a transcendent referent—that is, it refers to something beyond the horizon of human language and consciousness. O'Connor's understanding of symbol is rooted in her reading of St. Thomas, with whose *Summa* she spent twenty minutes every evening (*CW* 945). Like Thomas, O'Connor believed that human language can and does refer to God, though it does so through analogy and not directly. A literary symbol may likewise disclose the truth about God, although it always does so in an incomplete and limited way. John Desmond's succinct declaration is apt: "The doctrine of the analogy of being . . . provided the metaphysical basis for O'Connor's practice as a fiction writer" (31).

The view of symbol held by most modernists runs counter to this Scholastic understanding of analogy. For writers such as Joyce and Faulkner, the symbol is an invention of the artist that brings into human consciousness a world—or at least a scheme for comprehending the world—which did not previously exist. This view is presaged in Shelley's declaration that poets are the unacknowledged legislators of the world. Without the creative act of the poet no human world is possible. The writer is, at least potentially, a stand in for God, speaking a word that brings about order where previously chaos reigned. Although modernism is a term whose nuances continue to be disputed, Bradbury and McFarlane's generalization remains useful: "The world, reality, is discontinuous till art comes along, which may be a modern crisis for the world; but within art all becomes vital, discontinuous, yes, but within an aesthetic system of positioning. . . . There may be a poverty in the universe and a trauma in man, but the artist has the means to transcend both history and reality by the dispositions of his technique, creating

Joyce's 'luminous silent stasis of aesthetic pleasure'" (25–26). In the fiction of Joyce and Faulkner, human experience streams along in a kind of undifferentiated continuum until the shaping hand of art gives it direction and purpose; often this shape is epitomized in a symbol that provokes an epiphany in character and/or reader. But the shape thus given to experience and the understanding the symbol has elicited are temporary and likely to be superseded by the next bend in time's river. Thus, although the terms are tendentious, there is something to Michael Kreyling's claim that while O'Connor "privileges the text as doctrinal product," modernists tended to regard the text "as cultural process" (2).

By way of expanding upon Kreyling's point, I would like to employ alternative metaphors for these understandings of symbol. For a modernist such as Faulkner, symbol functions as does a kaleidoscope. In his narratives (which attempt to mirror human consciousness) one finds bits and pieces of odds and ends compartmentalized by the mind through association but otherwise unrelated and uncomprehended until with a turn and click of the apparatus a pattern suddenly emerges. The bits and pieces are temporarily and artificially (or should we say artfully?) held in place; a pleasing shape brings order to the randomness. That pattern (or, more accurately, one type of pattern) is the symbol, which gains its primary meaning from what it organizes rather than what it points to. The flow of experience requires another turn of the tube so that a new pattern can emerge. Alternatively, for a neo-Scholastic such as O'Connor, symbol functions in the manner of the chalice elevated by the priest after the wine has been consecrated. It points beyond itself to a mystery which is always the same—to an eternal, unchanging reality that recurrently manifests itself in the temporal flow. And although symbols themselves differ materially from context to context, they, too, remain formally the same, as do the wine and the cup from one church to the next. Thus the primary meaning of symbol is its referent, and the character of the symbol itself is permanent rather than temporary.

One must be careful not to exaggerate these distinctions: it is more accurate to think of particular symbols in the stories as occupying locations on a continuum rather than as residing in absolute categories. Modernist symbols such as the snow in Joyce's "The Dead" take their primary meaning from associations established in the story—with death and Irish nationalism, for example. However, at least one of these associations—that between snowfall and death—is not unique to the story. Insofar as an image reaches toward the archetypal it escapes temporality and comes closer to what the Scholastics called the anagogical. Like language in general, symbols must trade on public conventions in order to operate at any level. On the other side of the scale, where O'Connor is concerned, theologically minded critics in particular ought to remind themselves that literary symbols belong to the secular order. Thus even her most Eucharistic or Christological symbols must fit their local embodiment in the story. One may legitimately see a crucifix in the shape of the grandmother's distorted body at the end of "A Good Man Is Hard to Find." However, the corpse is also the form of a character particular to O'Connor's short story and thus is also dependent upon the story for shaping its meaning, as Louis Rubin urged thirty years ago.

In a sense, then, O'Connor's grandmother's body is as localized and autotelic a symbol as is Joyce's snow, and the two authors are playing by essentially the same rules for rendering symbols effectively. The difference is that for Joyce the ontological reach of the snow stops at the level of psychological and linguistic plausibility—what Kreyling called cultural product—whereas for O'Connor, meaning extends beyond the reach of history itself, disclosing the being of God. If snowfall has a universal symbolic resonance, it is as a psychological archetype. The symbolic significance of the crucifix comes from God's unique redemptive act—implausible and even shocking in its execution, but universal in its application.

Thus, given O'Connor's theological convictions concerning the completeness of God's revelation in Christ, her efforts to write fiction with anagogic significance do limit her in one way. In order for a symbol to make its way through analogy to the things of God, it must pass through Scripture and liturgy. That is, if, as O'Connor believed, God is already uniquely and finally revealed through the Church, then a literary symbol that has an anagogic depth will reflect the symbols of the church. To put it simply, O'Connor's most powerful images are religious; for Joyce and Faulkner, even when a symbol is religious, its meaning within the narrative is likely to be ironic. Part of O'Connor's genius lies in forging unexpected and unlikely Christian analogues: Hazel Motes's mortification of the flesh, Ruby Turpin's John of Patmos vision, Mr. Guizac's Christlike death. Joyce and Faulkner are more likely to deconstruct a Christian cliché. Faulkner's most successful extended treatment of a Christ figure is almost entirely ironic. The Joe Christmas of *Light in August* is a murderer whose lynching redeems no one; his tragedy serves only to condemn the hypocrisy of the racist order that victimized him. Similarly, in Joyce's story "The Sisters," the communion chalice becomes the symbol of death rather than "the cup of salvation"; it signifies the burden that broke the deceased priest's mind, and it literally rests on his bosom as the token of his passing.

By stretching toward a different level of meaning from the modernists, O'Connor establishes a different relationship to her readers. While O'Connor and Faulkner each place severe demands upon readers, the demands are quite dissimilar. For O'Connor, the purpose of symbol is to open the reader to mystery—specifically, the being of God, which is ultimately beyond our ken. Thus she hopes to confront us with something beyond ourselves, but something that is most decidedly "there," which we can understand more fully only by giving ourselves to it, as Hazel Motes is doing at the end of *Wise Blood*. For Faulkner, the purpose of symbol is to force us back onto our own resources, to empower us to replicate the artist's act of giving shape to formless flux. Perhaps the most obvious effect of this difference is that Faulkner's key symbols hide from us while O'Connor's hit us right between the eyes. To illustrate, I turn to two of the most famous scenes in southern literature, the conclusion of *The Sound and the Fury* and the climax of "The Artificial Nigger."

Readers who retain nothing else from Faulkner's own favorite novel remember how it ends—with Benjy bellowing with much sound and fury until his brother Jason throws Luster off the driver's seat of the surrey and turns it around so that it is traveling in the proper direction around the courthouse square. This ending seems fitting in many ways—for example, it amplifies the title in a surprising but appropriate manner, leading us to complete Shakespeare's line: "signifying nothing." The "idiot" who has the last word in this tale has nothing to tell us that will satisfy our desire for meaning. He himself is restored to passive equilibrium by the soothing but superficial order of his accustomed weekly route. But for the reader, who if she has kept up with Faulkner for three hundred pages is hardly an idiot, this level of orderliness is severely insufficient. Faulkner pushes us to look elsewhere to make sense of the Compson tragedy. And what I now take to be the key to this entire scene escaped me for twenty years. Benjy's howl is directed not merely at the violation of custom, but at the Confederate monument set in the middle of the square. When Luster goes left instead of right around the monument, Benjy, who looks to his right—since he is seated directly behind the driver he must look to one side or the other unless he wants to stare at the back of a head—is brought face to face with the Confederate soldier who sightlessly scans the horizon. Thus, symbolically, what horrifies Benjy is Lost Cause monumentalism. His protest resonates not only against the implosion of the house of Compson, but also against a culture that worships a dead past and thus has doomed itself.

The crucial evidence for this explication is laid out by Daniel Singal in *Faulkner: The Making of a Modernist,* to whom I am indebted. The fact that Luster goes left instead of right is plain, but for most readers this simply signifies an alteration of arbitrary habit. Much less noticeable is the phrase in the last sentence of the book: "[Ben's] eyes were empty and blue and serene again as cornice and façade flowed smoothly once more from left to right . . ." (321). The landscape would only move from left to right if Benjy were looking to the right, which we can safely assume is as much a habit as his other ritualized behavior. Returned to the prescribed route, Ben's gaze is directed to the courthouse and the objects lining the street. Until Luster's fateful error, Benjy had never faced the monument. In a novel that seeks to uncover the truth about the past, telling the same story four times, this fact is of major significance. Also important is the careful connection made between Benjy and the statue itself. In the paragraph that contains the only direct mention of the monument in this section, we are told that "the Confederate soldier gazed with empty eyes beneath his marble hand" (319). Six sentences later in the same paragraph the narrator says that "[Ben's] gaze [was] empty and untroubled" (320). At least so far as their gazes go, Benjy and the statue would seem to be twins. This verbal identification sets up the visual juxtaposition to follow and makes the statue the central if easily overlooked symbol in this scene.

Perhaps this interpretation seems strained, precious, and academic. But those who remain unconvinced of the monument's centrality would do well to reflect upon the fact that the strategy of deferral and deflection is standard practice for Faulkner. In this novel, the central character herself is missing. What usually sets off Benjy is hearing the word *caddy,* the name of the sister whose departure he has mourned for some twenty years. She is the silent center of the novel, and at least as they understand it, her sexual self-assertion has ruined her brothers' lives. But we never hear from her, except through them. Deferral of meaning, deflection among multiple narrators—these techniques are Faulkner's stock in trade. John T. Matthews detects in Faulkner's stylistic experimentalism an assumption about language: "The nature of language, Faulkner comes to suggest, forbids the illusion that any original idea, image, or sense can be embodied in words. Instead, *The Sound and the Fury* discovers, the fun of writing is in the play of failures, in the incompleteness, deferment, and repeatability of texts. The fiction veers away from resolution and completion in order to prolong its life. Accordingly, the novel makes two sorts of gesture toward silence, one toward the refusal to speak, the other toward deliberate mutations of the narrative's self-satisfaction" (87).

Matthews's remarks about the inadequacy of language help explain Faulkner's elliptical use of symbols. Symbol in his work is what Bradbury and McFarlane describe as "the hard objective centre of energy, which is distilled from multiplicity, and impersonally and linguistically integrates it" (50). Often when a symbol appears, as here at the end of *The Sound and the Fury*, it is there and it isn't. The reader is forced to posit it and contemplate it through implication. In the short story by that name, where is the rose for Emily? Even when one finds a crucial image directly presented in Faulkner's fiction, it is often an image of something in motion: Byron Bunch pursuing Lena Grove at the end of *Light in August*, Addie Bundren's peripatetic coffin in *As I Lay Dying*, the mobile rug in "Barn Burning" that makes its way to Jefferson from France, and then to Ab Snopes's cabin and washpot and back to Colonel Sartoris's porch.

Perhaps the most spectacular example of the moving symbol is to be found in the story Faulkner published both as "Spotted Horses" and as a section of *The Hamlet*. In the novel, the horses are a powerful image of the social disruption fomented by Flem Snopes. In the following passage, the wild horses unleash their fury upon the men who foolishly believe they own them after buying them at auction:

> The splotchy huddle of animals seemed to be moving before the advancing line of men like a snowball which they might have been pushing before them by invisible means, gradually nearer and nearer to the black yawn of the barn door. . . . Then an indescribable sound, a movement desperate and despairing rose among them; for an instant of static horror men and animals faced one another, then the men whirled and ran before the gaudy vomit of long wild faces and splotched chests which overtook and scattered them and flung them sprawling aside and completely obliterated from sight Henry and the little boy, neither of whom had moved though Henry had flung up both arms still holding the coiled rope, the herd sweeping on across the lot, to crash through the gate which the last man through it had neglected to close, leaving it slightly ajar, carrying all of the gate save the upright to which the hinges were nailed with them. . . . (333)

This final image of man and boy alone and miraculously unharmed in a sea of chaotic forces they cannot stem or control makes for a telling contrast to Mr. Head and Nelson's still contemplation of the statue at the climax of O'Connor's story, but more important is the fact that we have here a typical Faulkner image: one of motion. The symbol of the Confederate monument in *The Sound and the Fury* is static, of course, but we come to know it through motion—Benjy and Luster literally circumscribe it for us at novel's end.

O'Connor's symbols are often static by comparison—indeed, they are more than once images of the body in death. *Wise Blood*, the first truly O'Connoresque work, ends with Mrs. Flood contemplating the corpse of Hazel Motes. At the climax of "Greenleaf" is the image of Mrs. May impaled by the bull's horns. At the end of "A Good Man Is Hard to Find," The Misfit discourses over the deceased grandmother. To jump to a less fatal scene, "Parker's Back" ends with another defeated, bleeding body at rest. Of course one can think of exceptions—Harry Ashfield being swept under by the current in "The River" or Ruby Turpin's revelation—but the pattern is there. The demeaning lawn ornament named by the title of "The Artificial Nigger" certainly belongs to the category of broken bodies. Although it is a mere representation of a body, and a poor one at that, its brokenness is apparent. It is "pitched forward at an unsteady angle," an eye chipped and the smiling mouth "stretched up at the corners," giving the figure "a wild look of misery." But before touching on the content of this unlikely crucifix, I would like to dwell on the formal features of its presentation. I called Faulkner's strategy one of deferral; O'Connor's is one of confrontation. The statue is described from the point of view of Mr. Head, the failed Vergil to Nelson's Dante. Mr. Head is at a nadir so deep that he is indifferent to getting home, as he has for some hours longed to do. "Suddenly" something catches his attention, "like a cry out of the gathering dusk" (229). Benjy cries when he sees the unannounced monument, the presence of which we must deduce; metaphorically, this statue cries out to Mr. Head. The statue itself tilts toward the grandfather and grandson, "within reach" we are told, as though about to drop into their arms. O'Connor has both characters stop and stare at the object, which elicits the identical declaration from each of them in turn. And whereas Benjy emits a prelinguistic howl, the exclamations of Mr. Head and Nelson amount to an articulation of their experience in the city. In other words, the statue seems to bring them to understanding rather than driving them into a fury which signifies nothing.

Even more noticeable in the contrasting presentations is O'Connor's narrator's commentary. From Faulkner's narrator we get nothing: "Ben's voice roared and roared. Queenie moved again, her feet began to clop-clop steadily again, and at once Ben hushed. Luster looked quickly back over his shoulder, then he drove on. The broken flower drooped over Ben's fist and his eyes were empty and blue and serene again as cornice and façade flowed smoothly once more from left to right, post and tree, window and doorway and signboard each in its ordered place" (320–21). Flaubert would have been proud of such a passage; Caroline Gordon would have applauded. The narrator does not intrude; meaning is shown, not told. The opposite happens in O'Connor's story. After the climactic moment, the narrator tells us, among other things, "They stood gazing at the artificial Negro as if they were faced with some great mystery, some monument to another's victory that brought them together in their common defeat. They could both feel it dissolving their differences like an action of mercy" (230).

Interestingly, O'Connor had trouble with passages such as these in writing the story. The penultimate paragraph of the published story, which describes the "action of mercy" at some length, is entirely missing from earlier versions. She told Ben Griffith in a letter of 4 May 1955 that she reworked the ending of the story repeatedly, as the surviving manuscripts bear out (*CW* 931). Her additions could be described as a transition from the modernist sort of symbol to the Scholastic. And it seems to me that in this story, O'Connor has not yet mastered the new technique. That penultimate paragraph is jarring in context. It stands out as an interruption, an intrusion—an injection of "telling" into the poetics of "showing."

O'Connor's exchanges with Caroline Gordon over "The Artificial Nigger" reveal this conflict and suggest the way O'Connor reconciled it in her own mind. At this point in her career, O'Connor seems to have needed Gordon's approval. Gordon read drafts and gave detailed advice, usually throwing in a mini-lecture with illustrations from masters such as Henry James, whom Gordon affectionately refers to in one letter as "Uncle H.J." (19 February 1955). In the longest, undated letter on "The Artificial Nigger" from Gordon in the Georgia College and State University's O'Connor collection, she draws not on Henry James but on James Joyce. Gordon saw the technical problem of the story as one of tone. O'Connor needed to mix the high and the low more effectively, Gordon felt, and she especially wanted O'Connor to emend the beginning and end of the story, where she thought an elevated tone would do most to set off the more lowly, quotidian thoughts and dialogue of small boy and uneducated country man. She urged O'Connor to emulate the opening of Joyce's story "Araby," where according to Gordon, Joyce puts the unexceptional event of a boy's disappointment over an adult's failure to keep a promise in a context of universal significance by the tone he establishes at the beginning of the story. For the end of O'Connor's story, Gordon recommends as a model the final paragraph of "The Dead." Equally interesting is the fact that the final author Gordon praises for doing well the kind of thing she wants O'Connor to do is Faulkner. Despite her disappointment in *A Fable,* which had recently appeared, she tells O'Connor that at his best, Faulkner achieves exactly this edifying juxtaposition of the high and the low.

So much for Gordon's advice. What is more important for my case is the way O'Connor applies it. She uses Gordon's urging to elevate the tone as a license to introduce a didactic element in order to push the reader to what she

John D. Sykes Jr.

would in her essays call the anagogical level. In other words, O'Connor does not simply raise the level of her diction; she introduces authorial commentary meant to instruct the reader. And in terms of the New Critical demand for organic unity and in light of the practice of masters such as Flaubert or Chekhov or Joyce, this commentary is an artistic blemish, despite the fact that Gordon approved of it. O'Connor was to learn how to do this kind of thing more effectively—as, it seems to me, she does at the end of *The Violent Bear It Away*. But what is in my view an artistic flaw in this story points to a theological advantage of her view of symbol. Symbol, as she treats it, is denser and more likely to be a vehicle for revelation. Even if in this instance the narrator's commentary runs to a kind of explication that jars when set within the point of view of the character who has been touched by grace, O'Connor makes it clear that the symbol is worth this degree of investment. If explored, it will yield what she called mystery—a divine truth beyond human comprehension.

Indeed, O'Connor's symbols are typically divine in the sense of having a direct corollary in Christian iconography. O'Connor's crucial symbols are analogues to Christian symbols, and her hope is that her symbols will convey the same meaning as the original. Her symbols work typologically. And in this story, as in many of O'Connor's stories, the type that the story represents is the crucifix. This omnipresent element of Catholic worship is figured forth in every O'Connor story where we find a broken or wounded body, from "A Good Man Is Hard to Find" to "The Displaced Person" to "Greenleaf." And I would argue that in each of these instances, we are not simply being reminded of Jesus' death on a cross, but instead are being shown an utterly unexpected way in which a human being is joined to Christ through redemptive suffering. The suffering is a bridge from the victim to Jesus and thus to God; the symbol is a bridge from reader to divine revelation and thus to God's truth. And in most of her fiction O'Connor is mashing the crucifix in the reader's face the way that the nun's hug does to the unnamed girl in "A Temple of the Holy Ghost." What is different about the crucial symbol in "The Artificial Nigger" is that it encompasses race.

Needless to say, this is a vexed issue, one that has been trenchantly if polemically raised by Timothy Caron in a recent essay, "'The Bottom Rail Is on the Top': Race and 'Theological Whiteness' in Flannery O'Connor's Short Fiction." Caron finds it offensive that O'Connor would dignify the racist statuary by suggesting any positive connection to Jesus, and he accuses O'Connor of merely using black characters as a means for whites to achieve salvation. But before venturing a judgment of my own on O'Connor's racial attitudes, I think it worthwhile to note the primary contrast in the story between two ways that blacks are perceived by Nelson and Mr. Head. The first way is surprising, given the cultural context. Blacks are figures of knowledge and power. This association is especially strong for Nelson, for whom blacks represent the chief aspect of the city life of which he is ignorant. But it also holds for Mr. Head, who recognizes without acknowledging it that the blacks on the train and in the city are more worldly wise than he. In a neat reversal early in the story, Mr. Head and Nelson are escorted from the dining car by a black waiter while three dignified black passengers dine. Although Mr. Head saves face by insulting the waiter and drawing chuckles from the white diners, it is clearly he who is out of place. The crucial instant of black power, often commented upon by critics, comes when Nelson asks a black woman for directions and is nearly mesmerized by her, finding himself longing for her to pick him up and hold him "tighter and tighter" while he looks "down and down into her eyes" (*CW* 223). The woman's appeal seems to be both sexual and maternal; she also has knowledge Nelson needs, and her knowledge gives her immediate power over him. His feelings toward her seem to border upon awe. Indeed, the two principal characters must perceive blacks as figures of power in order for the decrepit statuary to have its effect at the story's climax. It is the contradiction between the powerful, mysterious people they have seen and the sad caricature they now behold that justifies the characters' reconciliation.

At the same time, Mr. Head and Nelson regard blacks as inferior to whites. Or at least they know they should so regard them, given the racist assumptions of their social world. This attitude is too common and expected to need illustration. What is less obvious and more important is the fact that given events in the story, this belief on the part of the two rural whites is manifestly false. Deeply ingrained though the notion of white racial superiority may be for Mr. Head and Nelson, it exists as a social expectation that they cannot live up to. This failure is what lies behind Nelson's first experience of racial hatred. When he is unable to identify the first black man he sees as a "nigger," Nelson is ridiculed by Mr. Head. Nelson turns his resentment against the "coffee-colored man" whom he misidentified, hating him with a "fierce raw fresh hate" for causing his humiliation (213). This experience also allows Nelson to understand "why his grandfather disliked them," implying that Mr. Head shares the poor white's resentment of blacks. The combination of fearful regard for the power of blacks and hateful resentment of them lays the foundation for their shock at the sight of the "artificial nigger." The grinning, dilapidated figure is a sad parody of the living black people they have encountered—an object of derision rather than a subject of substance. The statue's effect upon Nelson and Mr. Head is the result of the humiliation they perceive: what was mighty in their personal experience has been cast down in public display. Mr. Head's dismissive comment, "They ain't got enough real ones here. They got to have an artificial one" (230) is, like his earlier riposte to the waiter, an attempt to cover his own inadequacy with bravado.

The combination of power and humiliation that O'Connor builds into her characterization of blacks in this story is also what allows the statue to serve as a representation of Christ. Because O'Connor wants this symbol to suggest a "monument to another's victory" (230), she is at pains to avoid presenting blacks as helpless victims. Instead, what she means to convey is the notion of kenosis—the self-emptying in which power is forsaken as an act of sacrifice. For these reasons it is best to think of the "artificial nigger" itself not as a Christ figure, but more narrowly as a crucifix. This most definitive symbol of Roman Catholic devotion makes the humiliation of Christ its conceptual focal point, with the crown of thorns underscoring the irony of the public degradation. On the face of it, a crucifix would seem to deride the person it portrays. This is indeed how it strikes the samurai confronted for the first time by Christianity in Shusaku Endo's novel, for example. Examining a crucifix, he wonders how the foreigners can call such a man "Lord." He concludes, "If the Christians really worshipped this emaciated man, then their religion seemed an incredibly bizarre sort of heresy" (84). O'Connor is playing on exactly this irony in her use of the lawn statuary: what appears demeaning becomes, if the story has achieved its goal, a sign of victory. What she means to convey, then, is that blacks in the South as a group have served a Christ function, bearing the weight of sin on behalf of the region and thereby offering hope that the divisions of race will be healed, as this symbol of racism has brought these two white hicks together. In the letter to Ben Griffith, she writes, "What I had in mind to suggest with the artificial nigger was the redemptive quality of the Negro's suffering for us all" (*CW* 931).

If this interpretation is correct in its outline, then the symbol of "The Artificial Nigger" is oriented toward the future in at least two senses. First, and somewhat notoriously, O'Connor is a gradualist on racial matters, feeling that integration should not be thrust on the South too quickly, lest the social fabric tear from the shock, as Ralph Wood has explained in "Where Is the Voice Coming From?" One often finds reference in treatments of O'Connor to her refusal to meet James Baldwin in Georgia, a demurer recorded in a letter to Maryat Lee in *The Habit of Being* (329). She seems to have thought that a principled objection to legal segregation such as hers would eventually lead to a widespread acceptance of blacks' equality with whites, and that to force the white South to acknowledge that equality immediately would only drive the races further apart. But O'Connor's symbol is also forward-looking in an eschatological sense. It points to a divine fulfillment of history beyond human ken, just as the individual's reconciliation with God through Christ looks beyond death for its completion.

Here I think is a partial answer to a question that continues to puzzle me: why was O'Connor attracted to the work of Teilhard de Chardin, as she would be a few years after writing this story? Her other story about race, "Everything that Rises Must Converge," takes its title from Teilhard. One unironic meaning this title has for her is that racial reconciliation lies in the future, as Teilhard believed evolution and the progressive development of human consciousness pointed toward an ultimate unity in an omega point in the future. But racial reconciliation has certainly not happened yet in her stories—either in "The Artificial Nigger" or "Everything That Rises Must Converge." I have already mentioned Mr. Head's dismissive statement after the encounter with the statue. Of similar interest is the fact that in early manuscript versions of the story housed at Georgia College and State University, Mr. Head and Nelson are not even aware of what has brought them together. They do not know that it is the statue that has broken down the wall of hostility between them.

It seems to me that two judgments on O'Connor's racial views are justified. First, she was simply wrong about what her own Christian convictions demanded by way of social justice in her time and place. The civil rights movement that continued to unfold after her death demonstrated how positive change could be achieved through direct action, and many of those who participated in the movement did so in an attempt to follow Jesus. And even in terms of the story we have been considering, the fact that Nelson and Mr. Head could reach reconciliation between themselves by means of a racist statue without having their racism challenged is to me a theological weakness. However, on a second front O'Connor is profound and hopeful.

What Caron offers as a criticism, O'Connor would take as a compliment. He asserts that "O'Connor's theology led her to place salvational concerns over social justice . . ." (146n15). This is true. However, I would argue that for O'Connor "salvational concerns" do not eviscerate the desire for social justice; instead, they subsume it. To put the matter another way, loving God with all one's heart is what enables one to love one's neighbor as oneself. For O'Connor, the same sinfulness that generates social injustice has, more fundamentally, cut us off from God, so that God has had to take drastic action to rescue us from ourselves. It is this often covert rescue operation that O'Connor seeks to chronicle. Even racist hicks are the object of God's love, and they are being redeemed even when they do not know it. The chief symbol of "The Artificial Nigger" is primarily for the reader, so to speak. And the reader might well notice not only that the statue is a symbol of Christlike humiliation, but also that Nelson and Mr. Head, who are so much alike, also have much in common with the statue, whose forward-leaning posture they mimic, and which is "about Nelson's size" (229). The "action of mercy" the characters feel is dependent upon their identifying with the clownish brown figure. Ultimately, the Christ image, in whatever unlikely guise, is meant to be the form of us all—black and white. Her characters' opaqueness to it is a sign that for O'Connor the symbol brings its meaning with it, that it is effective—or at least powerful—whether or not the one opened to it understands it. The symbol works by analogy to the Eucharist, in which the body and blood of Christ are present in the bread and wine regardless of appearances—and regardless of the observer's awareness or beliefs.

To return at last to *The Sound and the Fury*, we have to do in Faulkner's case not with a figurative monument to another's victory, but with a literal monument to a defeat. The Confederate monument does not have race as direct referent; however, the significance of the monument inescapably includes race. When O'Connor searches for a cultural analogue to the humiliation of the cross, she finds a demeaning statue of a black man. When Faulkner wants a symbol of corrupting cultural domination he hits upon a memorialized white man. The marble soldier guards the sacralized and idealized past of the South as the dominant class wishes it to be remembered. With his eyes scanning the horizon, vigilant against another Yankee invasion, this guardian represents an attitude toward southern culture that does not bear looking into, as Benjy's bellows register. The truth about that past, and, even more, the way in which the myth of the past has paralyzed the present, is horrifying when you look it in the face, as Quentin Compson will disclose more fully in *Absalom, Absalom!*, when the issue of miscegenation emerges as central. Faulkner is acutely conscious that race lies at the heart of southern cultural categories. But notice the difference in direction, as we might say. Faulkner's great novels are backward looking in the sense of probing the past as a way of breaking its grip on the present.

One might even go so far as to say that the Confederate monument suggests a Christ figure—not in O'Connor's anagogic sense but in an ironic sense similar to the way Joe Christmas functions in *Light in August*. According to the Lost Cause religion that Charles Reagan Wilson describes in *Baptized in Blood*, the postwar South developed a theodicy in which the South was an innocent sacrificial victim "killed" in defense of a higher, nobler way that coincided with the ideals of the Founders. The South was the true America, and its defeat paradoxically demonstrated its righteousness. Jesus suffered and bled and died; the South suffered and bled and lost. This cast of mind also gives resonance to the phrase "the South will rise again." Wilson juxtaposes what he calls the myth of the Lost Cause to the theology of the Cause in this way: "The myth of the Crusading Christian Confederates had enacted the Christian drama, but without a resurrection and redemption to complete the myth. In the theology of the Lost Cause, one can see that Southerners still hoped the spirit of the suffering and dead Confederacy would one day have, in the words from a Confederate monument, 'a joyful resurrection'" (58).

The sort of monument Benjy is forced to confront became ubiquitous in the South, the period of greatest activity coming between 1890 and 1910, in Faulkner's boyhood (Wilson 18). The monument as described in *The Sound and the Fury* is actually a conflation of two statues Faulkner knew well, both having been erected in his youth. One stood in the courthouse square, as detailed in the novel; the other stood on the grounds of Ole Miss. The Ole Miss statue is the one with the shielding hand raised to the brow; Faulkner in effect moved the Ole Miss statue to the site of the courthouse monument in *The Sound and the Fury*. His own grandmother Faulkner was involved in the United Daughters of the Confederacy controversy that led to the erection of two monuments, installed by rival factions, one in 1906 on the campus, and the second the following year at the courthouse (Hines 21). To indicate the provenance of these statues in the South, I might note that the monument O'Connor would have known in Milledgeville was erected in 1912 and stands today at the corner of Hancock and Jefferson. These war memorials became a necessary demonstration of civic pride during the period when reactionary forces were pushing out the last vestiges of Reconstruction and reasserting white supremacy. It is no coincidence that the so-called Wilmington (North Carolina) Race Riot of 1898, which destroyed the only black newspaper in the country and amounted to a coup d'état on the part of white supremacists—occurred in the heyday of monument building (see Cecelski and Tyson).

But if we do read the monument this way—the monument all but hidden by Faulkner's prose—it becomes a thoroughly historicized symbol, and an ironic one. Making the Confederacy into a Christ figure is a huge mistake, a mistake more grievous than Luster's accidental turn to the left. Insofar as the marble soldier represents the resurrection hope of Lost Cause religion, Benjy's Easter confrontation with it draws out the blasphemous implications of such monumentalizing. Benjy has, after all, just been in Dilsey's church, where the Reverend Shegog preached about "de ricklickshun en de blood of de Lamb"

(295). Thus Faulkner's own treatment of the Confederate symbol is ironic. Faulkner is acutely aware that the Confederacy will not be resurrected—the South of the Compsons is a moribund culture, its only hope for progress lying in breaking out of the ritualistic circles that families like the Compsons have trod. Faulkner's fictional symbol allows the reader to pull together themes from the novel and make sense of them in a new way, but the meaning of this symbol is "accidental" as we might almost say—a meaning constructed by author and reader through the text itself. The meaning of the Confederate monument in *The Sound and the Fury* plays off of public meanings, generating an ironic valence that gives the symbol a meaning unique to this narrative.

Although some of these same things could be truthfully said of O'Connor's statue—lawn jockeys do not have any intended connection to Jesus—her use of the statue as symbol is unironic, even anti-ironic. Faulkner's point is, we might say, social deconstruction. He is demystifying civil religion—showing us that the marble man has feet of clay, so to speak. O'Connor's purpose is recovery. She wants to restore the symbol of the crucifix to its full transcendental significance, and seeing Christ in the lawn jockey is a way of defamiliarizing this ancient Christian symbol in order to restore its power. Faulkner mocks a monument; O'Connor glorifies dilapidated racist kitsch. This "nigger" is artificial—the product of artifice—but the symbol that it becomes by its connection to Christ is divine. Faced with the challenge of making her prose an occasion for religious revelation within the confines of a modernist aesthetic she largely accepted, O'Connor increasingly turned to this notion of the transcendently charged symbol as a way to negotiate the conflict. Even if, as I believe, "The Artificial Nigger" is not her most successful effort in this direction, it is an important step in the right endeavor and anticipates what she will do to near perfection in "Parker's Back."

Works Cited

Bradbury, Malcolm, and James McFarlane. "The Name and Nature of Modernism." *Modernism: 1890–1930.* Ed. Malcolm Bradbury and James McFarlane. Atlantic Highlands, NJ: Humanities P, 1978. 19–56.

Caron, Timothy P. "'The Bottom Rail Is on the Top': Race and 'Theological Whiteness' in Flannery O'Connor's Short Fiction." *Inside the Church of Flannery O'Connor.* Ed. Joanne Halleran McMullen and Jon Parrish Peede. Macon, GA: Mercer UP, 2007. 138–64.

Cecelski, David C., and Timothy B. Tyson, eds. *Democracy Betrayed: The Wilmington Race Riot of 1898 and Its Legacy.* Chapel Hill: U North Carolina P, 1998.

Desmond, John. *Risen Sons: Flannery O'Connor's Vision of History.* Athens: U Georgia P, 1987.

Endo, Shusaku. *The Samurai.* Trans. Van C. Gessel. New York: New Directions, 1997.

Faulkner, William. *The Hamlet.* New York: Vintage International, 1991.

———. *The Sound and the Fury.* New York: Vintage International, 1990.

Fitzgerald, Sally. "A Master Class: From the Correspondence of Caroline Gordon and Flannery O'Connor." *Georgia Review* 33 (Winter 1979): 827–46.

Fodor, Sarah. "Proust, 'Home of the Brave,' and *Understanding Fiction:* O'Connor's Development as a Writer." *Flannery O'Connor Bulletin* 25 (1996–97): 62–80.

Gordon, Caroline, to Flannery O'Connor, 19 Feb. 1955, and n.d. [1955]. Flannery O'Connor Collection, Georgia College and State University.

Hines, Thomas S. *William Faulkner and the Tangible Past: The Architecture of Yoknapatawpha.* Berkeley: U California P, 1997.

Joyce, James. *Dubliners.* New York: Penguin, 1976.

Kreyling, Michael. "A Good Monk Is Hard to Find." *Flannery O'Connor's Radical Reality.* Ed. Jan Nordby Gretlund and Karl-Heinz Westharp. Columbia: U of South Carolina P, 2006. 1–17.

Matthews, John T. "The Discovery of Loss in *The Sound and the Fury.*" *William Faulkner's The Sound and the Fury.* Ed. Harold Bloom. New York: Chelsea, 1988. 79–102.

O'Connor, Flannery. *Collected Works.* New York: Library of America, 1988.

———. *The Habit of Being.* Ed. Sally Fitzgerald. New York: Farrar, 1979.

———. *Mystery and Manners.* Ed. Sally and Robert Fitzgerald. New York: Farrar, 1962.

Rubin, Louis D., Jr. "Flannery O'Connor's Company of Southerners, Or 'The Artificial Nigger' Read as Fiction Rather Than Theology." *Flannery O'Connor Bulletin* 6 (1977): 47–71.

Singal, Daniel J. *William Faulkner: The Making of a Modernist.* Chapel Hill: U North Carolina P, 1997.

Sykes, John D., Jr. *Flannery O'Connor, Walker Percy, and the Aesthetic of Revelation.* Columbia: U Missouri P, 2007.

Wilson, Charles Reagan. *Baptized in Blood: The Religion of the Lost Cause, 1868–1920.* Athens: U Georgia P, 1980.

Wood, Ralph C. "Where Is the Voice Coming From? Flannery O'Connor on Race." *Flannery O'Connor Bulletin* 22 (1993–94): 90–118.

VIOLENCE, NATURE, AND PROPHECY IN FLANNERY O'CONNOR AND CORMAC MCCARTHY

Farrell O'Gorman

> There's no such thing as life without bloodshed.
>
> —Cormac McCarthy

> We are not living in times when the realist of distances is understood or well thought of, even though he may be in the dominant tradition of American letters.
>
> —Flannery O'Connor, "Some Aspects of the Grotesque in Southern Fiction"

Cormac McCarthy was raised a Roman Catholic in Tennessee, and his fiction abounds with the "distorted images of Christ" that Flannery O'Connor saw as particularly characteristic of the region they shared in common ("The Catholic Novelist in the Protestant South," *CW* 859). Yet he cannot be deemed a Catholic writer in the same way that she can. Unlike O'Connor, McCarthy has refused to elaborate on his views in lectures and essays, and for many readers the appeal of his fiction lies in the fact that it continually rearticulates religious questions with out giving clear answers to them. While his most recent novels seem to offer more sympathetic portrayals of Christianity than his earlier ones, McCarthy remains well characterized today by Robert Coles's 1974 description of him as "a novelist of religious feeling who appears to subscribe to no creed but who cannot stop wondering in the most passionate and honest way what gives life meaning" (90). Yet we do know at least two facts that can help to illuminate the religious motifs so prevalent in his work. We know that as a young man McCarthy struggled to reject his family's Catholicism.[1] And we know that in his view, "books are made out of books. The novel depends for its life upon the novels that have been written," so that we might well seek to understand the religious dimensions of his work in terms of intertextuality (quoted in Woodward).

Accordingly, I have argued elsewhere that reading James Joyce's *A Portrait of the Artist as a Young Man* and *Ulysses* alongside the two novels at the center of McCarthy's oeuvre, *Suttree* and *Blood Meridian,* can help us to better understand what Edwin T. Arnold has called the "mosaic" of McCarthy's fiction (1). That reading—both intertextual and intratextual—focuses specifically on the figure of the priest and speculates more generally on McCarthy's own quasi-Joycean identity as an apparently lapsed Catholic of Irish descent. In this essay, however, my first concern is with not McCarthy's priests but his prophets—and prodigals—in relation to those of O'Connor. My second, inextricably related concern is with O'Connor's and McCarthy's identities not only as religious writers exploring the relationship between violence and the supernatural but also as American writers exploring the relationship between violence and the natural, between violence and nature itself.

While O'Connor and McCarthy's similar regional backgrounds and their common penchant for violence have led a number of reviewers to casually link them as practitioners of a "Southern Gothic" mode of fiction, there is as yet little substantial scholarship comparing the two. Georg Guillemin has read McCarthy's early novel *Outer Dark* as indebted to both Faulkner's *Light in August* and O'Connor's *The Violent Bear It Away,* arguing rightly that McCarthy finally most resembles O'Connor in his tendency toward religious allegory. He also observes that the many instances of intertextuality linking McCarthy's novel with O'Connor's "in turn stand in intertextual relation with biblical elements": "Like the parody of the Eucharist in the scene of the child's murder in *Outer Dark,*" Guillemin writes, "Rayber's retarded child Bishop is murdered in a parodic baptizing scene" in *The Violent Bear It Away;* but in each case the murder only occurs after the child "has been thoroughly allegorized into a christchild" (31). Guillemin's analysis here, it seems to me, in fact turns more upon McCarthy's and O'Connor's typically Catholic emphasis on the sacraments than it does upon specific biblical parallels. But he is right to identify *The Violent Bear It Away* as a crucial intertext (or pre-text) for McCarthy's work. Tim Parrish has taken a different tack, linking O'Connor and McCarthy as common celebrants of not a Catholic but an American religion of violence.[2] Parrish's reading of O'Connor's "A Good Man Is Hard to Find" and McCarthy's *Blood Meridian* accordingly stresses that "redemption" is merely "an accident the grandmother stumbles into [in O'Connor's story], or something that the kid receives only from the reader [in McCarthy's novel]. Beyond these episodes, in the texts' extended universes, what comes next are assuredly more cycles of killing—with no redemption implicit in the process" (37). While I do not fully agree with Parrish here, he is right to posit The Misfit's murder of the Grandmother in "A

Good Man Is Hard to Find" as "[the truest] expression of the will to violence in American literature": "not even *Blood Meridian* quite matches it" (43).

McCarthy's recent novel *No Country for Old Men,* however, rewrites that murder, and understanding McCarthy's killer Chigurh in relation to O'Connor's Misfit—both insistently self-reliant males who engage in extended dialogues with their ultimate female victims—is crucial to understanding the role of the failed prophet therein. Here I will first demonstrate how *No Country for Old Men* can be read as the culmination of a series of intertextual links between McCarthy's prodigal prophets and those of O'Connor. Secondly, I will explain how prophecy's relationship to gender in this novel and in *Blood Meridian*— which itself rewrites a number of O'Connor's fictions, including "The River" and *The Violent Bear It Away*—as well as in these two writers' works more generally both reflects and reveals their broader concern with the relationship between violence, nature, and nature's God.

Prodigal Prophets: Good News, Bad News, or No News at All?

O'Connor's fiction, most notably her two novels, often features protagonists who are prodigal before turning prophet; McCarthy's does as well, though his grim Gnostic inclinations have generally led him to present failed prophets whose seeming call to find and deliver good news is ultimately overwhelmed by the bad news circulating in a physical world dominated by violence.[3] And McCarthy's prophets are consistently shaped in relation to O'Connor's.[4]

A word on terminology: I am defining a *prophet* here simply as one who speaks for God and, accordingly, carries *news* not otherwise accessible to the world. In the Old Testament, of course, such figures often seem to be primarily prophets of judgment and destruction and are often prodigal before embracing their prophetic calling (I use the term *prodigal* here as synonymous with *fugitive,* in the sense of being fugitive from divine calling or inherited religious tradition or both). In the New Testament, Christ culminates but also deviates from this line as the final prophet, *the* newsbearer who brings good news of final freedom from the familiar worldly cycle of sin, violent retribution, and death— though he is also something more, the Word, the Good News incarnate, who paradoxically must submit himself to the violence of the world before his message and gift of freedom from it is complete.

To briefly review O'Connor's prodigal prophets: in *Wise Blood,* Hazel Motes roams the streets of Taulkinham first denying every stranger who tries to identify him as a "preacher," then preaching his own prodigal Church Without

Christ, but finally blinding himself and living out his last days as a witness who silently communicates to his worldly landlady the message that another, invisible world exists; he does not speak of but rather becomes the "pin point of light" which might enable her to see the star over Bethlehem as something *new* instead of merely as a clichéd image "on Christmas cards" (*CW* 123, 131). Francis Marion Tarwater of *The Violent Bear It Away* flees from his home and his explicitly prophetic vocation after the death of his great-uncle only to circle back to both after his final rape by a Satanic figure who has stalked him all along. At the novel's conclusion, he embarks again for the city he has just left, this time to "GO WARN THE SLEEPING CHILDREN OF GOD OF THE TERRIBLE SPEED OF MERCY" (479). Haze and Tarwater fail to speak for God, and therefore to deliver any news, until they embody suffering and final redemption as opposed to merely "preaching" it; ultimately they resemble Obadiah Elihue Parker of "Parker's Back" when he, in his own unknowing and inarticulate manner, begins to participate in the body and the passion of Christ and thereby becomes the news that he carries.

Sarah Gordon, applying the terminology of Walker Percy's essay "The Message in the Bottle," has demonstrated how much of O'Connor's short fiction turns on the confrontation of a worldly character—a "castaway" on the "island" of the world, as Percy would have it—with a newsbearer, a prophetic figure with news from "across the seas," news previously inaccessible on the island. Robert W. Rudnicki, in *Percyscapes: The Fugue State in Twentieth-Century Southern Fiction,* has made a case for reading McCarthy's fiction in similar terms, albeit using a semiotic framework rather than a theological one. Rudnicki's analysis of McCarthy's *The Crossing* therefore highlights Billy Parham's dream of "a messenger [who] had come in off the plains from the south with something writ upon a ledgerscrap but [Billy] could not read it. He looked at the messenger but the face was obscured in shadow and featureless and he knew that the messenger was messenger alone and could tell him nothing of the news he bore" (*The Crossing* 82–83; Rudnicki 141). The context in this passage is not explicitly Judeo-Christian. But in much of McCarthy's work, it is.

McCarthy's ongoing concern with prophetic messengers begins at least as early as *Outer Dark,* wherein a seemingly supernatural and clearly unholy trinity hunts down a prodigal father—one whose spiritual blindness is countered both by the actions of his persistently maternal sister and, finally, by those of a physically blind man who is nonetheless a kind of seer.[5] But *Suttree* is McCarthy's first novel to clearly feature a failed prophetic protagonist. Cornelius Suttree is a fisherman who has forthrightly rejected the role of "fisher of men," in part because the Catholic priests who educated him have somehow failed to perform their own prophetic function (14). Roaming his old schoolhouse he encounters one such priest, who resembles a mere "piece of statuary. A catatonic shaman *who spoke no word at all.*" Leaving the school he looks back "to see the shape of the priest in the baywindow watching like a paper priest in a pulpit or *a prophet sealed in glass*"—an image which mirrors both a series of dead bodies sealed in glass throughout the novel and Suttree's own juxtaposed appearance in the "octagonal windowbay" of his boardinghouse "like a child in a pulpit in the dark of an empty church" (304–5, emphasis added; see O'Gorman 104, 106–7). Again, such scenes in *Suttree* seem to me best read in relation to Joyce: though the pairing of Christ-haunted intellectual Suttree with hapless bumpkin Gene Harrogate neatly parallels *Wise Blood*'s pairing of Haze Motes with Enoch Emery, the novel as a whole more obviously invokes *Ulysses.*

But O'Connor's work is directly alluded to in McCarthy's next novel, *Blood Meridian.* At the novel's beginning the protagonist, the kid, at least superficially resembles Hazel Motes as "his eyes lay dark and tunneled in a caved and haunted face" (*BM* 21); he is also like Motes in that he is homeless, a prodigal entering a new and nightmarish landscape where he seems hell-bent on doing some things he never has done before (*CW* 5). But McCarthy's kid is more insistently linked to Francis Marion Tarwater in his identity as a fourteen-year-old runaway whose mother has died in childbirth; his rape by a Satanic antagonist, the judge, at the novel's conclusion; and his persistent role in the failed baptism motif that runs throughout *Blood Meridian.* Unlike O'Connor's prodigals, however, the kid never assumes any prophetic function, despite having a few close calls—for example, when briefly separated from his gang of marauding scalp hunters, he comes upon a large burning tree, from which no message issues forth (215). And, near the novel's conclusion, the solitary kid once again adopts a guise reminiscent of Haze Motes, perhaps especially of the blind and largely silent Motes at the conclusion of *Wise Blood.* Here the kid clearly appears as a potential prophet:

> He had a bible that he'd found at the mining camps and he carried this book with him *no word of which he could read.* In his dark and frugal clothes some took him for *a sort of preacher* but he was *no witness* to them, neither of things at hand nor of things to come. . . . They were remote places for *news* that he traveled in and in those uncertain times men toasted the ascension of rulers already deposed and hailed the coronation of kings murdered and in their graves. Of such corporal histories even as these he bore no *tidings* and

> although it was the custom in that wilderness to stop with any traveler and exchange the *news* he seemed to travel with *no news at all,* as if the doings of the world were too slanderous for him to truck with, or perhaps too trivial. (*BM* 312, emphasis added)

Throughout *Blood Meridian* another character—the ex-priest Tobin—has functioned as the fading voice of a collapsed Christendom, while the villainous judge has served as a dark prophet of violence and determinism alike. By novel's end the kid seems ready to renounce violence itself, the worldly "news" the judge has delivered throughout, but it is exactly such news that he cannot escape. Immediately after the passage above, we are told that the kid "never saw the expriest again. Of the judge he heard rumor [i.e., news] everywhere" (313); and when he eventually finds himself compelled to kill a threatening boy—clearly a younger version of himself, much like the hitchhiker who confronts O'Connor's Mr. Shiftlet at the end of "The Life You Save May Be Your Own"—the judge immediately reappears to claim him once and for all (322–25).

Indeed, O'Connor's relevance to McCarthy's work seems, if anything, to have increased since he left the South for the West. Midway through the first novel of the Border Trilogy, *All the Pretty Horses,* the prodigal son John Grady Cole is unjustly imprisoned in Mexico alongside another prisoner who, like O'Connor's Misfit, "didn't know what crime he'd been accused of. He'd been told he could go when he signed the papers but he couldn't read the papers and no one would read them to him" (171). The meditation on the apparent injustice of Original Sin invited by this passage is extended further when Cole himself ultimately kills a man—albeit in self-defense, as with the kid in the final chapter of *Blood Meridian*—in prison. Once set free Cole is briefly positioned as a potential prophet when, attempting to regain his lost love Alejandra, he travels to her riding atop a truck with his hands outstretched "as if he were some personage bearing news for the countryside. As if he were some profound evangelical being conveyed down out of the mountains and north across the flat bleak landscape toward Monclova" (217).[6] But he fails in this mission and, once again, there seems to be little good news at the end of this novel, or, given Cole's death at the conclusion of *Cities of the Plain,* at the end of the Border Trilogy as a whole (no good news for or from Cole, that is: Billy Parham's is another story, one too complicated to address in full here).[7]

On a first reading, *No Country for Old Men* seems to continue McCarthy's pattern of failed prophets, with not the prodigal, Moss—who finds a bag of drug money and leaves his wife in order to keep it—but rather a lawman, Sheriff

Bell, coming closest to filling a prophetic role here. One particular scene in this tersely narrated novel clearly highlights Bell's identity in this regard. Just after Moss has been shot to death by Chigurh, the almost robotic killer who serves as the novel's villain, Bell prepares to inform Moss's wife, Carla Jean, of the bad news. Before doing so he stops in a coffee shop and reads the morning paper, as is his habit. Immediately impatient to know what bad news will appear in the evening paper, he asks his waitress when it will be available. She responds:

> I quit reading it and I made my husband quit readin it.
>
> Is that right?
>
> I dont why they call it a newspaper. I dont call that stuff news.
>
> No.
>
> When was the last time you read something about Jesus Christ in the newspaper?
>
> Bell shook his head. I dont know, he said. I guess I'd have to say it would be a while.
>
> I guess it would too, she said. A long while.

The narrative then shifts to Bell standing at Carla Jean's door: "He'd knocked on other doors with the same sort of *message*, it [i.e., reporting a death] wasnt all that *new* to him" (246–47, emphasis added). And in the chapter immediately following, Chigurh, returning Moss's briefcase of drug money to its owner, announces that he "would prefer not to be addressed as some kind of bearer of bad news" (251). Now, at the beginning of the novel, Bell himself has deemed Chigurh "a true and living prophet of destruction" (4). But finally Bell, too, is just such a messenger: he is a bearer of exclusively bad news. In a deeper sense, neither is a real prophet since they only deliver (or embody) the bad old news about violence, retribution, and death that is so disturbingly familiar, so mundane, that it is not really news at all—just as the waitress suggests.

What, then, would be *new*? News, perhaps, of love, and of the possibility of redemption; news of life rather than death. This is what the grandmother finally offers The Misfit at the end of O'Connor's "A Good Man Is Hard to Find." Though The Misfit presents himself as a prophet of self-reliant "meanness" and views his killing of the narcissistic grandmother and her family as inevitable, given the dictates of the world, he finally admits his anger at God and accordingly leaves himself vulnerable to the grandmother's one moment of true prophecy: when she touches him and calls him one of her own children, thereby planting the seed for The Misfit's transformation—in O'Connor's own words—into "the prophet he was meant to be" (*MM* 113). McCarthy's killer Chigurh, by contrast, does not feel anger at God but forthrightly models himself on a "God" whom he conceives of as ruthless and deterministic—and thereby becomes a kind of automaton himself. Accordingly, when near the novel's conclusion he confronts and engages in an extended dialogue with Carla Jean, he is not moved when she tells him that he can change: rather, he converts her to his own deterministic view immediately before he shoots her (254–60). He refuses to admit his capacity for change because doing so would entail admitting his vulnerability, which he steadfastly denies—even though the narrative itself reveals him to be vulnerable when he is hit and seriously injured by a car immediately after the shooting.

So: is there any good news in *No Country for Old Men?* If so, it is known only to Sheriff Bell's wife, Loretta. Bell flatly states at the conclusion that "the world I've seen has not made me a spiritual person. Not like her" (303). Bell has also told us from the beginning that he reads "the papers ever mornin. Mostly I suppose just to try and figure out what might be headed this way"—much as the grandmother first learns about The Misfit from the newspaper at the beginning of "A Good Man Is Hard to Find." But Loretta, like the waitress, has quit reading the paper (40). She reads the Bible instead and is last described reading the book of Revelation—an apocalyptic book, of course, but in the Biblical sense *apocalypse* is finally good news, the unveiling of a truly new world. So, while Carla Jean has failed to match the grandmother's final prophetic feat, perhaps Loretta won't. As elsewhere in McCarthy's fiction, women are here associated with the possibility of grace; in his most recent fiction, especially—at the end of *Cities of the Plain* and *The Road* as well as this novel—the good news which has always seemed to escape his prodigal males is whispered by or embodied in the actions of charitable females. It may well be that the violent American country McCarthy so often explores has been awaiting news not from old men but from old women. And it may be that reading McCarthy and O'Connor alongside one another can help us to better understand gender, as well as prophecy and violence, in the work of both.

No Life without Bloodshed: Nature, Mothers, and the Birth of Prophecy

In the work of O'Connor and, increasingly, of McCarthy alike, the prodigal or failed prophet seems to seek "news" only within himself and tries to force that news on the world, whereas the true prophet looks for and finds news outside of herself and communicates it with gentle persistence, almost silently—as Haze Motes does to Mrs. Flood at the end of *Wise Blood,* or Parker to Sarah Ruth at the end of "Parker's Back." Yet this assertion as it stands now is perhaps too pat, too unchallenging. For both O'Connor and McCarthy suggest that the true prophet must learn to read not only the Bible but also the book of nature; both recognize that nature, like the Bible, is not easy to read; and both recognize that nature, like the Bible, is often appallingly violent.

So it is that O'Connor's Misfit, murderously evil as he is, deserves to be taken seriously in his central contention that "I can't make what all I done wrong fit what all I gone through in punishment"—that is, that the universe he has been born into seems to be a grim prison-house where he is being unjustly tormented (*CW* 151). His violent anger at the world and whatever God might have made it mirrors that of figures in American literature ranging from Herman Melville's New England whaler Ahab to Walker Percy's southern-western gentleman-cum-frontiersman Lancelot Lamar, who echoes The Misfit and Ahab alike in his declaration that "Original Sin is not something man did to God but something God did to man" (222). In accordance with his grim vision of a violent and punitive God, Lance, like The Misfit, preaches a gospel of violence, of a mankind which properly devotes itself to the rape and murder which is in fact "the meaning and goal and omega point of *evolution*" (223, emphasis added). Here as elsewhere in the novel, Lance postures as a kind of scientist, and his scientism—while not itself endorsing the supernatural—is intrinsically bound up with his view that nature is a kind of limiting trap or prison, and "God" therefore its intrinsically inimical architect and warden. The violence that Lance and The Misfit and Ahab alike speak of and enact, then, is in their view finally not the work of humanity—it is first and foremost the work of nature, and of nature's God. And, indeed, from a certain point of view it might well seem that nature does trap these characters, along with McCarthy characters such as the kid and John Grady Cole, in a violent struggle for survival where only the strongest endure.

O'Connor's and McCarthy's participation in the longstanding dialogue in American letters regarding such concerns is furthered by consideration of how each addresses the question posed at the end of Robert Frost's sonnet "Design." Here the speaker initially describes a horrific, if minute, scene: a moth fallen prey to a spider. The speaker is horrified in part by the whiteness of both insects and by the fact that their encounter occurs amidst seeming beauty, atop a flower; but most fundamentally he is appalled by the predatory violence so obviously manifested in nature here, by creatures which have been *designed* such that they must conquer, rend, and devour other creatures. What, the speaker asks in the closing sestet, could have designed a scene such as this—a nature such as this? "What but design of darkness to appall?" he answers rhetorically. "If design govern in a thing so small" (198).

In the concluding couplet, the speaker suggests three possible answers to his initial question. Perhaps nature is so diabolically designed that only an evil intelligence could have created it (the dark Romantic's, and the Gnostic's, answer). Or perhaps there is no designer at all: no God, not even a lesser god or demiurge, on whom to place the blame (the literary naturalist's answer). Or—a final possibility—perhaps the speaker himself has somehow created the scene, and, realizing this, shrugs and walks away. Perhaps he's read too much into nature. Or—O'Connor and McCarthy alike would say—perhaps he hasn't read enough. Either way, this is in part the literary modernist's answer, one which ultimately encourages us to reread the text and nature alike.

O'Connor cannot adequately be defined as a literary modernist, just as her own understanding of nature finally cannot be separated from her belief in the supernatural. But what happens if we read her fiction looking at the natural world as closely as Frost's speaker has? We learn in "The River" that pigs are not "small fat pink animals with curly tails and round grinning faces and bow ties": instead, they have faces that are "gray, wet and sour" and bodies that are "long-legged and hump-backed" and marked by the ragged remnants of ears that have been bitten off; and if a little boy invades their territory, they'll run him over (*CW* 158–59). We learn that rivers, even when they shine with "the reflection of the sun . . . set like a diamond" on their surfaces, hold violence in their depths (161). We learn in "A Good Man Is Hard to Find" that the trees which initially sparkle in the silver-white sunlight outside Atlanta finally "gape like a dark open mouth" waiting to swallow us all—as does the larger natural order (146). Now, from a Christian or even a broadly humanistic perspective The Misfit's violence in this story must be attributed to his characteristically human misuse of his free will—to his sinfulness or even (some might argue) to his radically religious sensibility—but whatever we make of humans and their reasons for committing violence against other humans here, we still must confront a monkey, perched in a chinaberry tree, who is "busy catching fleas on himself and biting each one carefully between his teeth as if it were a delicacy" (142). We still, that is, must confront a violence which is simply and undeniably a part of the natural world. Due to her affliction with lupus, O'Connor knew in the most intimate way that nature—whether marked by violence in its order or its apparent disorder—is a killer.

McCarthy's statement about the impossibility of "life without bloodshed," to say nothing of his unfailingly violent fiction, bears witness to the same knowledge. And his own meditations on nature and violence clearly owe an important debt to Herman Melville, whom he has identified as one of his most favored predecessors precisely because the earlier writer so directly addressed "issues of life and death" (quoted in Woodward). *Moby-Dick* pointedly reveals Melville's own concern with the relationship between nature and violence—and with the deep proclivity of human beings for violence—when the *Pequod*'s African American cook Fleece makes a futile attempt to preach Christianity to sharks, only to then proclaim that his fellow humans seem "more of shark than Massa Shark hisself"; when Ishmael ponders Saturday meat-markets on land where "crowds of live bipeds star[e] up at . . . long rows of dead quadrupeds"; and when Queequeg proclaims that he "no care what god made shark . . . wedder Feejee god or Nantucket god; but de god what made shark must be one dam Ingin"—that is, a savage and accomplished killer (240–43). The most notable such killer on the *Pequod,* of course, is not an "Ingin," but the quintessentially modern Anglo-American Ahab. And what drives Ahab's own desire to kill is not simply his vision of the violence in nature, but his anger at the fact that he is not lord over that nature (which has already taken a bite out of him and still waits, he knows, to swallow him whole). As with Frost's speaker, Ahab looks at the natural order and sees a dark design at work—but goes a step further, declaring war on the Designer whose figure he sees in the Whale. Melville himself would elsewhere, in his grim depiction of the Encantadas or Galapagos Islands, tentatively posit Ahab's darkly Romantic and openly Gnostic vision of a nature so perverse that it seems to have been made "by a penal, or malignant, or perhaps a downright diabolical enchanter"—meditations perhaps not altogether inappropriate in Darwin's laboratory (78). But in the character of Ahab, Melville clearly shows that the danger of imagining a violent God of nature is that one will inevitably begin to resemble him and therefore to seek one's own absolute mastery over nature.[8]

O'Connor's work contains any number of characters who declare war on God, often specifically challenging, as with The Misfit or Ruby Turpin, the God revealed in the Bible. But others are more insistently at war with nature, a nature in which they might or might not see the hand of some God at work. Mr. Fortune in "A View of the Woods" fancies himself a Christian and refers to the Bible on occasion, but he sets himself squarely against nature—nature as manifested in the woods and in *family* broadly conceived, both his immediate family and the entire human gene pool, insofar as it is represented by the Pitts blood. Fortune dislikes the woods and his extended family for precisely the same reasons: both get in the way of convenience; both seem essentially useless; and both seem to breed irrational violence. And whatever we might make of the violence that takes place within the Pitts family itself here, this much is undeniable: Mr. Fortune, in his reaction to the violence he sees in nature and in family, ultimately turns to a greater violence himself and so ultimately destroys that which he meant to master. Though he does not openly posit any dark designer to the natural order (perhaps he jealously intuits one in the blood-drenched "someone" his granddaughter seems to glimpse in the woods), he follows Ahab both in his steadfast opposition to that order and in his repetition of the very violence which he seeks to eliminate (*CW* 537–38).

The most proximate model for Fortune and for other such O'Connor characters—Rayber of *The Violent Bear It Away* being the most fully developed—is to be found not in Melville but in Hawthorne, in Aylmer from "The Birthmark," whom O'Connor condemns so directly in her "Introduction to *A Memoir of Mary Ann*" (*CW* 830). Yet surely Melville co-established the American "tradition of the dark and divisive romance-novel" that O'Connor credited Hawthorne with, that tradition of the "realist of distances" whose gaze extends "beyond the surface, beyond mere problems, until it touches that realm which is the concern of prophets and poets." She hoped that in her own time this literary tradition—a broadly *prophetic* one, by her own account—had "combined with the comic grotesque tradition and with the lessons all writers have learned from the naturalists, to preserve our Southern literature for at least a little while" (*CW* 818–19). McCarthy's *Blood Meridian* might be read as fulfilling her hopes in all of these regards, but perhaps especially in its identity as a "dark and divisive romance-novel" in which McCarthy responds to Melville much as O'Connor did to Hawthorne. Furthermore, *Blood Meridian*—one of McCarthy's books "made out of books"—responds to O'Connor herself, particularly to *The Violent Bear It Away* and "The River." In doing so it provides a key to understanding, first, how McCarthy and O'Connor posit not only the reality of a nature that is violent but also the reality of a nature that is fertile, saving, and salving to the wounds depraved humans inflict on one another; and, second, how both tend to associate the former with a closed "masculine" aridity that refuses to recognize the existence of the supernatural and leads only to death, and the latter with a "feminine" fluidity that opens into the supernatural and gives birth to prophetic insight.

Blood Meridian foregrounds the violence of the natural world from its opening paragraph on: only "a last few wolves" remain in east Tennessee in

1847 because they have been hunted to the brink of local extinction by human beings—who, in this novel, often seem to be merely the ultimate predators. But the wolves are predators themselves, of course, and throughout the novel a snake-bit horse, a marauding bear, and a diphtheria epidemic further exemplify the fact that death and suffering are altogether natural—not merely man-made—occurrences. The violence of the natural world is perhaps emphasized all the more by the novel's primary setting, the deserts along the U.S.-Mexico border. When the kid and his initial gang of filibusters enter this region they witness that every morning "where the earth drained up into the sky at the edge of creation the top of the sun rose out of nothing like the head of a great red phallus," a phallus which proceeds to sit "squat and pulsing and malevolent behind them" (44–45). This figuring of the sun as a potential rapist calls to mind O'Connor's "Greenleaf," wherein the god-bull who eventually gores Mrs. May is consistently associated with celestial objects as well as with the natural world more generally. O'Connor's bull must ultimately be understood as a figure of Christ—the suitor-bridegroom who ultimately suffers and dies himself in the pietà scene that concludes the story—but *Blood Meridian*'s rapist-god of nature is the altogether malevolent judge, whom Tobin describes as mysteriously appearing in the middle of the desert much as the sun itself appears "out of nothing" above (125). Throughout the course of the novel the judge repeatedly rapes and kills children and, ultimately, the kid himself. Accordingly, this walking embodiment of masculine aridity—this pedophilic rapist-god of the desert—is best associated with the satanic stranger who dogs Francis Marion Tarwater's steps throughout *The Violent Bear It Away* and violates him just before the novel's conclusion.

Indeed, McCarthy's judge is straightforwardly identified as "the devil" by the Reverend Green, whom he upstages at a tent revival when he first appears in the narrative (7); and in the ex-priest Tobin's account he is clearly presented as an anti-Christ when he stands alongside a volcanic mount and delivers a perverse "sermon" to twelve scalp hunters who proceed to follow him "like the disciples of a new faith" (129–30). Throughout the novel as a whole, however, the judge is not necessarily—or not exclusively—the Satan conceived of in orthodox Christian tradition. Indeed, insofar as he is a seemingly supernatural personage whose primary attributes are judgment, jealousy, and domineering dedication to clearing a desert land of tribes that do not meet with his favor, he seems a perverse version of the Old Testament Jehovah, whom some ancient Gnostic sects conflated with the dark demiurge they saw as ruling the world of matter. Yet insofar as the judge seems human, he also resembles O'Connor's Rayber.

Farrell O'Gorman

Both are reductive devotees of science whose most essential violence springs from the fact that they want to be able to understand humanity and nature alike only so as better to control them. Rayber attempts to study and thereby cage first old Mason and then Francis Marion Tarwater inside his "head," where they "would be laid out in parts and numbers," figuratively dissected (341). The judge explicitly states that "whatever exists in creation without my knowledge exists without my consent": even "the freedom of birds is an insult" to him, and in order to better study such creatures he would prefer them either dead or caged in his own personal "zoo"—a "hell of a zoo," as one of the scalp hunters remarks, and one designed to include humans as well as animals (199).

The death-dealing aridity of both Rayber and the judge is perhaps manifested most clearly in that even as they preach that nothing exists apart from nature, they reduce nature to something human beings must inevitably conquer and destroy. Rayber seems straightforwardly Darwinian and affirmative regarding the natural order in his desire to teach young Tarwater about "his ancestor, the fish" (417); yet he sees the "majestic" woods around Powderhead only as potential lumber that might pay for something really useful, a "college education for the boy" (444–45). More disturbingly, Rayber views his mentally retarded son, Bishop, as a "mistake" of nature whom he wishes he had the courage to euthanize (403, 435). The judge preaches to his men that their "mother the earth was round like an egg and contained all good things within her"; yet immediately after doing so he proceeds to mine the earth and produce gunpowder in a bizarre ceremony that culminates with firing guns into a volcano—performing a figurative rape of the earth (Spurgeon 87–88). And as the god who seems to rule the world of *Blood Meridian,* the judge is properly implicated in the history of the West with regard to not only genocidal assaults on Native Americans but also the destruction of the buffalo, highlighted in the novel's final chapter (316–17). The judge has wiped the buffalo from the face of the earth much as Rayber would the trees around Powderhead. And like Rayber—like Hawthorne's Aylmer—the judge's general obsession with order and with eliminating undesirable forms of life marks him as a kind of eugenicist, though he points to nature itself as endorsing his view that humans must learn to separate weak children from stronger ones, must learn to "cull themselves," as wolves do (146).[9]

The judge's own endorsement of violence, then, is in fact altogether consistent with his identity as proto-Darwinian scientist. And that identity is further figured as destructively masculine and insistently inimical to a life-sustaining femininity. This characteristic of the judge and the desert world he rules is made

156

clear by the scene the kid encounters in the first of the many ruined Catholic churches he enters: he finds "an array of saints in their niches . . . shot up by American troops trying their rifles" during the Mexican-American War, most prominent among them "a carved stone Virgin" who "held in her arms a head-less child" (26–27). Immediately afterward the kid wades into a river to bathe himself "like some wholly wretched baptismal candidate," but emerges only to become subject to the faux-Christian doctrine of masculine self-reliance and Manifest Destiny preached by Captain White and his sergeant—both renegade American soldiers turned filibusters (27–35). This sequence is just one of many demonstrating how in *Blood Meridian* the kid constantly flees from women and water only to march further into the desert and the deadly embrace of the judge, whose doctrine of masculine self-reliance is the same as that preached by O'Connor's Satan in *The Violent Bear It Away*. A profound tension between figuratively gendered identities is at the heart of that novel as well: as Robert Donahoo has demonstrated, young Tarwater's "development—what O'Connor in her analyses of the novel sees as religious epiphany or 'salvation'—is linked to a movement not just toward acceptance of the feminine but toward emulation and submission to it" (97). Accordingly, old Mason Tarwater, the forthrightly prophetic character whom O'Connor identified as speaking for herself in the novel, is a mother as well as a father figure, one who sees that it is necessary to raise Francis Marion Tarwater not only to train him as a prophet but also be-cause Rayber is manifestly incapable of nurturing a child (*CW* 1108). As Mason puts it, Rayber wants to be able to control everything "in his head. You can't change a child's pants in your head" (378).

What old Tarwater wants most insistently, of course, is to make sure that all children are not only physically mothered but also baptized into Holy Mother Church. And baptism is directly linked to gender in *The Violent Bear It Away* in that, while the rebellious young Tarwater "wants 'drowning' to have a single, physical meaning—to be a masculine act," Bishop's ultimate drowning in the act of baptism in fact signifies "female fluidity as opposed to masculine aridity," thereby serving "to connect Bishop with that definite 'other,' the dead—for whom, Mason has reminded us, 'the world was made'" (Donahoo 102).[10] In keeping with her Catholic emphasis on the sacraments, O'Connor here depicts a nature that is not merely violent but also potentially fertile and saving, as in the act of baptism the natural substance of water opens into the supernatural and gives birth to prophetic vision in those who have eyes to see: after drowning Bishop, Francis Marion Tarwater looks into a well to see "two silent serene eyes" gazing back at him, the eyes of the dead, of Bishop or Mason or both calling him to his prophetic responsibilities (466). This reading also sheds light on "The River" and on the fact that—however darkly O'Connor's and McCarthy's fictions depict eugenicists and euthanasia advocates—both authors also suggest that physical death might not be the worst fate that could befall a child.

In "The River," young Harry Ashfield lives, as his surname suggests, in an arid urban wasteland where his neglectful parents have failed to nurture him and where he will eventually, inevitably, fall prey to demonic violence. He has previously been beaten up by one group of strange boys, and during the course of the story he is threatened by grim gray pigs that are explicitly associated with the swine into which Christ, in the Gospel of Mark, casts demons. Most disturbingly, the boy is ultimately stalked by the porcine and pedophilic old man known as "Mr. Paradise." And if it is in part nature (i.e., the pigs) which threatens him, it is also nature that saves him: Harry escapes a final violent degradation at the hands of the unbelieving old man when the river into which he has waded, the river in which he has recently been baptized, catches "him like a long gentle hand" and pulls him "swiftly forward and down" to his death (171). That hand must inevitably be linked to Mrs. Connin, the mothering babysitter who has introduced the boy to the river and Christianity alike and whose "pale spotted hand" reaches into the Ashfields' apartment to grab him at the very beginning of the story (154). So here the blood-red "River of Life" is explicitly associated with a maternal female, and perhaps with the womb itself—of which Harry has previously been ignorant, believing that "he had been made" by "a doctor named Sladewell," a "fat man" who "gave him shots and thought that his name was Herbert" (162, 160).

Yet Mrs. Connin has exposed this child of the modern city to not only the natural but also the supernatural, informing Harry that "he had been made by a carpenter named Jesus Christ" and leading him to the young preacher who, before he baptizes the boy, explains that the river flows all the way to "the Kingdom of Christ" (160, 163). Again, nature here is at once violent—as the pigs and Harry's drowning itself indicate—but also fertile, saving, and salving to the wounds humans inflict on one another. Harry's initial experience at the river, when he is baptized, promises a spiritual healing of the damage that has been done to him by his parents and the world at large; and when he returns on his own, the river saves him from the physical and spiritual damage imminently threatened by Mr. Paradise. O'Connor writes with the hope that Harry and the reader alike are—via Mrs. Connin and the preacher to whom she has introduced us—able to see the paradoxically violent and saving character of the natural world better than does the skeptical Mr. Paradise (whose habitual parading of his ugly cancer bears witness not only to his lack of faith but also to his vision of nature as *merely* violent). At story's end the old man stands "like some ancient water monster . . . staring with his dull eyes as far down the river line as he could see" (171). But O'Connor would maintain that the young boy who has escaped his grasp—and those readers in whom the river has given birth to prophetic insight—are able to see more deeply into and beyond nature, with the vision of the realist of distances.

Chapter 18 of *Blood Meridian* is a clear rewriting of "The River," one with a significantly different outcome, and this briefest of twenty-three chapters also provides a key to a proper reading of the entire novel. Here a character known simply as "the idiot"—who seems more severely mentally retarded than O'Connor's Bishop and who has long been kept caged and exploited by his brother—has fallen in with the judge's gang of scalp hunters. When they come to the banks of the Colorado River the ever-violent gang immediately begins to make an alliance with the local Yuma tribe in order to capture the ferry landing on the opposite bank; but as they do so a group of pioneer women encamped nearby takes notice of the idiot and proceeds to lambaste his brother, his "keeper," for treating him like an animal rather than a human being (256–57). The women roll the idiot's cage to the river, singing a hymn, then bathe the idiot and begin calling "him" (not "it," as he is elsewhere identified) by his proper name, James Robert. Wading into the river, one "swirl[s] him about grown man that he was in her great stout arms," like a mother, crooning to him. While no baptism proper takes place, the idiot somehow "sees hisself"—his better self, a purified self—in the river. The women burn the cage in which he has been kept like an inmate of the judge's hellish zoo, then dress him and feed him and put him to bed like a child.

But just as O'Connor's Harry-Bevel feels compelled to return alone to the river where he had been reborn, so too does James Robert, who likewise seems newly called to some form of dialogue with the divine: alongside the river he "hooted softly and his voice passed from him like a gift that was also needed so that no sound of it echoed back. He entered the water" and immediately began to sink. Observing this scene in the place of O'Connor's Mr. Paradise is the judge, who walks "stark naked" along the bank:

> . . . and he stepped into the river and seized up the drowning idiot, snatching it aloft by the heels like a great midwife and slapping it on the back to let the water out. A birth scene or a baptism or some ritual not yet inaugurated into any canon.

159

> He twisted the water from its hair and he gathered the naked and sob-
> bing fool into his arms and carried it up into the camp and restored it among
> its fellows. (258–59)

The idiot is no longer James Robert, no longer a "he" but once again an "it," a mere plaything of the judge—one kept for sexual purposes, as succeeding chapters make clear. The idiot therefore functions as an appropriate stand-in for the scalp hunters, its "fellows," and especially for the kid himself, all of whom are toyed with and ultimately destroyed by the judge for the sake of his own perverse pleasure. Whereas O'Connor depicts Harry-Bevel undergoing a violent natural death that simultaneously affords him a saving rebirth into the Kingdom of Christ, McCarthy depicts here a nightmarish vision of the fate of all those under the sway of the judge, all those who are born only into the violent desert world which he rules. This destructively masculine "midwife" in fact quashes both the idiot's and the kid's capacity for prophetic insight, denying them the knowledge of nature, God, and self they might acquire via feminine fluidity—or, to use a term that O'Connor might well prefer, Marian receptivity. The judge, that is, prevents those human beings who fall under his sway from experiencing and perceiving a created order that is life-giving as well as death-dealing, which is, as St. Paul says in Romans 8:22, "groaning in labor pains even unto now."[11]

And what makes *Blood Meridian* such a deeply horrific novel is this: unlike Mr. Paradise or The Misfit or Rayber or Mr. Fortune, unlike Ahab or Lancelot Lamar, the judge seems utterly triumphant in the end, his doctrine of murder-ously self-reliant individualism a true one. Yet—even leaving aside, for now, the more fertile landscapes suggested in the cryptic epilogue here—McCarthy surely means for us to see the judge as flawed. The judge straightforwardly maintains that while the human "heart's desire is to be told some mystery," there is in fact "no mystery." This claim is entirely consistent with the judge's reductively violent view of a nature that can and should be fully understood and controlled. But the ex-priest Tobin seems to speak for McCarthy himself when he whispers in response: "As if he were no mystery himself, the bloody old hoodwinker" (252; see O'Gorman 111–14). While the kid is unable to attain and articulate a full prophetic vision, the ex-priest here names the judge as the Prince of Lies—much as O'Connor might, since she affirmed that "the devil's greatest wile . . . is to convince us that he does not exist" (*MM* 112). This is not to say that McCarthy's viewpoint in the novel is necessarily a Christian one. Insofar as the judge is a Jehovah-like demiurge, he does seem to reveal McCarthy's own religious tendencies—at least at the time when he wrote *Blood*

Meridian—to be more darkly Gnostic than traditionally Christian.[12] Nonetheless, the judge's doctrine that life is war befits not only the Gnostic vision of Jehovah but also his identity as proto-Darwinist; and when the judge preaches that there is "no mystery," he is not Jehovah-like but rather speaking in contradiction to O'Connor's deeply orthodox assertion that "evil is not a problem to be solved, but a mystery to be endured" (862). McCarthy's judge follows, that is, in the path of O'Connor's most Satanic characters, those who seek to "correct" rather than accept the mysteries of the natural world—both its evils and the mysterious goods to be found there by those who hear God's voice and see with prophetic eyes. And even in this bleakest of McCarthy's novels there are, as we have seen, at least a few fertile landscapes promising natural good, and women who attempt to point to a good God's presence there.

It is impossible to look at human history and not see violence; it is impossible to look at nature and not see violence. And whether we read the Bible, read Darwin, or just read the newspaper, we might well reach the same conclusion: violence seems to be with us to stay. Of these three, only the Bible offers hope that it will some day come to an end, albeit not by human endeavor. And O'Connor, certainly, would have held with Walker Percy when, at the end of *Lost in the Cosmos,* he posed a choice between two future worlds: one, a brave new world where science seems to have ended both "the interminable quarrels of the Peoples of the Book" and—via eugenic strategies—human genetic imperfections; and two, a devastated version of the same old world humans have always found themselves in, a world where nature makes what seem to be mistakes in the form of imperfect children and where adults quarrel endlessly over religion, race, politics, and just about everything else (247). The latter world, O'Connor and Percy alike would maintain, is the one that God has given human beings, and it is there that they must seek grace and peace, by tending that which has been given to them—not by trying to force improvement on the species or on the world (both of which strategies are particularly tempting, perhaps, to Americans).

McCarthy's own sentiments may be surprisingly similar. His grim comment about the inevitability of bloodshed in nature takes on a profoundly traditionalist cast when read in full:

> There's no such thing as life without bloodshed. I think the notion that the species can be improved in some way, [so] that everyone could live in harmony, is a really dangerous idea. Those who are afflicted with this notion are the first to give up their souls, their freedom. Your desire that it be that way will enslave you and make your life vacuous. (Quoted in Woodward)

In McCarthy's view, then, souls prosper only when human beings accept some degree of natural inconvenience, including quarrelsomeness in their neighbors and limitation—not when human beings go too far in attempting to "correct" nature. And this statement might readily be connected with McCarthy's seeming jibes at the increasing acceptability of euthanasia and abortion in the late-twentieth-century United States in *No Country for Old Men* and—less directly—in *The Road*.[13] Here, in an ash-gray apocalyptic world where the judge seems to have had his way—where either violent natural forces (massive meteor strikes) or human technology (nuclear weapons) have wiped the beauties of nature from the earth and where many humans have turned to cannibalism to survive—a father and a son flee across the barren landscape. The narrative follows the path not of the hunters, as in *Blood Meridian,* but the hunted, and lingers not so much on scenes of violence as on those moments when the man and the boy are able to establish some simple semblance of peaceful domesticity: sharing meals, trying to remember good things from the past, the man cutting his boy's hair (128). Here the father must also serve as mother, for his wife has committed suicide rather than face the horror of this seemingly hopeless world; and he is careful to keep two bullets in his gun, one for himself and one for the ten-year-old whom he fears to leave behind.

But when he is finally dying himself, the father gives his son life. In his last hours, looking with irrational hope and love at the boy who will live beyond him, he speaks not to the son but to no one, or perhaps to God: "Look around you, he said. There is no prophet in the earth's long chronicle who's not honored here today. Whatever form you spoke of you were right" (233). The ambiguity of this statement extends beyond the question of the addressee: when the man says "you were right," does he mean to emphasize the prophesied destruction of the world or the prophesied survival of the good? His very last words answer the question. Speaking directly of another boy they had glimpsed earlier in the narrative, but indirectly of the son himself, the father says in parting: "Goodness will find the little boy. It always has. It will again" (236).

And it does. In the most straightforwardly hopeful ending McCarthy has ever written, another man and another family appear to take the boy in, to protect him and raise him. And this family is, furthermore, one of religious conviction:

> The woman when she saw him put her arms around him and held him. Oh, she said, I am so glad to see you. She would talk to him sometimes about God. He tried to talk to God but the best thing was to talk to his father and

he did talk to him and he didnt forget. The woman said that was all right. She said that the breath of God was his breath yet though it did pass from man to man through all of time. (241)

The possibility that the boy and this woman's daughter might help to repopulate the earth with human "goodness" is clearly left before the reader. The hope of completely restoring the natural world seems a much more remote possibility. Yet nonetheless McCarthy chooses to end *The Road* with a reminder of the goodness of that world, of how "once there were brook trout in streams in the mountains," trout who had on their backs "vermiculate patterns that were maps of the world in its becoming": "In the deep glens where they lived all things were older than man and they hummed of mystery" (241).

These final images of humans and nature alike, of the rich mysteries contained in each, suggest that perhaps McCarthy has at this point in his career become somewhat like old Mason Tarwater at the beginning of *The Violent Bear It Away:* "He had known what he was saving the boy from and it was saving and not destruction that he was seeking. He had learned enough to hate the destruction that had to come and not all that was going to be destroyed" (333). Perhaps he—like O'Connor—is finally not as concerned with the violence God might seemingly do to us as with the violence we do to each other and to God's creation, however flawed it may often seem. Both suggest that if we read that creation correctly we might find unexpected goods even in the most seemingly horrific scenes, whether those scenes are shaped by human agency—or not. I want to close by connecting O'Connor and McCarthy in this regard to one last American writer, Annie Dillard. Both, I think, finally read the natural world much as Dillard does in *Pilgrim at Tinker Creek,* looking squarely at its seeming horrors and its beauty and finally refusing to draw a line between the two. Meditating on the apparent cruelty of nature, Dillard describes witnessing a feeding frenzy of sharks who "roiled and heaved" in crimson waves, and—unlike Frost's speaker in "Design"—she forthrightly presents this bloody scene as a manifestation of divine "power and beauty, grace tangled in a rapture with violence" (10). Certainly that is what O'Connor describes in her work, too—not because she wishes to posit a God who is violent, but because she sees a world that is violent and affirms that a loving God is present even there. Whether or not McCarthy is able to affirm such good news remains an open question. But the women who close his most recent novels, and the loving father who finally gives his son life rather than death at the end of *The Road,* suggest that he is at least open to the possibility of hearing it.

Farrell O'Gorman

Notes

1. Knoxville friend Bill Kidwell claims that Catholicism "embittered" McCarthy; his second wife, Anne DeLisle, that the young writer "felt guilty because he couldn't encompass [his family's Catholic beliefs] in his works" (quoted in Gibson). The bitterly lapsed Catholicism of McCarthy's most clearly autobiographical protagonist, Cornelius Suttree, suggests both the veracity of such claims and the inevitable conclusion that the family's faith—along with McCarthy's education at Knoxville's Catholic high school—left an indelible mark on the writer's imagination. The following comments by Don DeLillo, a writer of McCarthy's generation who has praised his fiction, seem as if they might be applied to McCarthy as well: Despite his own current distance from the church, DeLillo says, "I think there is a sense of last things in my work that probably comes from a Catholic childhood. For a Catholic, nothing is too important to discuss or think about, because he's raised with the idea that he will die any minute now and that if he doesn't live his life in a certain way this death is simply the introduction to an eternity of pain. This removes a hesitation a writer might otherwise feel when he's approaching important subjects, eternal subjects. I think for a Catholic these things are part of ordinary life" (quoted in Passaro).

2. Parrish identifies valuable contexts for further joint consideration of O'Connor and McCarthy, briefly citing Richard Slotkin's argument that "'regeneration through violence' is the dominant theme of American history" but relying primarily on Harold Bloom's study of U.S. Gnosticism in *The American Religion*, which despite its generally pro-Gnostic bent "dissects better than any book on the American imagination the blessed landscape of the American's murdering soul" (37).

3. Daugherty firmly establishes McCarthy's engagement with Manichean Gnostic thought in *Blood Meridian;* see also Arnold on Jacob Boehme's influence on *The Crossing* in "McCarthy and the Sacred." Such readings do not place McCarthy in an orthodox Christian framework but do correct earlier claims that his fiction is simply nihilistic or "purely naturalistic" (Cawelti 169).

4. Cawelti is close to the mark in his general claim that McCarthy's "characters, like O'Connor's, are 'god-haunted,' and his novels are secular allegories of driven souls fleeing from the devil and seeking salvation in a realm across the borders of good and evil where it is increasingly difficult to distinguish between the holy and the diabolical"—yet "the possibility of Christian revelation" is not clearly "held out" to McCarthy's characters as it is to O'Connor's (168–69).

This 1997 assessment seems valid with regard to McCarthy's work up until that time, at least.

5. See Spencer regarding *Outer Dark*'s "unholy trinity" (both he and Guillemin, I think, are reductive in their claims that the novel simply "parodies" the Bible). See Metress regarding the blind seer and the novel as a whole as indicative of McCarthy's knowledge of and engagement with apophatic theology.

6. The word *evangelical* derives from the Greek for "good" and "messenger."

7. See Arnold's "McCarthy and the Sacred" and Ambrosiano for nuanced readings of McCarthy's engagement with Christian tradition in *The Crossing*.

8. William B. Dillingham demonstrates Melville's familiarity with Gnosticism in relation to Ahab's "heresy" in chapter 4 of *Melville's Later Novels* (Athens: Univ. of Georgia Press, 1986).

9. The judge's deadly obsession with a sterilizing hygiene is clear when he routes "small life from the folds of his hairless skin" and proceeds to hold up "one hand with the thumb and forefinger pressed together in a gesture that appeared to be a benediction until he flung something unseen into the fire before him" (93). Here as elsewhere in the novel the judge appears as both a mad scientist and a dark priest.

10. Donahoo's distinction between "feminine fluidity" and "masculine aridity" builds on Showalter.

11. Casarella, building on the work of Hans Urs von Balthasar and others, presents Marian receptivity as necessary for observers of the natural world to counter a modern "Anglo-American intellectual milieu" wherein "the dominant view of nature is atomistic and the dominant view of biological life accords with Darwin's most draconian interpretation of the survival of the fittest" (25). This milieu, of course, is that belonging to the judge.

12. *Blood Meridian* presents such a nightmarishly violent vision of the real that it arguably becomes anti-Gnostic: how many readers can say that hell is in fact not only possible on earth but identical to earth, as seems to be the case here?

13. In *No Country for Old Men*, Sheriff Bell recounts his conversation with a woman who complains about "right-wing" politics: "*She kept on, kept on. Finally told me, said: I dont like the way this country is headed. I want my granddaughter to be able to have an abortion. And I said well mam I dont think you got any worries about the way the country is headed. The way I see it goin I dont have much doubt but what she'll be able to have an abortion. I'm goin to say that not only will she be able to have an abortion, she'll be able to have you put to sleep. Which pretty much*

ended the conversation" (196–97). Bell himself is a habitual doomsayer and not a simple spokesman for McCarthy, but throughout the novel he is portrayed as flawed primarily in his lack of hope that right can prevail—not in his sense of right and wrong itself.

Works Cited

Ambrosiano, Jason. "Blood in the Tracks: Catholic Postmodernism in *The Crossing*." *Southwestern American Literature* 25.1 (Fall 1999): 83–91.

Arnold, Edwin T. "McCarthy and the Sacred: A Reading of *The Crossing*." Lilley 215–38.

———. "The Mosaic of McCarthy's Fiction." Hall and Wallach 1–8.

Casarella, Peter. "Waiting for a Cosmic Christ in an Uncreated World." *Communio* 28 (Summer 2001): 1–35.

Cawelti, John. "Cormac McCarthy: Restless Seekers." *Southern Writers at Century's End.* Ed. Jeffrey J. Folks and James A. Perkins. Lexington: UP of Kentucky, 1997. 164–76.

Coles, Robert. "The Stranger." *New Yorker* 50 (26 Aug. 1974): 87–90.

Daugherty, Leo. "Gravers False and True: *Blood Meridian* as Gnostic Tragedy." *Perspectives on Cormac McCarthy.* Ed. Edwin T. Arnold and Dianne C. Luce. Jackson: UP of Mississippi, 1999. 159–74.

Dillard, Annie. *Pilgrim at Tinker Creek.* New York: HarperCollins, 1998.

Donahoo, Robert. "Tarwater's March Toward the Feminine: The Role of Gender in O'Connor's *The Violent Bear It Away.*" *CEA Critic* 56.1 (Fall 1993): 96–106.

Frost, Robert. "Design." *Selected Poems of Robert Frost.* New York: Holt, Rinehart, and Winston, 1963.

Gibson, Mike. "He Felt at Home Here." *Metro Pulse* 11.9 (1 Mar. 2001). http://www.metropulse.com/dir_zine/dir_2001/1109/t_cover.html.

Gordon, Sarah. "The News from After: A Note on Structure in O'Connor's Narratives." *Flannery O'Connor Bulletin* 14 (1985): 80–88.

Guillemin, Georg. "'Books Made Out of Books': Some Instances of Intertextuality in *Outer Dark.*" *Proceedings of the First European Conference on Cormac McCarthy.* Ed. David Holloway. Miami: Cormac McCarthy Society, 1999. 28–34.

Hall, Wade, and Rick Wallach, eds. *Sacred Violence.* Vol. 1, *Cormac McCarthy's Appalachian Works.* El Paso: Texas Western, 2002.

Lilley, James D., ed. *Cormac McCarthy: New Directions.* Albuquerque: U of New Mexico P, 2002.

McCarthy, Cormac. *All the Pretty Horses.* 1992. New York: Vintage, 1993.

———. *Blood Meridian.* 1985. New York: Vintage, 1992.

———. *The Crossing.* 1994. New York: Vintage, 1995.

———. *No Country for Old Men.* New York: Alfred A. Knopf, 2005.

———. *The Road.* New York: Alfred A. Knopf, 2006.

———. *Suttree.* 1979. New York: Vintage, 1992.

Melville, Herman. "The Encantadas." *Billy Budd and Other Stories.* New York: Penguin, 1986.

———. *Moby-Dick.* New York: W. W. Norton, 2002.

Metress, Christopher. "Via Negativa: The Way of Unknowing in Cormac McCarthy's *Outer Dark.*" *Southern Review* 37.1 (Winter 2001): 147–54.

O'Connor, Flannery. *Flannery O'Connor: Collected Works.* Ed. Sally Fitzgerald. New York: Library of America, 1988.

———. *Mystery and Manners: Occasional Prose.* Ed. Sally Fitzgerald and Robert Fitzgerald. New York: Farrar, Straus, and Giroux, 1969.

O'Gorman, Farrell. "Joyce and Contesting Priesthoods in *Suttree* and *Blood Meridian.*" *Cormac McCarthy Journal* 5.1 (Spring 2005): 100–117.

Parrish, Tim. "The Killer Wears the Halo: Cormac McCarthy, Flannery O'Connor, and the American Religion." Hall and Wallach 35–50.

Passaro, Vince. "Dangerous Don DeLillo." *New York Times Magazine,* 19 May 1991. http://www.nytimes.com/books/97/03/16/lifetimes/del-v-dangerous.html.

Percy, Walker. *Lancelot.* 1977. New York: Farrar, Straus, and Giroux, 1999.

———. *Lost in the Cosmos.* 1983. New York: Farrar, Straus, and Giroux, 1996.

———. *The Message in the Bottle.* 1975. New York: Farrar, Straus, and Giroux, 1997.

Rudnicki, Robert W. *Percyscapes: The Fugue State in Twentieth-Century Southern Fiction.* Baton Rouge: Louisiana State UP, 1999.

Showalter, Elaine. "Representing Ophelia: Women, Madness, and the Responsibilities of Feminist Criticism." *Shakespeare and the Question of Theory.* Ed. Patricia Parker and Geoffrey Hartman. Methuen: New York, 1985. 77–94.

Spencer, William C. "Cormac McCarthy's Unholy Trinity: Biblical Parody in *Outer Dark.*" Hall and Wallach 83–91.

Spurgeon, Sara. "The Sacred Hunter and the Eucharist of the Wilderness: Mythic Reconstructions in *Blood Meridian*." Lilley 75–102.

Woodward, Richard B. "Cormac McCarthy's Venomous Fiction." *New York Times Magazine,* 19 Apr. 1992. http://www.nytimes.com/books/98/05/17/specials/mccarthy-venom.html.

SHIFTLET'S CHOICE:
O'CONNOR'S FORDIST LOVE STORY

Doug Davis

In the opening pages of Flannery O'Connor's short story "The Life You Save May Be Your Own" (1953), the tramp Tom T. Shiftlet arrives at the hardscrabble farm of Lucynell Crater and her daughter of the same name, a "large girl" with "pink-gold hair and eyes as blue as a peacock's neck." Entering the Craters' yard, Shiftlet pauses for a moment to admire the sunset. Turning to approach the two ladies, his gaze passes over a pump and some chickens before settling on a shed in which he can make out "the square rusted back of an automobile." It is love at first sight. Tom T. Shiftlet can not keep his eyes off of that car. "You ladies drive?" he asks, and in the conversation that follows he makes his proper introduction—not to the Craters but to the car that has kept his gaze and which he addresses modestly with downcast eyes:

> "That car ain't run in fifteen year," the old woman said. "The day my husband died, it quit running."
>
> "Nothing is like it used to be, lady," he said. "The world is almost rotten."
>
> "That's right," the old woman said. "You from around here?"
>
> "Name Tom T. Shiftlet," he murmured, looking at the tires. (*CW* 172–73)

Shiftlet will ultimately get Mrs. Crater's Ford, but only by marrying her handicapped daughter. By story's end he will have abandoned his new wife at a roadside diner, driving off to Mobile, Alabama, as fast as he can in his true love—the stolen Ford.

"The Life You Save May Be Your Own" is a story about a man who falls in love with a car. For many mid-century American authors it may have remained just that. Yet in O'Connor's hands this innocent, all-American scenario becomes a grotesque story about desire deflected in terrifying, inhuman ways that reveals the unspoken political truth of postwar America's consumer society. O'Connor presents Tom T. Shiftlet as a new kind of American who inhabits an alienating world in which the regime of mass production has collapsed the boundary between man and machine in ways both personal and physical. O'Connor figures this collapse in the inhuman image of Shiftlet himself, a man she describes not only literally as in love with an automobile but also figuratively as part automobile himself. Shiftlet is O'Connor's model modern American, a conflicted figure driven to find meaning and satisfaction in things but also driven by a sense that the things he desires are essentially meaningless. The story of Shiftlet's choice of a Ford over his wife is a fable about the terrifying kind of person that the American worker has become: a consumer.

As critics such as Roger N. Casey, David R. Mayber, Brian Abel Ragen, and Deborah Clarke have observed in their respective analyses of O'Connor's automotive imagery, O'Connor is a keen observer of American car culture. Cars play a central and often critical role in a great many of O'Connor's stories, propelling her characters through her plots and signifying their fealty to American consumer culture and its secular materialist ways.[1] Many of O'Connor's characters are eager participants in America's postwar car culture. They have profound relationships with their automobiles, projecting their hopes and dreams upon them, putting their faith in them, preaching atop them, sleeping and eating in them, experiencing divine visions in their presence, killing with them, dying besides them, and even, in the case of "The Life You Save May Be Your Own," resurrecting them. As Jon Lance Bacon and Ralph C. Wood observe, the car is one of the main symbolic means by which O'Connor demonstrates the perils of buying too thoroughly into the whole "American Way of Life" (Wood 15–22; see also Bacon 38–41).

In this essay I turn O'Connor's story inward upon the subject who inhabits the American way of life and its automobiles—Tom T. Shiftlet, model American—and read "The Life You Save May Be Your Own" as a politicized technocultural fable about not only what the American Way of Life is but also what the American worker and consumer have become. O'Connor's close observance of America's car culture stands out strikingly in this particular story when it is read as a representation of the industrial regime that produced postwar American car culture, Fordism. Tom T. Shiftlet is O'Connor's model of the Fordist man. He is her prescient, deeply alienated image of the emergent postwar hybrids that people her era of machinic coupling and desire. Shiftlet is a real man of his mass-industrial times. His love for his car is the most natural thing about him, and love it truly is.

O'Connor turned the focus of her story upon the people who inhabit Fordist culture as she revised the story's title through the stages of its publication. When O'Connor sent a draft of "The Life You Save May Be Your Own" to her agent, Elizabeth McKee, it initially bore the working title "The World Is Almost Rotten" (*HB* 44). The working title looks unambiguously outward, locating Shiftlet in a modern world that matches his own rotten actions. O'Connor later changed the title to the one we have now, and the final title looks more ambiguously inward, taking a personal interest in Shiftlet and the choices he makes.[2] Yet in addition to addressing Shiftlet, who first sees the phrase "The Life You Save May Be Your Own" on a sign warning him to drive carefully as he makes his dash for Mobile, the final title also addresses the reader herself, who is likewise hailed by O'Connor's titular "you." You and Shiftlet have something in common; you are both subjects of the same things. The retitled story published in the spring 1953 issue of the *Kenyon Review* puts its readers in a subjunctive mood, prompting them to consider possibilities and look to the future, both Mr. Shiftlet's and their own. Its uncertainties are questions that can be addressed to every modern American reader who encounters O'Connor's contemporary American fable about the man who chose a car over his wife. Where are you going? More important, what have you become?

At face value, the situation O'Connor presents in "The Life You Save May Be Your Own" reads like a humorous grotesque built from broken bodies, mean perceptions, and comic reversals. A one-armed drifter schemes to marry an impoverished deaf and possibly mentally handicapped girl in order to steal her mother's car. The girl's mother, "ravenous for a son-in-law" (*CW* 177), turns out to be just as calculating as Shiftlet, scheming to marry her feeble, aging daughter to the only person who would have her, "a poor disabled friendless drifting man" (*CW* 179). When Shiftlet decides to abandon the sleeping Lucynell at the roadside diner after driving with her for only one hundred miles, he strips her of whatever dignity she had left by telling the counter boy that she's a hitchhiker. Mr. Shiftlet soon gets his grotesque comeuppance, though. After dumping his wife, he feels a pang of social responsibility and picks up a hitchhiker of his own, a young boy on the run from home. Shiftlet strikes up a conversation with the boy about the emotional value of mothers of all things. It's only fair that the hitchhiker responds to his tenderness with verbal terror, telling Shiftlet that "My old woman is a flea bag and yours is a stinking pole cat!" and then jumping from his car. The sorely pained Shiftlet feels "the rottenness of the world was about to engulf him." He cries out, "Oh Lord! Break forth and wash the slime from this earth!" (*CW* 183). By story's end, the rottenness of the world rebalances. The rain, along with the story's joke, falls in the final paragraph on him.

This grotesque comedy of ill manners can certainly be read as a humorous satire aimed at heartless materialists. However, as Patricia Yaeger discusses in *Dirt and Desire,* the grotesque is also a serious political category in literature, especially literature written by the women of the American South. "Grotesque bodies provide a particularly condensed and useful figure of thought for presenting a set of problems plaguing the South," Yaeger writers, for the monstrous figure "offers, among other advantages, a way of previewing what is known but not thought—a set of unacknowledged political coordinates." The grotesque image thus functions, firstly, as a "semiotic switchboard," "a prose technique for moving background information into the foreground of a novel or story" (25). Grotesque images can display the reality of a situation when neither characters nor narrator describe them. For example, a child's grotesque impersonation of adults engaging in acts of violence depicts the unspoken brutalities of slavery in *Uncle Tom's Cabin* (26). Grotesque images of hybrid bodies, in turn, register cultural shifts. For example, the changing public role of women finds its grotesque analog in the hermaphrodite who challenges men to judge her in O'Connor's short story, "A Temple of the Holy Ghost." In a similar manner, O'Connor's "Everything That Rises Must Converge" marks the breaking down of traditional social boundaries between races by the identical purple hats worn by Julian's white mother and the black woman who kills her (31–32).

The grotesque image of the one-armed, wife-abandoning Shiftlet racing away in his stolen Ford is a revealing figure in both of these senses, bringing to the fore the new realities of postwar America's political economy and the alienated consumers who inhabit it. Shiftlet is a new kind of man in a mass-produced world. His choices reveal, in their own grotesque way, Fordist culture's own hybridizing tendencies to not only break down the boundary between men and machines but also to redirect the productive desire for meaningful labor to the consumptive desire for mass-produced goods. Shiftlet's choice of Ford over family is, in short, the grotesque image of America's postwar economic assumption.

In her 1963 lecture, "The Catholic Novelist in the Protestant South," O'Connor foregrounds the importance of the grotesque to faith-based literature such as her own by noting its ability to unmask assumptions and reveal unspoken political truths. She fears a time in the not-too-far future when southern writers will turn to writing about "men in grey flannel suits" and lose their "ability to see that these gentlemen are even greater freaks than what we are writing about now" (*CW* 861). When she gave the lecture, that time had not yet come and O'Connor thus urges her audience to appreciate anew the significance of the southern grotesque:

> It is to be hoped that Catholics will look deeper into Southern literature and the subject of the grotesque and learn to see there more than what appears

on the surface. Thomas Mann has said that the grotesque is a true anti-bourgeois style. Certainly Catholicism is opposed to the bourgeois mind. (*CW* 862)

As Jon Lance Bacon discusses in his essay "A Fondness for Supermarkets," these are provocative sentiments to utter, especially in the midst of the cold war. They mark O'Connor's willingness to "participat[e] in a nationwide debate regarding the status of individualism under corporate capitalism" (28) and link her with other critics of the American way of life such as C. Wright Mills and Marshall McLuhan, each of whom "expressed a desire to resist a consumerist ideology that dovetailed with the reigning political consensus" (36).

Shiftlet is the figure through whom O'Connor most decisively figures her resistance to the reigning political consensus. His choice of a Ford car marks him as a character created by a very specific and influential kind of bourgeois mind. In his writings on Americanism and Fordism in his *Prison Notebooks,* Antonio Gramsci singled out the Fordist factory as an exemplary product of the bourgeois mind. His interpretation of Fordism and its spiritually deadening aspects dovetails with O'Connor's own antibourgeois sentiments, especially as expressed in "The Life You Save May Be Your Own." Gramsci analyzes the "new industrialism" as an "American phenomenon, which is also the biggest collective effort to date to create, with unprecedented speed, and with a consciousness of purpose unmatched in history, a new type of worker and of man" (215). Shiftlet is that new kind of man, in all his technological embodiments and false sentiments.

Fordism collapses traditional boundaries between labor and consumption alongside those between man and machine to create its new type of man. Henry Ford successfully applied the techniques of Taylorism to the assemblyline, matching workers' motions to the machines they worked at, thus greatly increasing the efficiency of mass production while driving costs down (Harvey 125). This allowed him to raise wages to the point that his workers could afford to buy the same products whose components they were repetitively assembling. In this way Ford did something almost magical for American capitalism: he closed the loop between mass production and mass consumption, integrating his workers simultaneously into the assembly line and the market.

As David Harvey describes, Ford's true innovation

was his vision, his explicit recognition that mass production meant mass consumption, a new system of the reproduction of labor power, a new politics of labor control and management, a new aesthetics and psychology, in

short, a new kind of rationalized, modernist, and populist democratic society. (125–26)

Ford closely monitored the purity of his workers' lives, sending inspectors from
his company's sociology department to police their personal behavior, not for
his workers' welfare but to maintain the efficiency of the assembly line. As
Gramsci observes of the industrialists' puritanical-seeming motivations:

> It is certain that they are not concerned with the "humanity" or the "spiri-
> tuality" of the worker, which are immediately smashed. This "humanity and
> spirituality" cannot be realized except in the world of production and work
> and in productive "creation." They exist most in the artisan, in the "demi-
> urge," when the worker's personality was reflected whole in the object cre-
> ated and when the link between art and labor was still very strong. But it
> is precisely against this "humanism" that the new industrialism is fighting.
> (216)

The new industrialism that came to flower in postwar Fordism constitutes what
Harvey identifies as "a total way of life. Mass production meant standardization
of product as well as mass consumption; and that meant a whole new aesthetic
and a commodification of culture" (135). Fordism's technocultural integrations
reach through culture and into the body as well, blurring the line between not
only machine and worker but human being and mass-produced technological
product, the deficiencies of the former being made up for by the purchase of the
latter (Clarke 49). Thus, as one reader of "The Life You Save May Be Your Own"
observes, the one-armed Shiftlet "sees the car as a way to make him whole and to
make him mobile" (Casey 87). In Fordian terms, a man is what he drives.

O'Connor's grotesque driver, Tom T. Shiftlet, registers these integrations
of mass-industrial consumption. Yet while the author makes her fictional driver
a monstrous thief, when it came time for O'Connor and her mother to buy a
car, she made the same choices as most other American consumers. O'Connor
spent her early childhood in Savannah around cars and saw automotive tech-
nologies come and go; in the 1920s and 1930s, her cousin Katie drove her
around town in the last electric car in the city (Cash 17). O'Connor didn't
get a license to drive until 1958 (*HB* 291) and pled ignorance as to the difference between a bumper and a fender.[3] However, throughout her writing career
O'Connor knew the importance of the car not only as a status symbol but also
as a cultural formation in its own right, a whole way of life.

O'Connor's personal experience with cars illustrates how they become not only a part of one's life but also an extension of one's body. As objects of conspicuous consumption, cars can reflect the character of their driver. For instance, when it came time for her family to purchase a car, O'Connor wrote to Betty Hester in a letter of 20 August 1958 that her mother "will not have one that looks like an Easter egg so we are looking for a black one" (*HB* 291). The car that arrived carried mortal connotations, being "black, hearse-like, dignified, a rolling memento mori." It came with family connections as well: "Brother Louis got it for us in Atlanta from a man named Young who called up to sell it to us and told us that he loved Brother Louis just like he was one of his brothers and made a slight reduction in price." Like any new car buyer, O'Connor was eager to show off her family's new purchase to Hester, writing that "the next time you arrive at our gate, I shall meet you in it and drive you up" (*HB* 294).

Cars are not only objects of conspicuous consumption but also extend the human body while integrating it into vast technoscientific systems. The driver becomes both a consumer of a mass-produced industrial product (itself produced by the laboring man-machine hybrid, the assembly line) and also a kind of laboratory technician in her own right possessed of the skills to combust gas and operate gears. O'Connor's family cars are no exception to this technoscientific integrative process. As the sociologist of science Bruno Latour describes, modern technological civilizations develop by incorporating pieces of laboratory practice into the business of their citizens' everyday lives. The high-tech world is riddled with "black-boxed" technoscientific networks, largely taken for granted and given little thought, that reproduce scientific experiments throughout society every time a technological device does whatever it is supposed to do.[4] Ultimately, the citizen of a high-tech state must conform to regimes of scientific praxis, for their societies have been engineered, in effect, into vast laboratories (Latour, "Give Me a Laboratory," 166–67). These networks and expert scientific practices disappear from consciousness and integrate themselves into modern lives through a process that Latour calls "delegation." Machines and other artifacts do work once done by people. In this way, the human world efficiently incorporates nonhumans into its cultures, routinely employing the "congealed labor" otherwise known as technology by delegating sundry tasks to machines and artifacts, all without too much thought about the vast scientific and engineering networks that produce and sustain those things (Latour, *Pandora's Hope,* 189).

These processes change how people live by breaking boundaries between nature and culture, humans and nonhumans, and bodies and machines. They make people and their machines increasingly complementary and even inter-changeable. In her correspondence with Hester, O'Connor illustrates how she automatically accepted the technology of the car as an augmentation of the human body and freely delegated several of her own actions to it, such as shift-ing and steering. Indeed, with the latest high-tech accessories, she remarks that the car they purchased could even extend life itself. In her letter of 19 July 1958, she writes, "I am now persuading my mother to buy a car with automatic trans-mission and power steering. I figure this will add some years to her life as well as making it easier on me" (*HB* 291). When they purchased another new car in 1963, O'Connor matter-of-factly explains to Hester how its new feature, power brakes, augments her weak legs and allows her to drive because "they are so positioned that you don't have to lift your foot to put them on" (*HB* 533). Out in the writer's everyday world, machines and bodies mesh naturally and the ne-cessity for a car, once granted, becomes a given.[5]

Because writing about the car as an augmentation of the body and a means to extend life appears so very natural to a contemporary readership, O'Connor must adopt grotesque literary means to foreground how thoroughly the car and its hybrid states of being have penetrated American culture. O'Connor registers the integrations of man, market and machine through the grotesque hybrid imagery that she uses to describe her cars and drivers. O'Connor began using such imagery to reveal American culture's attachment to cars in her novel *Wise Blood,* her first prolonged study of the car's significance to American culture. Before considering how O'Connor uses hybrid imagery in "The Life You Save May Be Your Own," it is instructive to see how O'Connor registers her culture's attachment to its automobiles—and by extension its integration into the entire regime of Fordist mass consumption—in a similar way in that earlier work. In *Wise Blood* O'Connor shows how thoroughly cars have integrated themselves into American culture in two ways: at the level of plot by the amount of faith Hazel Motes puts into a car that is truly a piece of junk; and at the level of imagery by how fleshy and sexualized, how human, Haze's car turns out to be.

The Essex not only becomes an object of Haze's philosophy but also be-comes a kind of human character in the novel. The language O'Connor uses to describe how Haze's car behaves also describes how people behave. The Essex sounds and acts alive. It makes a "high growling noise" as it moves (*CW* 40) and its windshield wipers make "a great clatter like two idiots clapping in church" (*CW* 41). At one point, Haze enlists the help of a one-armed man to push-start his car after it stalls; after several hundred feet Haze knows that the Essex has started because it "began to belch and gasp and jiggle" (*CW* 71–72). As Linda

Rohrer Paige observes, at one point the Essex even "imitates the sexual act itself" (331):

> The Essex had a tendency to develop a tic by nightfall. It would go forward about six inches and then back about four; it did that now a succession of times rapidly; otherwise Haze would have shot off in it and been gone. He had to grip the steering wheel with both hands to keep from being thrown either out the windshield or into the back. It stopped this after a few seconds and slid about twenty feet and then began at it again. (*CW* 87–88)

Small wonder, J. O. Tate muses in "The Essential Essex," that O'Connor chose a brand name with such an obviously erotic pun (53–57).

While O'Connor humanizes the car in her prose, Hazel Motes attaches philosophical meaning to the Essex. The inflated value he places in it is a sign of how thoroughly he rejects the supernatural. But the grotesque metaphors that O'Connor uses to describe the Essex also illustrate how cars have more than philosophical appeal and become part of human life. Haze wants more than transportation from his car; he wants to live in it. To use Latour's term, Haze wants to "delegate" the work of housing to his car, telling the man he purchases it from that "I wanted this car mostly to be a house for me . . . I ain't got any place to be" (*CW* 41). As a house, the Essex will of course have to deal with Haze's bodily functions, perhaps some he has not thought about. But those become apparent as soon as Haze takes his car out for its first ride. As he sits in his stalled car at the top of a hill and blocks the road, the truck driver who confronts Haze tells him, "Will you get your goddam outhouse off the middle of the road?" (*CW* 43).

Tom T. Shiftlet, like Hazel Motes, is what Marshall Bruce Gentry identifies as "A Philosophical Criminal with a Car" (46). Yet while Haze chooses to live in his Essex to make an explicit philosophical statement about how little he needs the supernatural, Shiftlet chooses the Ford because he *desires* it, and he uses his philosophy to get it. Shiftlet wants the Ford to be a part of his life. Much as O'Connor uses humanized imagery to describe the Essex as a part of Haze's life in *Wise Blood,* she uses mechanized imagery to describe Shiftlet as part of the Ford's life. The language of man and machine becomes interchangeable. As soon as the Craters meet Shiftlet, he begins to identify himself in automotive terms. As the story progresses, the lines between the man carrying the toolbox and the car with the square rusted back begin to blur. At first this blurring is metaphorical and proceeds at the level of puns, but it swiftly turns to an expression of love.

Consider Shiftlet's name: Tom T. Shiftlet. It is an evocative name. For starters, it indicates that Tom is shiftless, insofar as he hasn't made anything of his life. It likewise indicates that he is shifty. Yet his middle initial also evokes a car, the Model T, which resonates with the car he covets, a Ford. Furthermore, his last name is a pun, playing off of the car's gear shifter. In one of his philosophical spiels, Tom tells Mrs. Crater that she cannot know who he is and then proceeds to list a series of names that could be his, most of which are automotive puns:

> I can tell you my name is Tom T. *Shift*let and I come from Tarwater, Tennessee, but you never have seen me before: how you know I ain't lying? How you know my name ain't Aaron *Sparks*, lady, and I come from Singleberry, Georgia, or how you know it's not George *Speeds* and I come from Lucy, Alabama. (*CW* 174; my emphases)

Through these puns, O'Connor recapitulates the history of automotive engineering: couple a gear shifter with a spark plug in a gasoline engine and get a car capable of speeds much greater than any O'Connor's cousin's old electric car could attain.[6]

Peering under the car's hood, Tom identifies the car as a 1928 or 1929 Ford, making it a Model A, the replacement for the Model T, which was discontinued in 1927 (Casey 86). After he promises to fix the car, Shiftlet lies to Mrs. Crater in such a way that he turns the history of Fordism on its head; he informs her

> that the car had been built in the days when cars were really built. You take now, he said, one man puts in one bolt and another man puts in another bolt and another man puts in another bolt so that it's a man for a bolt. That's why you have to pay so much for a car: you're paying all those men. Now if you didn't have to pay but one man, you could get a cheaper car and one that had had a personal interest taken in it, and it would be a better car. (*CW* 177)

Of course, the exact opposite is true about the car that he means to repair; it is as much a product of the assembly line as the Model T that preceded it. Indulging in nostalgia, Shiftlet describes the way he thinks a car ought to be built, a way that is an expression of the person who built it.

But that's not the way things are in Fordist America, nor is it Shiftlet's intention to accurately tell Mrs. Crater the history of Fordism. Rather, his praise of her old car is instead a form of flattery. It is a part of the way that Shiftlet, a man who identifies himself with aspects of cars, seduces not Mrs. Crater's daughter, but Mrs. Crater's car, flattering it and its owner. He is wooing the car. To complete his wooing, he sleeps with the car, paints it up nicely with a jaunty yellow stripe, and ultimately gives it a new life away from the Crater farm. Mrs. Crater is of course complicit in this process; it is her idea to have Shiftlet sleep in the car in the first place, her reasoning being that she is "advanced" (*CW* 176).[7]

Where Hazel Motes wished—but ultimately failed—to delegate all the business of living to his Essex, Shiftlet almost effortlessly delegates the mysteries of the human heart to the Ford assembly line. Shiftlet is one of O'Connor's many lost souls, possessed of a sense that something is wrong in the world but dispossessed of the means to fix it, or even identify it. Since Shiftlet can't come out and identify what ails him, the reader must look at the story's grotesque hybrid figure, the choice he makes, to see what background information it is moving into the foreground. As John Desmond observes, Shiftlet is suffering from "spiritual malaise" (55), an emptiness that drives him "in his endless inhuman quest for the perfect world" (59). Desmond attributes Shiftlet's malaise to the idealistic dualism of his personal philosophy. Yet O'Connor's hybrid imagery suggests his malaise has a more material source. The "inhuman" thing that is really driving him on his quest, after all, is his car.

Shiftlet is a man driven to seek personal satisfaction in mass-produced commodities, the very kind of satisfaction that is the engine that makes the American economy go. O'Connor, however, presents this kind of satisfaction as a grotesque choice. Unable to fix his spiritual malaise, Shiftlet fixes the next best thing, a Ford car, which will allow him to at least live fully in his Fordist world; after all, "his spirit," as he tells Mrs. Crater, "is like a automobile: always on the move, always" (*CW* 179). Yet while Shiftlet's spirit may be satisfied by the car, there is a material part of Shiftlet, a human part, that feels the emptiness of his choice and is aware that *something* has smashed the world's humanity and spirituality. His world *is* almost rotten. And so he drives on.

It is O'Connor's grotesque hybrid imagery that reveals what that something is: Shiftlet in his Ford, the working man lost on the road of postwar Fordism's commodity culture. Showing up at the Craters' farm with a tool box, Shiftlet identifies himself as a laborer. He equates being a man with the kinds of jobs he can do. He responds to Mrs. Craters's doubts about him by telling her, "the best I can tell you is, I'm a man; but listen lady . . . what is a man?" (*CW* 175). The only thing the reader then learns about this man is that he is "a carpenter." Indeed, the only part of Shiftlet's personal history that the reader ever learns is the succession of jobs that he has held as a singer, railroad foreman, undertaker, and soldier (*CW* 175). But even though he shows up at the farm as a worker bearing his tools, this worker is wounded and incomplete. Shiftlet's labors do improve the farm. He even fixes Lucynell by teaching her to say her first word. But despite his stated intentions, he will not stay on the farm. Once he sees that car, Shiftlet turns into a thieving, monstrous consumer more in love with things than people. The farm he leaves is the past; he is the future, the very model of what the American worker has become.

Model Tom has another, more personal history preserved in O'Connor's early drafts of "The Life You Save May Be Your Own." These fragments clearly mark him as a product of his technoscientific commodity culture. As Jan Nordby Gretlund explains, the unpublished material gives Shiftlet psychological depth. Knowing his motivations, he becomes a more sympathetic character. In place of the published version's moral cipher, we find a man who "has been conditioned by his environment." Gretlund speculates that O'Connor eliminated Shiftlet's backstory deliberately so as to shift her readers' focus away from its social critique and towards its "consideration of human culpability" (76). If O'Connor did suppress her story's political dimension in favor of its moral one, it is not surprising that the story's element of social critique emerges to the foreground primarily in its grotesque hybrid figure of car and driver. However, this is far from the case in the early drafts, wherein the reader learns precisely why Shiftlet makes the choices he does. In Shiftlet's unpublished backstory collected in folders 153a and 154a in the manuscript archive in the Flannery O'Connor Collection at Georgia College and State University, the reader learns very clearly who Shiftlet really is: an amalgam of Thomas Edison and Henry Ford. In his own mind, he is the rightful maker of the industrial world he inhabits.

"[In] his heart," O'Connor writes in her unpublished draft, the young Shiftlet "felt that he could change the world" (quoted in Gretlund 83–84). The boy is the product of a grotesque parody of a progressive scientific upbringing. His mother had hired a phrenologist to evaluate his character, a scientist whom O'Connor describes monstrously as "an eyeless old man in a brown tail coat. His head was as naked as a vulture's and the same shape. His nose, long and thin and blue, overhung a scar which gapped in the middle to expose a gold and a black tooth, side by side" (quoted in Gretlund 79). After the gruesome Dr. Sparks has sized up Shiftlet's head, he offers Mrs. Shiftlet the following advice: "*make* him do nothing! Let him do what he pleases" (quoted in Gretlund 82). As Gretlund observes, the phrenologist's "claims for phrenology parody the modern belief in the omnipotence of science and the human intellect" and his advice mocks "one of the principles of modern education" (Gretlund 75). Shiftlet, for his part, soon chooses to stop going to school.

Instead, he chooses to become a self-made man and announces to his mother his intention to be the inventor of an ultimate thing to which humanity could delegate just about *everything*. To which his mother replies,

> "What thing?"
>
> "Like a car," he said, "only like a submarine too and a airplane at the same time so you can ride anywhere you want to go. It'll dig a hole in the ground too," he said, "straight down or anyway you want to go, and you can live in it a nobody'll ever catch you."

Shiftlet calls this miraculous device "a infiblat." In addition to promising to take over the duties of most other machines, Shiftlet imagines the infiblat will also "make the duties of religion unnecessary." He then demonstrates his total identification with the machine he proposes to build by *becoming* the infiblat, jumping up on his bed as "he waved his arms wildly and went 'Blll-aaaaaaaattttttttttatatatataaaaaaaatt!' and frightened his poor mother to death" (quoted in Gretlund 83–84).

Shiftlet keeps his world-transforming inventor's spirit as he grows up, even though he never invents a thing. Even after he gets his arm blown off in a foxhole, he remains a futurist called to go faster and faster, seeing the world's "unifying principle" as speed (quoted in Gretlund 85). As O'Connor describes him, he lets his mind run on automatic, never thinking about what he has done until after he has done it. Even his morality becomes a machine, a device built to withstand pressure. In the published version of the story, Shiftlet enigmatically declares to Mrs. Crater, "I'm a man . . . even if I ain't a whole one. I got . . . a moral intelligence!" (*CW* 176). The phrase moral intelligence had originally been used by mid-century literary critics such as John Crowe Ransom and Yvor Winters.[8] O'Connor gratefully received a copy of Winters's *In Defense of Reason* from Cecil Dawkins (*HB* 286–87), wherein Winters articulates his moral theory of poetry. Winters argues that poems are "a realization of spiritual control." A poem exhibiting a controlled moral intelligence is "not a safety valve, by which feeling is diverted from action" in an attempt to escape the pressure of that feeling, but rather a controlled means to contemplate feeling so as to arrive at objective truth (Winters 21–22). O'Connor employs Winters's phrase "safety valve" in one of her story's unpublished alternate endings (collected in folder 154a) to describe Shiftlet's moral intelligence in mechanical terms, writing that it was built without indicators or releases but was nevertheless capable of with-standing enormous pressures.

In that unpublished ending, the controlled moral intelligence of Tom T. Shiftlet finally succumbs to too much pressure and explodes. It turns out he really is Aaron Sparks of Mobile, Alabama. He arrives at his home, where his wife and three kids await him. In his absence, his wife has bought a new television on the installment plan. When he enters his sons' bedroom, he finds them seated as if in church worshipping the television while watching lady wrestling. This makes Aaron Sparks blow up. He seizes a baseball bat, smashes the television, smashes his wife on the head, and hits the road once again.

In this version of O'Connor's story, Shiftlet returns home to Mobile look-ing for satisfaction in the institutions of family and home and marriage. He finds nothing there, much as he found nothing worth staying for at the Craters' farm. The institutions of marriage and family don't exist in any meaningful way for a Fordist man such as Tom T. Shiftlet whose labors and desires are part of the machinery of mass production and consumption. Only life at the wheel of his stolen car offers him any relief, and this may be because the Ford is the one thing that he has been able to fully take a personal interest in, the one thing he truly built that is a reflection of him. While his description of the old Ford Model A as a car that "had been built in the days when cars were really built" by "one man . . . that had had a personal interest taken in it" is a false piece of nostalgia, he ultimately makes it come true by being the one man to take a personal interest in the car and make it run again. The Ford becomes his infiblat. When he drives the Ford out of Mrs. Crater's shed, he wears "an expression of serious modesty on his face as if he had just raised the dead" (*CW* 178). Stealing the resurrected Ford allows him to live with the two contradictory impulses that drive him as a Fordist inventor-missionary of speed through a mass-produced technoculture that welcomes consumers, not missionaries. He *really* wants the car, this em-blematic yet essentially meaningless product of Fordist culture; at the same time he just as dearly wants to believe the lie that the Ford car is the product of per-sonal interest, that it contains true meaning and value. When O'Connor's model Fordist man sits at The Hot Spot diner with the sleeping Lucynell, the choice he faces is not really between his wife and his car at all. It is a choice between the value of two things he has rebuilt. On the one hand, he has fixed Lucynell's voice, allowing her to blurt out "Burrttddt" (*CW* 177). On the other hand, he has brought a car back to life, allowing him to go anywhere in America and be anyone. The choice Model Tom makes is terrifying and inhuman, but it is the only natural choice for a man in his situation.

Notes

1. "The Life You Save May Be Your Own" is often read as a critique of the depredations of modern American consumer culture. As Jan Nordby Gretlund argues in his analysis of the story's unpublished early drafts, Shiftlet's tale should be read as a satirical account of "what modern society does to us" (73). In this line of critique, Shiftlet's choice is not only morally wrong, it is unnatural; the car is a fetish in a tale of "perverted love" (Burke 49) and Shiftlet's choice is but one of many ways that O'Connor uses "the detritus of an industrial society which lives out of time" to foreground the banality of "the modern environment" (Tate, "Uses of Banality," 15, 17). Shiftlet's Ford, much like Hazel Motes's Essex in *Wise Blood,* becomes, as J. O. Tate puts it, "a symbol of every exploitation associated with industrialism, corporate capitalism, and the New" ("Essential Essex," 53).

2. The original title of "The Life You Save May Be Your Own" was "Personal Interest" (Gretlund 76).

3. In the version of "The Life You Save May Be Your Own" published in the *Kenyon Review,* O'Connor has Shiftlet start his car by stepping on its clutch, an error that she corrected in later published drafts (*HB* 148).

4. Latour discusses his "actor-network" theory of technological civilizations in two studies of how Louis Pasteur integrated vaccination into French society: his article "Give Me a Laboratory and I Will Raise the World" (1983) and his book-length study, *The Pasteurization of France* (1988).

5. Of course this doesn't mean one has to like it. While O'Connor recognized the necessity of a car (especially given her deteriorating health and the advancing age of her mother), she never took to driving, writing to Hester in 1963, "I still hate to drive unfortunately" (*HB* 533).

6. The first names Tom, Aaron, and George also have major religious connotations, referring to Thomas Aquinas, the model priest, Aaron brother of Moses, the great spokesman, and St. George, the model martyr.

7. O'Connor moved Shiftlet closer and closer to his current hybrid automotive state as she drafted the story, first having him sleep with the animals and then with the tools before having him sleep in the car. In an early draft of this story preserved in Folder 153a in the Flannery O'Connor Special Collection at Georgia College & State University, O'Connor originally had Shiftlet sleeping in the farm's milking parlor. However, she then crossed that line out and replaced it with a handwritten mention of the farm's tool shed.

8. My thanks to Ralph Wood for pointing out this connection to me.

Works Cited

Bacon, Jon Lance. "A Fondness for Supermarkets: *Wise Blood* and Consumer Culture." *New Essays on Wise Blood.* Ed. Michael Kreyling. New York: Cambridge UP, 1995. 25–50.

Burke, William. "Fetishism in the Fiction of Flannery O'Connor." *Flannery O'Connor Bulletin* 22 (1993–94): 45–52.

Casey, Roger N. "Driving Miss Flannery: Automobiles in O'Connor's Short Stories." *Journal of Contemporary Thought* 4 (1994): 85–97.

Cash, Jean W. *Flannery O'Connor: A Life.* Knoxville: U of Tennessee P, 2002.

Clarke, Deborah. *Driving Women: Fiction and Automobile Culture in Twentieth Century America.* Baltimore: Johns Hopkins UP, 2007.

Desmond, John F. "The Shifting of Mr. Shiftlet: Flannery O'Connor's 'The Life You Save May Be Your Own.'" *Mississippi Quarterly* 28 (1974–75): 55–59.

Gentry, Marshall Bruce. "O'Connor's Legacy in Stories by Joyce Carol Oates and Paula Sharp." *Flannery O'Connor Bulletin* 23 (1994–95): 44–60.

Gramsci, Antonio. *Prison Notebooks, Volume II.* Trans. and Ed. Joseph I. Buttigieg. New York: Columbia UP, 1996.

Gretlund, Jan Nordby. "Mr. Shiftlet, Chapter Two: An Introduction to 'The Shiftlet Fragment.'" *Flannery O'Connor Bulletin* 10 (1981): 70–86.

Harvey, David. *The Condition of Postmodernity: An Enquiry into the Origins of Cultural Change.* Oxford: Blackwell, 1989.

Latour, Bruno. "Give Me a Laboratory and I Will Raise the World." *Science Observed: Perspectives on the Social Study of Science.* Eds. Karin D. Knorr-Cetina and Michael Mulkay. London: SAGE, 1983. 141–69.

———. *Pandora's Hope: Essays on the Reality of Science Studies.* Cambridge: Harvard UP, 1999.

———. *The Pasteurization of France.* Trans. Alan Sheridan and John Law. Cambridge: Harvard UP, 1988.

Mayer, David R. "'Ain't Adjusted to the Modern World': Flannery O'Connor and the Automobile." *Kansas Quarterly* 21.4 (1989): 67–74.

O'Connor, Flannery. *Collected Works.* New York: Library of America, 1988.

———. *The Habit of Being: Letters of Flannery O'Connor.* Ed. Sally Fitzgerald. New York: Farrar, 1979.

Paige, Linda Rohrer. "White Trash, Low Class, and No Class at All: Perverse Portraits of Phallic Power in Flannery O'Connor's *Wise Blood.*" *Papers on Language and Literature* 33 (1997): 325–33.

Ragen, Brian Abel. *A Wreck on the Road to Damascus: Innocence, Guilt, and Conversion in Flannery O'Connor.* Chicago: Loyola UP, 1989.

Tate, J. O. "The Essential Essex." *Flannery O'Connor Bulletin* 12 (Autumn 1983): 47–59.

———. "The Uses of Banality." *Flannery O'Connor Bulletin* 4 (1975): 13–24.

Winters, Yvor. *In Defense of Reason.* Denver: U of Denver P, 1947.

Wood, Ralph C. *Flannery O'Connor and the Christ-Haunted South.* Grand Rapids: William B. Eerdmans, 2004.

Yaeger, Patricia. *Dirt and Desire: Reconstructing Southern Women's Writing, 1930–1990.* Chicago: U of Chicago P, 2000.

Part Three

THEORIZING
O'CONNOR'S
VIOLENCE

O'CONNOR AS MISCEGENATIONIST

Marshall Bruce Gentry

A variety of positions on the topic of O'Connor and race have been presented reasonably. I can agree with Timothy P. Caron that O'Connor's southern religiosity ironically led her into problems on the subject of race, or with Julie Armstrong's whiteness-studies approach to O'Connor's works, in which Armstrong finds some stereotyping. I also agree with Margaret Earley Whitt when she suggests that O'Connor's racial views became increasingly enlightened, and with Ralph C. Wood on the subject of race when he says that whatever O'Connor's personal struggles with racial issues, her Catholicism guided her fiction toward an enlightened stance. I appreciate Wood's pointing out "the anthropologists' claim that everyone is at least the forty-fifth cousin of everyone else" (93). Perhaps we can all agree that O'Connor struggled with race and that she was more enlightened than a lot of people.

In this reconsideration of O'Connor and race, I intend to avoid what some reasonably consider an unfair shortcut—references to O'Connor's letters, essays, and interviews. Instead I will focus on the fiction. My thesis, which I think is original, is that Flannery O'Connor, a "white" writer of Irish ethnicity, writes as a miscegenationist, that she advocates race-mixing more than she would be comfortable acknowledging.[1] For those who find my claim as startling as I have at times—after all, the Supreme Court did not throw out state laws against miscegenation until after O'Connor's death—let me review three sources of encouragement.

One is a book I am attempting to gain permission to publish: Clif Boyer, formerly of the Georgia College Library, has prepared a double-column, single-spaced index—of well over two hundred pages—to O'Connor's *The Complete Stories.* While waiting for permission for Boyer to quote in this index virtually every word of *The Complete Stories,* I flip through the index from time to time, and I am impressed by O'Connor's color palette, her use of complex colors, compound or hyphenated colors, such as, of course, rat-colored (*CS* 83), but also chocolate purple (88), dead-silver (294), dried yellow (93), fox-colored (314), freezing-blue (289), gold sawdust (242), gray-purple (241), "a green that was almost black or a black that was almost green" (99), green-gold (164), mole-colored (96), monkey white (61), polluted lemon yellow (85), sticky-looking brown (277), sweet-potato-colored (169), toast-colored (285), tobacco-colored (218). Of course one might say that O'Connor had a sharp eye for shades of color because she was a painter and a visual writer. But did she learn to notice and enjoy colors mixed and in flux because she was a writer, or was she a good writer because she was inclined to mix colors, to notice the mixing of color all around her? I assume O'Connor noticed a mistake constantly being made—the separating into mere black and white of a wide range of colors, racial and otherwise. (I am emphasizing black-white race-mixing here, though it is also true of course that O'Connor notices the mixing of Native Americans with other races.) When O'Connor describes skin, she seems to enjoy noting gradations of color, mixes, changes: burnt-brown (*CS* 121), cinnamon (215), coffee (254), gray (415), purple (414), red (198), tan (255), yellowish (198). O'Connor records the ways "white" skin isn't white, the ways that changes in skin from white to other colors often mark the emotion of revelation: "white" skin in O'Connor is mottled (41) or speckled (161). The Judge is "clay pink" (218), Mr. Cheatam "nearly the same color as the unpaved roads" (237). "White" people are given names like Ruby, Red Sam, Tanner. I particularly like the way O'Connor makes white an unnatural color in this description: Old Tarwater's "skin between the pockmarks grew pink and then purple and then white and the pockmarks appeared to jump from one spot to another" (301). And notice how many colors Julian's mother's face is in "Everything That Rises Must Converge": "her florid face" (485) becomes "an angry red" (492), then "unnaturally red" (495), and then she is "purple-faced" (495) and seems "almost gray" (495), and then Julian's mother's face is transformed into "a face he had never seen before" just before the "tide of darkness seemed to be sweeping her" away from Julian (500). It is in that final darkness that Julian and his mother converge.

Another source of encouragement for looking at O'Connor as a race-mixer is an article in which O'Connor is compared to Latino writer Richard Rodriguez. Farrell O'Gorman proposes what he (and Rodriguez) call a "brown" reading of O'Connor. O'Gorman stops just short of saying that O'Connor endorses race-mixing, apparently because for O'Connor to do that would be to take a political stand (45n11). But O'Gorman and Rodriguez agree on an erotic impulse in O'Connor's art that has something to do with relations between different races.[2] In a sense, I am proposing that, while O'Connor would sign no petition, she endorsed miscegenation in all sorts of ways, however apolitically, symbolically, fantastically. I will avoid repeating O'Gorman's readings here, but it is clear that O'Gorman and Rodriguez show us how O'Connor's Catholicism could give her interesting insights on race.

A third source of encouragement for treating O'Connor as a race-mixer is Patricia Yaeger's *Dirt and Desire,* because for Yaeger so much of southern women's writing is about race, even—or especially—when the writing is about everydayness. There are many inspiring ideas in Yaeger's book, but most relevant here are those in which Yaeger builds on "the historical association of African Americans with earth or dirt" (37) and on the idea that " . . . in modern southern culture, both white and black women have been fastened to dirt—defined as its source and charged with its removal" (275). For Yaeger, race is the elephant in the living room that southerners fascinatingly try to ignore, and ignoring the topic in a certain way becomes a way to talk about the subject. While white women writers "use dirt to explore the possibilities in a fantasied self-blackening," according to Yaeger, " . . . black women use dirt as a means of transcendence, a way of changing the meaning of blackness altogether" (275). I am inclined to accept the suggestion that O'Connor's references to dirt imply an indirect discussion of race.

Before I go any further with my attempt to reveal miscegenationism in O'Connor's fiction, I should explain what I assume is going on in Flannery O'Connor's psyche. I have already noted that I find things in the fiction that would make O'Connor, generally a gradualist on the subject of civil rights, uncomfortable. How can this be? My answer has to do with how the parts of the psyche other than the conscious intellect are involved in the creation of fiction. Some literary criticism is written as if everything O'Connor ever wrote were a sort of term paper, in which everything there is intended and almost everything has its documentable source. I assume that when O'Connor writes fiction, she communicates ideas and feelings from all sorts of places in her psyche. She probably would not have become a great writer if she had not been comfortable with the idea that there are important things in her fiction of which she is completely unaware.

These assumptions about O'Connor's psyche come from watching my wife, Alice Friman, as she writes and as she teaches poetry writing. One of Alice's basic lectures as she teaches creative writing is particularly applicable to the study of O'Connor. This lecture is based on Alice's adaptation of something called the Johari Window, created back in the 1950s by Joseph Luft and Harry Ingram while researching group dynamics. Here, as I understand it, is Alice's version:

> Imagine a window divided into four panes.
> The first pane conveys things about the writer that the writer knows and that others know too.

The second pane conveys things about the writer that the writer does not know but that others do know. This is about the writer's blinders.

The third pane conveys things about the writer that the writer knows but that others do not know. This one is about the writer's secrets.

The fourth pane conveys things about the writer that the writer does not know and others do not know.

The creators of the Johari Window, who are not highlighting art, apparently consider it healthy to have the first pane grow, to increase awareness all around and reduce what is hidden. In a writing class, Alice's lecture leads to the conclusion that the course involves learning about oneself and one's classmates, involves sharing secrets. As paradoxical as it may seem, creative writing comes primarily from the fourth pane. One needs to be prepared to work at getting in touch with memories, desires, fears. All four kinds of communication happen in creative writing, whether one likes it or not. When you write, the reader sees you through all four panes. Artistry is a matter of coordinating and controlling (just enough) the different sorts of communication—*not* of shutting down any of them. We communicate things we do not know we are giving away. We communicate through what we hide. We communicate mystery.

So while I think O'Connor may have been aware of *some* of what I believe exists in her fiction, her full awareness is far from necessary. I also assume that some *part* of O'Connor's psyche wished to communicate another substantial portion of what I am pointing out in this essay.

My claim about miscegenation is supported in the fiction almost explicitly in a couple of places. For example, there is the explicit promotion of miscegenation by a heroic, arguably Christlike character—Mr. Guizac, the displaced person. Then there's the title "Everything That Rises Must Converge." One need not make this title a double entendre to say that the story suggests different races must and should converge. So the point for debate is really whether there is a sexual convergence involved. When Julian thinks about presenting a "suspiciously Negroid" fiancé to shock his mother (*CW* 494), are we to see such a relationship as a sign of hope for the future? Are we, on the other hand, to think that O'Connor has some sympathy for the claim pronounced by Julian's mother, that blacks can "rise, yes, but on their own side of the fence" (488)? According to Julian's mother, for blacks to rise on the same side of the fence as whites is the same as intermarriage, for she almost immediately adds, "Suppose we were half white. We would certainly have mixed feelings." When Julian answers, "I have mixed feelings now" (488), is O'Connor praising or blaming this mixedness about race-mixing? What are the motives behind the miscegenationist fantasizing here?

I would like now to imagine some opposition to my idea that O'Connor endorses literally the mixing of races. Perhaps the joining of races occurs at an abstract, nonphysical level. Maybe Julian's fantasy of interracial marriage is motivated so much by a desire to shock that all value disappears from his imagined miscegenation. A Bible passage regularly cited in discussions of various othernesses in O'Connor's works suggests that O'Connor might not literally think of race-mixing when she thinks of convergence. Here is Galatians 3:27–28:

> For as many of you as have been baptized in Christ, have put on Christ.
> There is neither Jew nor Greek: there is neither bond nor free: there is neither male nor female. For you are all one in Christ Jesus.

What does this mean practically for a writer of O'Connor's persuasions? Did Flannery O'Connor see a saved character as beyond all differences, as able or required to drop all earthly distinctions? When Mrs. Shortley asks about the Polish Guizacs, "You reckon they'll know what colors even is?" (*CW* 287), does this imagined ignorance carry a hint of the virtue of color-blindness? Sometimes I think O'Connor goes for such a treatment. There is Hazel Motes, finally an emptied, washed-out character if ever there was one: beyond gender, beyond race, beyond sect, beyond humanity. Even his clothes lose their color in the end. Or I think of Ruby Turpin, who sees finally "that even [her] virtues were being burned away" (*CW* 654). I understand why some readers might feel Ruby's vision makes her temporarily leave behind any racial characteristics; her moment of redemption might change her in a way that has nothing to do with the habits she will return to after the story ends, of being a very white lady with ongoing racial prejudices.

But back to the passage from Galatians. I think it makes more sense to say that for a color-obsessed, visual writer like O'Connor, the best way to put into fiction the notion of overcoming differences is to combine races rather than ignore race. Instead of reading O'Connor as saying that her characters could stop being members of any race, it makes more sense to read her as saying her characters could combine colors, could experience more than one race. I think that we find this suggestion again and again in O'Connor, amazingly in spite of the fact that no O'Connor character ever explicitly states a desire to become racially mixed or to intermarry.

Now for examples: I am going to dash through a series of works here, suggestively and speculatively rather than thoroughly. Back to "The Displaced Person": We might have doubts about whether O'Connor really endorses a marriage between Mr. Guizac's relative and the yellow-skinned farmhand Sulk. Maybe we are simply to note Sulk's generosity and Mrs. McIntyre's lack of generosity. The more interesting endorsement of miscegenation in this story, to my mind, has to do with Mrs. Shortley, who knows Mr. Guizac to be the great miscegenator, who imagines him to be promoting mixing, not only on the farm but also throughout the English language (because Polish is a dirty language and it dirties the body of English words). Mrs. Shortley does nothing to stop Guizac. Her moment of religious insight coincides with her realization that her refusal to tell Mrs. McIntyre about Mr. Guizac makes him more likely to succeed with his plan for miscegenation. Her orgasmic death scene thus suggests her own participation in Mr. Guizac's browning the world.

"Greenleaf": Once we accept Patricia Yaeger's notion that dirt (even in Georgia) is symbolically black, Mrs. Greenleaf's religious mud-wallowing becomes a sexual union with a black Jesus the story endorses. And the Greenleaf bull, which is amazingly described as "squirrel-colored" (*CS* 253) and attributed to a black owner—at least until Mrs. May learns the bull belongs to the Greenleaf boys—is surely by the end of the story a miscegenator who disturbs "the breeding schedule" (*CW* 504)—as well as being Christ, of course. The goring can be interpreted as a redemptive miscegenation.

Back to "Revelation": Along with this story's final image of Mrs. Turpin's burning, there are numerous suggestions that race-mixing is a bridge to heaven. "You have to have a little of everything" (*CW* 638), Mrs. Turpin claims proudly, and there is probably some connection between this source of pride and her sense that she is always just about to become black, a sense she has most noticeably in her dream fantasy of being offered a choice by Jesus about whether to be born black, and in her dream of the collapse of the hierarchy of races and classes, through the muddying action suggested by the words "moiling and roiling" (636). I would also say that most of the story's talk about animals suggests a concern with race-mixing. Caring for pigs is equated by a character in the story with loving blacks, and O'Connor uses this equation. Mrs. Turpin's insistence that her pigs are clean and upstanding ironically confirms the equation of pig and black—or of the pig and race-mixing. And when Mrs. Turpin goes to the pigpen at the story's end, she sees shoats whose color is suggestive of some mixing: "tan with liver-colored spots" (651). Her husband Claud's earlier descriptions of "white-face cattle" (636) and "white-faced niggers" (641)—both supposedly bred into higher status—reinforces the use of animals to talk about race. So when Mrs. Turpin asks God, "How am I a hog and me both?" (652)—even though Mary Grace called her only a hog—I see Mrs. Turpin embracing a revelation of herself as mixed in all sorts of ways, including race.

Here is one more speculation: does purple in this story hint at miscegenation? Another way that Mrs. Turpin becomes nonwhite is through her wound. Mary Grace's attack makes Mrs. Turpin's face red at first (*CW* 646), then later a green shade of blue (648), so one might conclude that her face has a stage at least of purple. Mrs. Turpin's husband, Claud, the man whose jokes link race and animal, the man whose white brains could easily be scattered over a highway with the brains of blacks (653), is said to have a purple swelling on his leg (633) from a cow's kick, and he is kicked once again on the leg during the story (646) by Mary Grace, whose acne-blue face (635) turns "almost purple" with anger just before she begins her attack (644). What I am speculating my way toward is that Mr. and Mrs. Turpin as purple parents figuratively give birth to purple Mary Grace—or perhaps that Mary Grace and Mr. Turpin introduce Ruby to her purple shading—and that all of them know they are somewhere between white and black. The fact that Mrs. Turpin contemplates baby pigs and a pregnant sow in the pigpen suggests that her own potential as a mother is on her mind here.[3] The punch line to this speculative train of thought, I hope, is that after shifting purple away from its traditional association with royalty, O'Connor redeems the color by making her use of it—in relation to the Turpins and Mary Grace—key to the final revelation. What starts this greatest revelation is literally "a purple streak in the sky" (653). It may seem that all my emphasis on figurative language overstates the suggestions of physical race-mixing, but let me finish this discussion by recalling that the story satirizes Mrs. Turpin when she imagines race superficially, when she thinks she could be "herself but black" without significant change (636). To some extent, the story insists the race talk be real.

On to "A Circle in the Fire": Yaeger suggests that whites can be the source "of pollution" in racial terms, as in this story (262, 296n6). If one accepts that the boys' destruction of the farm triggers the female characters' redemption, along with the idea that Mrs. Cope experiences race-mixing as the boys nakedly set fires, then we have something of a fresh explanation for that puzzling line about Mrs. Cope having a look that "might have belonged to anybody, a Negro or a European or to Powell [one of the boys] himself" (*CW* 251). These three angels of redemption can burn away parts of Mrs. Cope in a fashion suggestive of Mrs. Turpin's burning, but that does not prevent Mrs. Cope's crossing the racial line, profoundly, by being polluted by three boys who are, ironically, freshly washed.

Back to "Everything That Rises Must Converge": Everybody in this story is potentially everyone else's double. Racial barriers are crossed constantly. The color purple works here to equate Julian's mother and the black mother through their hats, and the mothers swap sons. What I might add to discussions of race in this story is inspired by Leanne E. Smith, who points out that " . . . it is the [black mother's] pocketbook, more than the hat, that . . . bluntly teaches a lesson that Julian wants his mother to learn about changing societal norms" (49). The purple crowns, I would agree, are less important than the mothers' contrasting pocketbooks. Julian's mother has a pocketbook that once dispensed nickels but now only pennies (*CW* 498), and at the end of the story she drops and forgets the purse (499). The black mother has "a mammoth red pocketbook that bulged throughout as if it were stuffed with rocks" (495). Usually the black woman's pocketbook is treated by critics as a political statement, but I would also suggest—even if one has not recently reread the section of "The Comforts of Home" about Sarah Ham's sexual pocketbook—that both purses in "Everything That Rises Must Converge" can also impress one as being about sexual power. Julian's mother, with her fantasies of being close to blackness in the person of her mammy, is on her way out; the black mother, who suggests crossing racial lines through the clothes she chooses for herself and for her son, also suggests that part of her power to make her choices comes from sexuality. The black mother suggests miscegenation so strongly that she makes us see how superficially Julian is able to think about it. When the black mother first displeases Julian by sitting beside him, we are told, "He could not see anything but the red pocketbook upright on the bulging green thighs" (496). Julian's response, of course, is to wrench his focus as soon as possible away from the pocketbook and toward the identical hats. Julian cannot face—until perhaps the very end of the story—what convergence must be.

While we are on the subject of O'Connor's making black women into sex symbols, let me address "The Artificial Nigger," where Nelson encounters a black woman whom he asks for directions. Nelson might see her primarily as a maternal figure, but she is also sexual, and he quickly feels "as if he were reeling down through a pitchblack tunnel" (*CW* 223). This tunnel image suggests not only the sewers of Atlanta and a pathway to hell but also surely the woman's womb, the woman's vagina. So I agree that her sexual symbolism is something O'Connor is using. It is all one-sided, of course—in no sense does the story imply that the black woman desires anything about Nelson—but the conclusion seems unavoidable that this story is saying Nelson would be better off if he could stay in touch with blacks, could return to his birthplace, which, as Mr. Head reminds him, is a city full of blacks. I now typically read this story in conjunction with *The Violent Bear It Away*, where, after the white boy returns to his country home, it is even clearer that he will have to return to the city, probably to confront black people constantly. Yaeger notes as significant the fact that young Tarwater finally "smears his face with dirt" (265; *CW* 478), suggesting perhaps a bit of "racial protest" (Yaeger 265). One has to infer from a story like "The Artificial Nigger" the full range of discoveries that await Tarwater back in the city.

"The Enduring Chill": Here Asbury fantasizes about communion with black workers in a way that would cause "the difference between black and white [to be] absorbed into nothing" (*CW* 558). Not quite the right fantasy, Asbury: too abstract, too bloodless. His Leda-and-the-swan moment at the story's end is successful, but primarily because of an earlier symbolically miscegenationist fantasy played out in more clearly physical terms. It is important that in one of Asbury's dreams, he imagines being brought back to life by a "violently-spotted" cow who is "softly licking his head as if it were a block of salt" (564). This seemingly silly detail sets up the crucial basis for Asbury's enduring chill: the source is Bang's, a venereal disease of cows, which Asbury contracted by drinking milk in hopes of achieving communion with blacks.

"Judgment Day": Throughout this story I feel O'Connor wants to allow Tanner to cross the racial line in a way the old man cannot consciously admit. The physical argument for miscegenation that I find most persuasive in this story is Dr. Foley, the wave-of-the-future, multiracial owner of the land on which Tanner squats with his black friend Coleman Parrum. Dr. Foley "was only part black. The rest was Indian and white" (*CW* 680). Tanner knows that his own actions require acceptance of Dr. Foley as a symbol of necessary convergence, and Tanner finally decides, probably along with his author, that there is value in working for Foley, thus becoming "a nigger's white nigger" (685). Of course Tanner learns this lesson, becomes "tanner," by living in New York City, symbolically the land of miscegenation.

Is it perverse to compare Tanner's desire to cross the color line with Enoch Emery's? If, as Timothy P. Caron has suggested, Gonga the Gorilla is a symbol of the black race (39), I am prepared to agree that Enoch wants to become black as he turns himself into Gonga. One way I differ from Caron—and from most readers, I must admit—is on the extent to which I think O'Connor is satirizing Enoch. I believe that insofar as Hazel Motes is the protagonist emptied of race in *Wise Blood,* Enoch Emery is the character embodying miscegenation in *Wise Blood,* perhaps fully successfully.

I have heard people I respect say we have overdone our talking about race. I have tried to suggest here that race, rather than being a tangential topic for O'Connor, is intertwined with all the rest of her important themes. One could continue on the train of thought I have been riding in these considerations, perhaps in a religious direction. Maybe we should read O. E. Parker as a character who crosses the color line as he colors himself; of course this reading makes the face of Christ the final step in Parker's transition to a different race status. Or maybe we should follow John D. Sykes Jr., who sees in "A Temple of the Holy Ghost" evidence that for O'Connor, Christ is always of "two 'natures'" (89). If we agree with Sykes that Christ is like O'Connor's hermaphrodite, then it may be that combining opposites in all sorts of ways is a path toward the sacred. Seeing the divine as essentially a matter of mixture makes me think that it may even be appropriate to reconsider the significance of those multicolored peacocks.

On the other hand, I should note that the course of my speculations here makes it easy to overstate the value of miscegenation in O'Connor's fiction. Certainly the history of racial oppression gives ample evidence of race-mixing that both results purely from, and reinforces, white racist domination. And there is ample evidence of race-mixing that has resulted in little or no benefit to humankind, or that benefits only whites. Critic bell hooks tells the story of overhearing a conversation, among white boys in New Haven, Connecticut, about the value of having sex with "as many girls from other racial/ethnic groups as they could 'catch' before graduation" (23).[4] One of their misguided goals, according to hooks, was "to make themselves over, to leave behind white 'innocence' and enter the world of 'experience'" (23). O'Connor created such a young man in Julian of "Everything That Rises Must Converge," I think, and probably was critical of his motives. But there is still the possibility that O'Connor's talk about race-mixing is motivated primarily by a desire to benefit whites. One might look at O'Connor's endorsement of miscegenation as primarily biological, with insufficient attention to changing behavior.

I return eventually—and repeatedly—to the idea that, however much O'Connor may have endorsed miscegenation in the various ways I have been sketchily speculating about here, those endorsements tend toward the indirect, the veiled, the cautious. When O'Connor thought about her own racial awareness, she probably saw in herself a bit of the impracticality of Asbury Fox in "The Enduring Chill"—somebody who means well but who needs years of work. O'Connor knew there were answers she did not have.

We are left with this question: to what extent shall we see O'Connor's writing as simply timid, and to what extent shall we also see her writing as surreptitious?

Notes

1. The title of this essay, which may appear outlandish, uses a word that comes from a Civil War hoax: a couple of journalists apparently tried to sabotage Abraham Lincoln's reelection in 1864 by trying to trick him (and other Republicans) into endorsing their pamphlet which created the term "miscegenation" and praised race-mixing as a panacea. See "Miscegenation, a Story" and "Miscegenation Hoax."

2. Rodriguez says all sorts of interesting things in his book *Brown,* such as, "The future is brown . . ." (35); "I do not hesitate to say into a microphone what everyone knows, what no one says. *Most American blacks are not black*" (134); and "White is an impulse to remain ignorant of history" (139).

3. William Meyer Jr. introduced me to this idea.

4. I thank Beauty Bragg for introducing me to hooks's essay.

Works Cited

Armstrong, Julie. "Blinded by Whiteness: Revisiting Flannery O'Connor and Race." *Flannery O'Connor Review* 1 (2001–2): 77–86.

Boyer, Clif. "Flannery O'Connor: *The Complete Stories* Index." MS. Georgia College and State University Library, Flannery O'Conner Collection.

Caron, Timothy P. *Struggles Over the Word: Race and Religion in O'Connor, Faulkner, Hurston, and Wright.* Macon, GA: Mercer UP, 2000.

Friman, Alice. Personal interview. 5 Apr. 2005.

hooks, bell. "Eating the Other: Desire and Resistance." *Black Looks: Race and Representation.* Boston: South End, 1992. 21–39.

Johari Window. http://www.businessballs.com/johariwindowmodel.htm. This is one of many Web sites that describe the basics of the Johari Window.

"Miscegenation, a Story of Racial Intimacy." *African American Registry.* http://www.aaregistry.com/african_american_history/1483/Miscegenation_a_story_of_racial_intimacy.

"The Miscegenation Hoax." http://www.museumofhoaxes.com/miscegenation.html.

O'Connor, Flannery. *The Complete Stories*. New York: Farrar, 1971.

———. *Flannery O'Connor: Collected Works*. Ed. Sally Fitzgerald. New York: Library of America, 1988.

O'Gorman, Farrell. "White, Black, and Brown: Reading O'Connor after Richard Rodriguez." *Flannery O'Connor Review* 4 (2006): 32–49.

Rodriguez, Richard. *Brown: The Last Discovery of America*. New York: Viking, 2002.

Smith, Leanne E. "Head to Toe: Deliberate Dressing and Accentuated Accessories in Flannery O'Connor's 'Revelation,' 'A Late Encounter with the Enemy,' and 'Everything That Rises Must Converge.'" *Flannery O'Connor Review* 6 (2009): 40–55.

Sykes, John D., Jr. "Two Natures: Chalcedon and Coming-of-Age in O'Connor's 'A Temple of the Holy Ghost.'" *Flannery O'Connor Review* 5 (2007): 89–98.

Whitt, Margaret Earley. "1963, a Pivotal Year: Flannery O'Connor and the Civil Rights Movement." *Flannery O'Connor Review* 3 (2005): 59–72.

Wood, Ralph C. *Flannery O'Connor and the Christ-Haunted South*. Grand Rapids, MI: Eerdmans, 2004.

Yaeger, Patricia. *Dirt and Desire: Reconstructing Southern Women's Writing, 1930–1990*. Chicago: U of Chicago P, 2000.

"THE HERMENEUTICS OF SUSPICION": PROBLEMS IN INTERPRETING THE LIFE OF FLANNERY O'CONNOR

W. A. Sessions

I

In the 1950s, down at Andalusia on the front porch, I once told Flannery about a wonderful African American gospel singer during that time, performing mostly in the South, Sister Rosetta Tharpe. Sister Rosetta Tharpe had a great performance piece she belted out that I liked to sing: "Strange things is a-happening every day!" That was all over fifty-four years ago—I first met Flannery O'Connor in May of 1956—and the first line of that gospel song is as good an emblem as any for what I want to say. I have obviously never ceased to discover, especially about Flannery O'Connor, that "strange things is [still] a-happening"—and more now than before—"every day." It seems crucial to bring to bear on O'Connor studies at this point some of these surprises, especially as they have related to the life of Flannery—and I call her "Flannery" because that is how I first knew her. These surprises often come in the form of problems in interpretations of O'Connor's life, not least in dealing with problems that come from my own limited interpretation of that life I knew so long ago and that I find, like so much of life, mysterious. Of course, problems in understanding actual life histories, as opposed to mythic re-creations, are as old as Exodus and Plato's *Phaedo*. So why should interpreting Flannery O'Connor's life be any different? The danger always after a certain point in understanding any life, especially that of a person who lived with a special depth, is, like the accounts in Exodus and *Phaedo*, that another process takes over. Idealizations of the actual life take place, but idealizations fail to reveal the negative along with the positive.

It is not, of course, that Flannery is either Moses or Socrates, but her life too, for better or worse, has taken on the making of a cultural and anthropological narrative not always related to her actual life. That life, difficult enough in itself to comprehend—as I should certainly know—has now been raised, like a number in algebra, exponentially. It is even used to interpret culture. In fact, one might say that, in this first decade of the new millennium, the life of this young woman who lived for a relatively short time in the middle of the last century has begun to accrue, for better or for worse, exactly what certain life accounts in the alchemy of human history often develop: a mythology.

How or why is another issue, but the evidence is there. Neil Scott's almost 1,100-page annotated reference guide (2002) to criticism on Flannery O'Connor's literary work is already becoming a bit dated, and the O'Connor critical and cultural vortex Scott once tabulated keeps on spiraling, not least increasingly into the legendary. Indeed, for a surprising number of readers, it appears that encountering Flannery has become more than literary appreciation or recognition of the power of her language. To take the simplest case, the Hollywood actor and director Tommy Lee Jones required the cast of his recent film, *The Three Burials of Melquiades Estradas* (2006) to read as preparation Flannery's stories, essays, and letters, along with the Old Testament book of Ecclesiastes.

A quick comparison shows how far in forty years the mythology has moved. Could one, for example, expect such "preparation" from a Eudora Welty story or even a Faulkner novel? I suspect not with the same guru-intensity and hardly the same first-name familiarity with "Eudora" or "Bill," as "Flannery" is used by countless O'Connor aficionados, not least the young prize-winning novelist Jonathan Franzen and his editor Paul Elie, who call O'Connor "Flannery," although Paul was born, for example, the year after Flannery died. For better or worse, we are in myth-making land. In the same way, it is impossible to take seriously some recent statistics without reaching something of the level of a myth. With her small canon, is it possible that Flannery O'Connor now ranks as the seventh greatest twentieth-century American writer; fourth greatest twentieth-century fiction writer in the United States; top American woman fiction writer ever; second greatest American woman writer (after that other regional anchorite, Emily Dickinson); twelfth greatest American writer of all time; the eighth greatest woman writer of all time (Burt 298)? What has happened? Can this be little Mary Flannery O'Connor from Savannah and Middle Georgia? Can anything good come out of Nazareth?

Here are two quotations from the last decade that illustrate the range of Flannery O'Connor in American culture, the one from a famous rock star, Bruce Springsteen, the other in 2000 from a West Coast black woman revolutionary, Guerilla Girl Alma Thomas:

> There's this movie *Wise Blood* [John Huston's film of Flannery's first novel].
> One of my favorite parts was the end, where he's doin' all these terrible
> things to himself; and the woman comes in and says, "There's no reason for

it. People have quit doing it." And he says, "They ain't quit doing as long as I'm doing it." (Percy 38)

Flannery could never have predicted that those who soon would need her more than air would be the very readers and writers who'd been so marginalized she couldn't imagine them as part of her audience. It is her embattlement as a believing writer in a secular world and the morality of her aesthetic standards that have instructed generations of artists who have been "othered." Whenever I reread *Mystery and Manners,* I picture dozens of artists underlining, writing in the margins, changing the word Catholic to Asian, lesbian, Latino. This is an irony I feel Flannery would relish in time. (Thomas 76–77)

What adds more of a stage for this mythologizing is that the last decades have also seen, beyond Neil Scott's bibliography, the surprising internationalizing of O'Connor. I choose four random examples from among the plethora from almost every country in Europe to Turkey, Japan, and Latin America. First, in Paris in spring 2005, the *Nouvelle Figaro Litteraire* paired O'Connor with Flaubert and Rousseau as well as with Hemingway and Fitzgerald but mentioned O'Connor more often in a discussion of new directions in the novel. A second example is that of the Japanese 1994 Nobel Prize novelist Kenzaburo Oe, who has written one whole novel, *An Echo of Heaven,* in which a young very liberated Japanese woman models her life on Flannery O'Connor, and Flannery's actual life forms the plot of the novel and the reason for its meditation on the meaning of suffering in a postmodern world. I should also add that in his Nobel lecture, Oe specifically mentions O'Connor and the influence of what he calls her "habit of life," an influence discussed at length in Oe's 1999 interview at Berkeley. A third amusing example is that of a Norwegian novelist who completed an Internet novel called "Flannery's Bear," in which the Scandinavian author with the euphonious name "Ulf Wolf" reinvents the person of O'Connor (with surprising factual detail) as the center of a postmodern contemporary fantasy. The fourth example reveals one of many recent allusions to Flannery among key religious figures. Over a year ago, the Archbishop of Canterbury, Rowan Williams, gave the Clark lectures at Trinity at Cambridge, one of the most prestigious series in the United Kingdom, and his third and final lecture was completely on Flannery O'Connor as one of the spiritual voices of the modern world, with again a precise knowledge of her life in Milledgeville, Iowa, and the letters. But even Williams's loving study of Flannery involves her art, her fiction, her life, and letters more than points of ideology. It is obviously the mythic figure being identified, what the life—and the work as life—have become.

II

One of the proofs of this mythologizing has been precisely this idealizing, positive and negative, of Flannery herself, life, and work. Myth—any kind of myth from Athena to Brad Pitt—requires the idealization of character—generally heroes or villains. Nuances and any *blending* of direct positive and direct negative need not apply. Critical idealization demands an argument, and it is the degree of this idealization (how totally negative and how totally positive) that for many determines the argument. The result of how negative and how positive ultimately sets, in many critical readings of Flannery O'Connor, her value as a writer, even as an artist, and more often than not, her worth as a human being. In other words, what I am arguing is that, for better or worse, Flannery's life has become a paradigm for all kinds of idealistic projections, including those of her own making. These projections may be fiercely positive just as they are as fiercely negative. But idealistic they are, and based not on ambiguity such as is natural to any human being or any work of art, but on an absolute arrived at outside of Flannery's creative work and, for that matter, outside her actual life.

A better term for this act of idealistic projection is interpretation, and interpreting an artist's work means understanding it and understanding not just the meaning of the art but the art itself—at least for a writer like Flannery O'Connor, who announced early at Iowa "I want to be artist" and did not mean a painter, cartoonist, or engraver. Flannery saw herself with a vocation as a maker of language, metaphor, and story—old-fashioned enough but focused just on that. Above all, Flannery saw her work as one with her time and universal enough for any time, so that in the 1950s, when the critic Granville Hicks asked O'Connor if her work were relevant in 1950, she replied: "1950, 2050, or 5050!"

That means, it seems to me, that Flannery would have expected her work to attract criticism neither passive nor indifferent. She would not have been surprised that her readers have generally been enthusiastic or repelled, and the systems of hermeneutics or interpretation have been negative or positive from the start. Martha Stephens and Josephine Hendin appear early on the scene with what both the twentieth-century French theorist Paul Ricoeur and the German philosopher Hans Georg Gadamer name "a hermeneutics of suspicion." Ironically, this hermeneutics has generated some of the best discussions of O'Connor. The defense has not only strengthened a positive hermeneutics for reading O'Connor but led to new territory because of the dialectic between negative and positive readings. Most of all, in a paradox, the readings that have emerged have been much deeper of Flannery's own fiction than her own definitions and particularly than her own dreary even flat explanations of her stories and fiction.

At its worst, however, O'Connor criticism of this kind—the hermeneutics of suspicion—has the "gotcha" mentality that pervades all criticism in any area and, since the eighteenth century, journalism of all kinds. The problem is that the "gotcha" mentality is often essentially ignorant except for the facts of the attack. Often, the attacker is relatively clueless about basic facts of O'Connor's life, education, customs, traditions, and, most of all, to use Marx's term, the ideology she held. Added to that, a number of these "gotcha" critics loaded with "suspicions" and heavy on regurgitated theory are also generally ignorant and unsophisticated about recent facts of culture and history, much less anything beyond fifty years. The actual texts of Flannery's fiction are referred to, if at all, to prove the theory—never to engage their own powerful ambiguous life.

Two examples illustrate such problems. One critic, eager to identify Flannery's racial position with that of the evangelical Protestant white South, remarks, "As a devoted reader and student of the Scriptures herself, O'Connor uses the Bible as her primary [and then the critic quotes from *Mystery and Manners*] instrument to plumb Christian meaning." The critic's assertion is highly doubtful given the fact that for Flannery, the Eucharist, the Catholic Mass, was always the central "instrument to plumb Christian meaning." Nothing, certainly not the Bible, would supersede what O'Connor considered the Real Presence. In fact, the author misquotes O'Connor in her essay and also gives the wrong page. What O'Connor actually writes is, "The Catholic writer may be immersed in the Bible himself, but if his readers and his characters are not, he does not have the instrument to plumb meaning—and specifically Christian meaning—that he would have had if the biblical background were known to all" (*MM* 204–5). Neither the word "primary" nor its meaning as "primary" is in the passage. What collapses is the author's argument built on the identity of O'Connor and white racist evangelical Protestant experience through the faulty major premise of Bible as central to Christian experience of both. Flannery may or may not be accused of racism. Her Bible reading—a late experience in her life, in fact—was never primary for plumbing Christian meaning. O'Connor's text won't support the charge.

Critics like Josephine Hendin, John Hawkes, and Claire Kahane often "see the 'demonic' in O'Connor's work." What is wrong with this? The art is just where the demonic should be. The fact that ideologically Flannery did believe in the active existence of the Devil would be of no importance if she had not translated this belief into fiction, art. This translation and activation of the diabolic came because she first had models. Not least was her French model, the novelist Georges Bernanos, in teaching her how to dramatize the "demonic" and the realistic with an ambiguity that makes it actual and surprising.

The result of careful craftsmanship is that The Misfit is genuinely scary. No one would have to take her ideas seriously to find the knock-out power of diabolical characters in O'Connor. They are there because she has written them that way. The ideology may or may not have kept Flannery from being Stephen King, but the art made the difference, not the ideology. In fact, I agree with Michael Kreyling's statement in a July 2007 public lecture: "I question the special truth status of *any* art work."

At this point, it should be noted that Flannery herself wrote in a tradition whose hermeneutics always moved in suspicion. Most of her aesthetics and theory are jam-packed with attack mechanisms, and violence in an O'Connor story is genuinely creepy and authentic, if nothing else. Critically, the hermeneutics of suspicion was, like Flannery's narrative violence, in the great tradition of the negative in the West. Particularly, Flannery saw her roots ideologically in an artist and myth-maker like Charles Baudelaire and heeded his call "*epater le bourgeoise*" and beyond it, in Milton's great phrase (and pun) in *Areopagitica:* "the wayfaring / warfaring Christian." At Iowa identifying with Baudelaire and the French, Flannery also leveled an attack, in the same Romantic nineteenth-century reaction, against "progressive liberalism"—as had Marx, Nietzsche, Levi-Straus, and not least Freud. She too did not believe in a "liberal" solution to history. Such an attack has its first moment in the West at the very time that the original synthesis of the Middle Ages broke up, and Petrarch followed his contemporary and master, Dante, to be followed by Erasmus and then Luther. Whatever she learned from Gilson and Maritain about St. Thomas, Flannery knew her essential hero was Haze Motes, to be reproduced in The Misfit and finally in Obadiah Elihue Parker. This hero was as broken as Baudelaire and believed more in possibilities of terror than solutions to history.

III

And with this reproducing of the Romantic negative polemic (and in the case as well of the positive Romantic hero, a mode also applied to Flannery), it should be no surprise that we are also back in the literary method of the old nineteenth-century Romantic formula of criticism and interpretation—now almost two hundred years old as method and still going strong. In this kind of formulaic criticism that would by Flannery's death be known as the Old Historicism, idealizing the writer—including attacking her—does not so much focus on the art as explain it by the writer's life, the writer's character, the writer's world. Two examples of how this critical method works: if we want to understand the poem "Tintern Abbey," we have to read and understand the journeys of Wordsworth and his sister in the English Lake country (their bills at the local inn will help to explain the poem as well as personal references to the trip in the poem); if we want to understand the life of Shakespeare, the more we know about thatched roofs or Elizabethan staging or the Elizabethan World Picture or personal references in the plays, the more we can determine the correctness and justice of Shakespeare's political, social, moral, and religious principles.

Of course, we are reading a mythology here and not literature or if literature, primarily through myths of the writer, the artist as a young man (or old man or old woman, whatever). For many Romantics, the thrill of the master is in the work and makes the work have any value at all. How much of *Mrs. Dalloway*, we often ask, is really Virginia Woolf? Conversely, in the hermeneutics of suspicion, the work exists to support what the other incriminating evidence shows about the master: the emperor has no clothes on. The master is a crook, a fraud, a pervert of some kind and, by implication, the art is not complete or of value because the life is not pure.

Now, it will be clear to any serious O'Connor reader, such a tight connection between artist's life and value of art is the exact opposite of Flannery's idea of art, as she often explains to Betty Hester, the woman called "A" in the letters in *The Habit of Being*. Betty particularly was steeped in an older form of literary criticism and thought the writer's art always contained a template of autobiography. So did on another occasion Erik Langkjaer. Erik was then a young Danish man who was traveling across the South in the early 1950s representing a book company. He and Flannery developed a close friendship. In 1955 Erik believed that their friendship and its termination had been the source for a story in her second book, *A Good Man Is Hard to Find*. Flannery explained at length that their friendship was not the basis for "Good Country People." At no point did O'Connor believe, with the famous nineteenth-century French critic Sainte-Beuve, that literature comes directly from life (as, on the contrary, Erik, a person of considerable sophistication, thought that this story did, and quoted Sainte-Beuve in a letter to me). On this point, I agree with Cormac McCarthy, who has deliberately quoted his master Flannery O'Connor: literature begins with literature, art with art, not with life.

By now we might examine just where Flannery's theory of the artist and the writer does come from. It will explain her reaction to Betty and Erik, among others. Of course, as everyone knows, Flannery was a product of the New Criticism that came in the late 1940s and 1950s as the Old Historicism began to fade. The writer as artist came into style again. The power of this criticism remained all through Flannery's life, but shortly after her death, especially after Stephen Greenblatt and Stanley Fish produced their first works, the New Historicism appeared—and has remained the dominant literary critical method.

This new critical method of the New Historicism has had enormous influence in American literature and on O'Connor studies. Once more, critics and scholars gained cachet with a simple formula: if you know the history, sociological data, political currents of a period (the Cold War, for example), or an ideology like Marxism or like the recent psychoanalytic theory of Jacques Lacan or the feminist theory of Julia Kristeva, that combine a variety of disciplines and focus on issues of choice—once you have such back-up theory or data, you can interpret the writer herself by the simple act of reading her in her times, with very little attention to the actual art. In the writer's personal responses and choices in the face of social and political phenomena or psychological or cultural breakdown, one can determine not only the value of the art but the value of the maker, the writer, and therefore of the myth of the maker.

IV

Flannery's concept of art, however, did not necessarily originate in the superior moral being of the artist. Good writing for her represented something she considered beyond personal morality: the skill and craftsmanship and insight with enough perception of beauty to shape a work of art. Flannery's belief about this origin rose not only from Jacques Maritain's *Scholasticism and Art* but (a fact not often noticed) from St. Thomas's definition of a prophet as Flannery discovered it and explained it to Betty. The truth and quality of a prophecy determined the worth of the prophet, not the personal degradation or the moral probity of the prophet herself. The other great unnoticed source for Flannery's concept of art derives from the Catholic Church's definition of the efficacy of a sacrament. That is, for Flannery and in the eyes of the church, the efficacy of a sacrament does not depend on the moral being of the priest who gives it or as he gives it. The priest (or married deacon for that matter) may or may not be in a state of grace when he dispenses the sacrament. It is enough that already he himself possesses both the sacrament of ordination and the clerical faculties, although it is certainly hoped that he will be worthy as priest or deacon in every sense.

So where determines the efficacy of the sacrament? The answer is in one of the oldest teachings of the Church—"*ex opere operato*": the efficacy of the sacrament derives from the one receiving the sacrament, from the state with which she receives the sacrament. This is the key point St. Paul makes in his First Letter to the Corinthians 11:27, where the Apostle admonishes the first Christians about the proper taking of the Bread and Wine, for Flannery, the living Body and Blood of Christ.

So, in this definition of an artist, Flannery or any other writer does not have to be moral or politically correct or even sane to create the power of the literary text. The efficacy—the truth—of the literary text is in the reader, not the writer. The artist is merely setting up and performing the ritual. When Joyce Carol Oates compares Flannery and Dostoevsky as political conservatives, she is not denouncing their art but IS implicitly praising the efficacy of their literary texts. Only in the art itself, the making of a special kind of beauty—what Hans-Georg Gadamer calls "The Relevance of Beauty"—does O'Connor see the function of any artist as artist, writer as writer. This is the truth or, if you want, the prophecy that through art, through beauty, is passed on.

Missing this crucial point in Flannery's theory of aesthetics, the "gotcha" critical mentality keeps berating her for not being a perfect Catholic or Christian or citizen or woman—too much a product of her time and not a hero in defiance like a female Luther. Such a hermeneutics of suspicion would even vitiate the art itself by the failed life.

Before we lament too strongly, however, this type of hermeneutics of suspicion and see its genuinely vicious nature, let us consider its value. That can be done by considering the opposite. If the negative idealization produces an attack, the positive idealization has its own action: biography breeds the heroic.

In this mythology, Flannery O'Connor was a prophet in her time. She is a literal prophet (for some, self-recognized) amid the disasters and breakdowns of the twentieth century. Her life of physical and mental suffering demonstrates the actual carrying forth of an increasingly clear prophecy in her life. Her Sibylline utterances, in this idealization, have made her a voice for all time.

There is a step further in this positive ratio of idealization. It also has nothing to do with the beauty of O'Connor's art, except as to recognize such beauty as an accidental proof of personal holiness. What counts in this argument as first is a formulaic clear-cut meaning beyond the ambiguity and irony and paradox of any art. There must be a clarified doctrine, belief-system, even ideology. The mythologized figure of the writer—suffering here like Edgar Allan Poe or even the syphilitic Baudelaire—becomes the instrument of meaning because the suffering life justifies the myth that illustrates the doctrine. The art, the novels and stories, the constant humor do not explain or enhance values as firmly as Flannery's positive social, communal, and cultural role. She is the hero to be imitated, her art ancillary. Given this idealized hermeneutics of appreciation that Kierkegaard discusses, what is more natural than that there is a step, in this idealized perspective, even beyond the Oedipal figure of Flannery O'Connor redeeming society? In no surprise, I know a young millionaire in Atlanta determined to see a process of canonization in Rome initiated for her. He will use his resources so that the procedure, once begun at the Vatican, say, sometime later in the twenty-first century, will, to the resounding cheers of millions of Latin Americans, Africans, Europeans, and Asians, canonize in Rome as a saint of the universal Catholic Church the American author Flannery O'Connor.

V

Whether I project an absurdity or make a prophecy, I have problems here. I find the hermeneutics of appreciation as formulaic as the hermeneutics of suspicion. Both have been used, in my argument, without any irony (and therefore neither will last as a method of interpretation because they are not open to the paradox or surprise of new argument). Most of all, neither understands the place of language and art itself in reading Flannery O'Connor. That is, Flannery O'Connor may indeed be a saint a hundred years from now, with her litany being sung in the vast churches of Africa and Asia and Latin America, but I hope over diverse and diffuse continents her stories will also be read (and I'm with Elizabeth Bishop that they will be) for their language, their irony, their humor, their high jinks and farce, and most of all, for their opening through startling images into the depths of human life. There not even Flannery's politics, failed or noble, or her religious forms, for that matter, remain except as metaphors.

As is obvious, I have real questions about abstractions and positive and negative idealizations. They pretend to set formulas of existence for Flannery's life, when she has provided none—except—and this is the exception that makes the rule for me—in the images of human life she created in narratives told with metaphors and analogies and powerful language. Where else can we or would we find the formulas of human life but in stories, in the art Chekhov set forth that shows morality and even eternity without *demanding* it of the reader? This is what Raymond Carver understood instinctively about both Flannery and Chekhov: the vitality and actuality of the art trumps any theory or ideology, even Flannery's, however such a belief-system of hers may be constructed. There are readers and critics who instinctively understand this triumph of art, even the ideological. Louise Westling appears to understand this complexity in O'Connor:

In her complex and troubling presentation of mothers and daughters in the farm stories, Flannery O'Connor has inadvertently presented a poignant and often excruciating picture of the problems these women have in living together, of female self-loathing, powerlessness, and justified fear of masculine attack. (174)

This is prefaced by a tribute: "Clearly O'Connor's fiction is an achievement of the first order in literary terms, and at its best it provides the mysterious and exalting experience of all great art" (173–74).

So, three cheers, if you want, for Flannery as saint—and shame, if you want, on Flannery for having made bad choices as a woman and as a social and political observer in awful times—and most of all, for being an imperfect human being, what she kept telling Betty (and most of her good friends) she was! Why couldn't, these critics of suspicion keep asking, she have been a less ambiguous person and made heroic political decisions? But, in fact, do we read Homer and Shakespeare, for that matter, for their archaic brutal Greek politics and Elizabethan lack of resistance to tyranny or, on the other hand, do we read them for their social virtues or redemptions even by an eternal community? No, we read them for what they wrote. That is usually where we first begin and, if we love the text enough, where we return.

Remembering my singing Sister Rosetta Tharpe's song to Flannery on the front porch at Andalusia, I see full circle: "Strange things is a-happening every day!" And what is happening is this strange, almost incredible—at least for me, her friend of fifty years, process by which Flannery is becoming a myth and a legend, whether attacked or praised. Viewed as a maker of parables, Flannery has become, from thousands and thousands of perspectives, a mythic woman for all seasons. It is all pretty grand, this being a personal object of attack and, more frightening, of special veneration. I'm not sure I like it all at all.

Works Cited

Burt, Daniel. *The Literary 100: A Ranking of the Most Influential Novelists, Playwrights, and Poets of All Time*. New York: Checkmark, 2001.

Caron, Timothy P. *Struggles Over the Word: Race and Religion in O'Connor, Faulkner, Hurston, and Wright*. Macon: Mercer UP, 2000.

Gadamer, Hans-Georg. *The Gadamer Reader: A Bouquet of Later Writings*. Ed. Richard E. Palmer. Evanston: Northwest UP, 2007.

————. *The Relevance of the Beautiful and Other Essays.* Cambridge: Cambridge UP, 1986.

Kreyling, Michael. "Flannery O'Connor and the Art of Believing: Caroline Gordon, Jacques Maritain, and Teilhard de Chardin." NEH Summer Institute. 16 July 2007.

Oe, Kenzaburo. *An Echo of Heaven.* Tokyo: Kodansha International, 1996.

O'Connor, Flannery. *Mystery and Manners: Occasional Prose.* Eds. Sally and Robert Fitzgerald. New York: Farrar, 1969.

Percy, Will. "Rock and Read: Will Percy Interviews Bruce Springsteen." *DoubleTake* (Spring 1998): 36–43.

Ricoeur, Paul. *Hermeneutics and the Human Sciences.* Cambridge: Cambridge UP, 1981.

Scott, Neil. *Flannery O'Connor: An Annotated Reference Guide to Criticism.* Milledgeville: Timberlake, 2002.

Thomas, Alma Guerrilla Girl. "Flannery and Other Regions." *In Celebration of Genius.* Ed. Sarah Gordon. Athens, GA: Hill Street, 2000. 73–78.

Westling, Louise. *Sacred Groves and Ravaged Gardens.* Athens: U of Georgia P, 1985.

Williams, Rowan. *Grace and Necessity: Reflections on Art and Love.* London: Continuum, 2005.

MADNESS AND CONFINEMENT IN MICHEL FOUCAULT AND FLANNERY O'CONNOR

William Monroe

Among the strangest of bedfellows, Michel Foucault and Flannery O'Connor are social critics whose work exposes the force inherent in medical culling and legal incarceration, whether perpetuated by the European Enlightenment or a small southern town. Foucault unmasks the socially edifying function of asylums and confinement in his influential *Madness and Civilization,* recently retranslated and published as *History of Madness.* O'Connor depicts the community-sustaining effects of imprisonment in narratives such as "Revelation," *The Violent Bear It Away,* and—our main focus here—a story explicitly about criminal insanity, "The Partridge Festival."

Associating O'Connor's fictions with the social critique of Foucault makes her work relevant to an entirely new audience of readers, critics, and theorists, an audience who rightly sees the intellectual discourse of the last century strongly influenced if not dominated by what Paul Ricoeur calls the "hermeneutics of suspicion." I want to suggest that O'Connor and Foucault have ground similar critical lenses for their quite dissimilar readerships. Both thinkers help us see the connection between progressive, optimistic knowledge systems and the confinement of those whose very presence calls those systems into question. As Ricoeur says, the intuition that unites the critiques of Marx, Nietzsche, and Freud, is a simple reversal: *truth is lying* (31). A similar intuition lies at the political heart of the work of Foucault and is present as well in Heidegger and Derrida. Like these and other Big Thinkers, O'Connor wants to reveal the world's hypocrisy and show the punitive costs of its conventions and arrangements.

What makes O'Connor's regional stories more intellectually complex and provocative than Foucault's grandiose histories is her self-awareness, her ability to tease out the sentimentality of her inclination to suspect and condemn. Like Foucault, O'Connor had ample opportunities from childhood on to observe and experience spaces of confinement and methods of social control. And she was as ready as Foucault to mock the righteous and scandalize the beneficiaries of the status quo. But unlike Foucault, she would not celebrate aberration in order to shame civilization and its "too-contents." Instead, she weaves a skepticism of her own critical hermeneutics into her fiction.

Progressive thought from the Enlightenment to the present day has sought institutional solutions to the problem of madness, by building more and bigger places of confinement, for instance. Foucault's solution is as ambitious and masterful as the construction of huge asylums: like Marcuse and Laing as well as his hero Nietzsche, Foucault redefines madness as a revolutionary strategy worthy of reverence, a specifically aesthetic gesture that indicts the world and reveals its lies and guilt. The ethical claim of *Madness and Civilization,* according to James Miller, is that madness should be valued as a way of "winning back access to the occluded, Dionysian dimension of being human." Its core insight is a simple reversal: "The man called 'mad' is innocent. It is society that is guilty" (117). O'Connor's stories resist such a simplistic solution. Madness is for her not an apocalyptic *jouissance* but an affliction. It is not a problem to be solved by more and bigger asylums; at the same time, it is not a mere social construction that can be eliminated by a neat theoretical reversal of derangement and citizenship (*MM* 209). My hope is that an admittedly brief glimpse at the insights of Foucault will help us understand more clearly the significance of O'Connor's trenchant social criticism and to recognize the stories of this "lady writer from Georgia" as more empirical and tough-minded than the historical anthropology of one of the most influential thinkers of the twentieth century.

I

In *Madness and Civilization* Foucault makes the claim that the period of the Enlightenment in Europe effected a transformation in the way deviancy was managed. Whereas Medieval and Renaissance society allowed beggars, thieves, and lunatics to congregate in public areas such as the city gates, seventeenth- and eighteenth-century communities incarcerated their deviants in ever-larger prisons and asylums. Foucault explains how a belief in Cartesian rationalism and a celebration of individual autonomy led to such strategies of isolation and restraint. The presence of a deviant person among other fallen but functional creatures may be an inconvenience; in a would-be perfect world, deviancy is a scandal that must be corrected or hidden. A hallowed belief in reason and human perfection means that madness and "the presence of the inhuman" created embarrassment, a massive, collective shame. "Feeble-minded" human beings scandalized Enlightenment claims of universal vitality and competence

(*Madness and Civilization* 68). Thus the motive to help the mentally ill or disabled, while apparently altruistic, was actually rooted in shame, Foucault argues. He links the desire to cure with the need to correct, expel, or incarcerate living reminders of failure and fragility (7). The confidence of a progressive and enlightened order depends on the absence of the criminal and the madman. The prison, the hospital, and the asylum go hand-in-hand with enlightened, progressive, egalitarian societies.

The sociologist Erving Goffman develops similar observations about "total institutions" in *Asylums,* published in 1961, the same year as "The Partridge Festival" and *Folie et deraison,* the first French edition of *Madness and Civilization.* Goffman adds boarding schools, concentration camps, and orphanages to prisons, hospitals, and asylums—all, he says, are total institutions because they use regimentation to strip the individual of volition and control. O'Connor was simultaneously fascinated and terrified by such institutions, including the Catholic orphanage in Savannah not far from her childhood home and the Boys Reform School that virtually abutted Andalusia. Foucault's valuable contribution, developed more fully in *The Birth of the Clinic,* is that such institutions, as *edifices,* serve not merely to contain and demean those who are incarcerated but also to instruct those who are "free." They become markers not of the divide between *health* and illness but between *normality* and illness, a very different distinction. Huge buildings such as the Hôpital Général in Paris were as educational as they were operative: by signifying what happens to the mad, they instructed and comforted the normal majority. Visiting asylums became a great source of public entertainment, titillation, and, presumably, reassurance. According to Foucault, 96,000 people a year visited "Bedlam," the Bethlehem Hospital in London. Yet visiting was not really necessary: these ostentatious embodiments of power and knowledge educated passers-by at the same time they implicated them in a legally and medically authorized strategy of incarceration.

Foucault's contribution, then, is that "houses of confinement" are needed not only to contain abnormality but also to define it. Those whose behavior challenged the narrative of universal progress—an illusion that buttressed social, political, and economic practices and institutions—had to be quarantined, yes, but they also were needed as case studies and embodied cautionary tales. Incarceration does more than create the order and tranquility that make progress possible; Foucault claims that prisons and asylums are required for the inculcation of a way of knowing, a communal mind-set, an *episteme.*[1] The episteme of a community or historical moment is an unexamined knowledge system, a way of seeing and being seen, that exudes power through its political, social, and economic arrangements; for those who lack extraordinary critical acumen, an episteme or way of knowing is simply the way things are. Foucault follows Nietzsche in his assertion that knowledge is always purposive and purpose is always self-interested. Thus a way of knowing is not a simple will to truth; instead, an episteme is a system of meaning that is motivated by a will to power, a striving for superiority, domination, and control. Historical persons think they see things as they are but actually see only what a particular *knowledge/power* matrix allows them to see.[2] Since, according to Foucault, our very reality derives from power and the threat of force, including the possibility of incarceration, modes and methods of confinement become rubrics of meaning and determiners of reality.

II

Flannery O'Connor was no stranger to confinement. The Flannery O'Connor Childhood Home in Savannah contains a number of family artifacts, including Mary Flannery's "Kiddie Coop," a squarish protective crib for infants and toddlers.[3] According to the docent, Regina Cline O'Connor was concerned about Mary Flannery being bitten by mosquitoes and would place her in the coop, a shallow box with screen panels, when they sat in their walled garden. As her precocious and willful daughter grew older, Mrs. O'Connor chose Mary Flannery's friends for her and made Lafayette Square off-limits: that sandy, treeless lot was a place of sticks and balls, of boys and dangerous games. After school Mary Flannery was to walk straight home from St. Vincent's Academy at St. John the Baptist Church or from Sacred Heart School on Bull Street, staying on the sidewalk and keeping well clear of the lawless "no man's land" in the middle. We usually think of force as phallic and intrusive; it can also be a confining matrix.

Flannery's yearning for freedom developed as she did. After an adolescence under the roof of Miss Mary Cline, an aunt who ruled the roost at 431 Greene Street, O'Connor left Milledgeville—flew the coop—as soon as a scholarship to the University of Iowa would allow her to do so. It took a "dread disease," the first onset of lupus in 1950, to drive her back to Milledgeville and the Clines. She did not return permanently until 1952, when Sally Fitzgerald revealed to her the severity of her medical condition. Most of her writing life was spent with her mother on a farm that belonged to Regina's brother, Louis Cline, who visited from Atlanta on the weekends. Milledgeville was known as "a bird sanctuary," as Flannery wryly pointed out in several of her letters, and out at Andalusia, Flannery herself was like one of the exotic birds she raised, well cared for but confined. It is true that she made frequent trips to the Sanford House, the

Piggly Wiggly, and Sacred Heart Church in town, but always with her mother. She did not get a driver's license until late in her life (when Regina was hospitalized with pneumonia) and even afterwards drove rarely. As Robert Donahoo has noted, her letters are filled with appeals to friends, acquaintances, and those with whom she had merely exchanged some correspondence: come see me. In December, 1955, she wrote to Fred Darsey, an inmate who had escaped from Milledgeville State Hospital earlier that year and fled to New York City: "Christmas doings in the city must be quite something . . . Christmas in the country," she reports somewhat wistfully, "is like any other day." She had lived in Iowa City, at Yaddo, on Broadway on the upper west side in Manhattan, and in Connecticut with Sally and Robert Fitzgerald. Life in these stimulating locales had its annoyances, but she did not choose to return to her family and she knew what she was missing. Back home, contending with lupus erythematosus, she remembered the freedom of a normal life.

As safe refuge for O'Connor, Andalusia was literally an asylum, both home and house of confinement. Moreover, the proximity of Andalusia to institutions of incarceration may have sharpened her awareness of physical and psychic modes of confinement. It is clear from her letters to Darsey that the huge state hospital was a prominent factor in her imagination, as indeed it was for all of Baldwin County and middle Georgia (Monroe B14). Perhaps this proximity, combined with her experience of a constricting illness, led O'Connor to anticipate Foucault's insights about society's willingness to use legally and medically authorized force to maintain the status quo.[4]

Also like Foucault, O'Connor understands how authorized force—power—is linked to ways of knowing. In "Revelation," for example, Ruby Turpin's reality consists of the functional stratification of society into demographic and socio-economic groups:

> Sometimes Mrs. Turpin occupied herself at night naming the classes of people. On the bottom of the heap were most colored people, not the kind she would have been if she had been one, but most of them; then next to them—not above, just away from—were the white-trash; then above them were the home-owners, and above them the home-and-land owners to which she and Claud belonged. Above she and Claud were people with a lot of money and much bigger houses and much more land. (CW 636)

Ruby's world, perhaps an O'Connor parody of the theory of the "great chain of being," depends on implied threats of force and incarceration. Ruby seems completely unaware that it is a social and political order and a way of seeing that is on the verge of imploding under the weight of its inability to place and contain "abnormalities." Specifically, her knowledge/power system cannot accommodate the data points presented when a black man begins to acquire property and when those with "good blood" suffer financial setbacks:

> The complexity would bear in on her, for some of the people with a lot of money were common and ought to be below she and Claud and some of the people who had good blood had lost their money and had to rent and then there were colored people who owned their homes and land as well. There was a colored dentist in town who had two red Lincolns and a swimming pool and a farm with registered white face cattle on it. (636)

Sheer complexity, the surplus of possibilities even in her small Southern town, threatens Ruby's episteme and her stable world.

The first act of "Revelation," read with a lens ground with the insights of Foucault, is a story about the restoration of order and meaning through incarceration, an action that at once defines, justifies, stigmatizes, and instructs. Mary Grace—one of those "Mary *Blank*" caricatures of Mary Flannery herself—is a character who mentally unmasks the knowledge/power system that serves Ruby Turpin and her own "stylish" mother so well. Silently but fiercely assessing the smugness of Ruby, Mary Grace sits in the waiting room of the doctor's office, increasingly frustrated with her mother, who seconds and affirms Ruby's celebration of the status quo. Mary Grace holds a massive book, and though probably a textbook, the title has the anthropological sound of a Foucauldian tome like *The History of Sexuality* or *The Order of Things*. When *Human Development* hits Ruby squarely in the forehead, many readers have thought of the blows directed to bourgeois society by Marx, Freud, and Nietzsche as well as Foucault.

In O'Connor's world, houses of confinement stand ready to carcerate those like Mary Grace whose rage gives the lie to Ruby's smugly optimistic mind-set. The final provocation is Ruby's song of thanksgiving for her many blessings:

> When I think who all I could have been besides myself and what all I got, a little of everything, and a good disposition besides, I just feel like shouting, "Thank you, Jesus, for making everything the way it is. It could have been different." For one thing, somebody else could have got Claud. At the thought of this, she was flooded with gratitude and a terrible pang of joy ran through her. "Oh thank you, Jesus, Jesus, thank you!" (644)

Connecting class-serving social arrangements with the will of the Almighty is an age-old tactic used by apologists for European aristocrats and American slave-owners alike, not to mention those who cleave to market capitalism as a kind of religion. Having absorbed the mantra—*truth is lying; society is guilty*—we may be tempted to shout hallelujah in support of Mary Grace's explosive rage. For her trouble, her violent expression of an inarticulate "cultural critique," Mary Grace finds herself in a straightjacket with a needle in her arm while a character described as "the white trash woman" observes, "that there girl is going to be a lunatic" (647). She calls Ruby "an old wart hog from hell" because she has broken out of the religious way of knowing, having realized that Ruby's religion depends on force and stratification. Mary Grace's gesture is honest and based in fact, yet it marks her as a social deviant and a handy victim. What happens when your attitude and actions challenge the social order, including the modal distribution of scarcities, not the least of which is Ruby's hyper-desirable husband, Claud? In this situation, as in others depicted by O'Connor, you are hauled off to a nuthouse.

In "Revelation" the action by the doctor and nurses is sudden and instinctive; but in *The Violent Bear It Away,* O'Connor elaborates the premeditated collaboration of medical knowledge with power and vice versa. For several weeks Old Tarwater had been preaching on the sidewalk outside his sister's house, condemning her modern, up-to-date, and eminently normal way of living. In order to silence her brother and end the embarrassment of his condemnations, she "works a perfidy" on him, as he describes it; that is, through premeditation and planning, she has a court order drawn up to have Tarwater committed to the state asylum. The only requirement: a medical doctor must be persuaded that Old Tarwater's prophesying is symptomatic of insanity. In a scene reminiscent of the deception and incarceration of Blanche Dubois, Tarwater is lured inside his sister's house where a doctor and two orderlies are hiding behind a door. After he realizes that his blood relation has set a trap for him, he goes into a rage, and it takes both orderlies, the doctor, and two neighbors to subdue him. The doctor declares that Tarwater is not only crazy but dangerous, and he, like Mary Grace, is taken "to the asylum in a strait jacket" (CW 369). Looking back on his confinement, Old Tarwater would tell his grand-nephew, "Ezekiel was in the pit for forty days, but I was in it for four years" (369). Thus in O'Connor does knowledge align itself with power.

In *The Order of Things* Foucault suggests that the "human sciences" are by their nature modes of confinement. Disciplines such as psychology, sociology, and criminology are knowledge systems that allow society to maintain control over its "inmates," to incarcerate mentally, emotionally, and spiritually in the very process of analyzing and explaining. And again, O'Connor has evoked a similar intuition in her novel. Her distaste for "social-sciencey" explanations is well known, but nowhere is it more powerfully evident than in the rendering of the intellectual Rayber and his capture of his uncle—not in a literal house of confinement, but within his scientific theory. When Tarwater discovers that his nephew has written an article on him in a "schoolteacher magazine"—we call them scholarly journals—he "felt that he was tied hand and foot inside the schoolteacher's head, a space as bare and neat as the cell in the asylum" (CW 378). Like the prophets of old in whose line he sees himself, Tarwater's nonconformity has been trapped and contained, not physically, but by a system of knowledge: "His eyeballs swerved from side to side as if he were pinned in a strait jacket again. Jonah, Ezekiel, Daniel, he was at that moment all of them— the swallowed, the lowered, the enclosed" (378). "The world believes that madness can be measured," Foucault says, "and justified by means of psychology" (538). For him, Nietzsche, Van Gogh and Artaud are mad prophets whose "excess" challenges the world's categories, its "efforts and discussions," just as Old Tarwater's prophesying challenges his nephew's science and his sister's "modern" way of life.

It is important to remember that the forceful apprehension and incarceration of Mary Grace and Old Tarwater is perpetrated by their attacks on upstanding citizens who simply want to go about their business without being vexed by abnormal language or behavior. Throughout the O'Connor oeuvre, in fact, we find arrangements of confinement based on systems of knowledge that quarantine the odd and the unwanted. For example, blacks are invariably "placed" by the Jim Crow hierarchy articulated by Ruby Turpin. As Mr. Head says of blacks in "The Artificial Nigger," "they rope them off" (CW 217). O'Connor's depictions of the old can also be viewed as scenes of confinement. Both "The Geranium" and "Judgement Day" depict the exile and confinement of old men in apartments "owned and operated" by daughters. Such an arrangement is a symmetrical reversal of Flannery's own situation, and it is telling that she revisited this version of confinement throughout her writing life.[5] Finally and most remarkably, throughout her writings there are those who are physically or mentally afflicted. Freaks, lunatics, idiots, and inassimilable outsiders are murdered, abandoned, or contained—in boxcars, refugee camps, reform schools, prisons, asylums, even carnivals, and, as we will consider in more detail, in an outhouse with a goat.

III

O'Connor's most detailed treatment of confinement in the sense elaborated by Foucault is "The Partridge Festival." The two main characters, Calhoun and Mary Elizabeth—another Mary *Blank* character—embody the cynicism of late adolescence and a Nietzschean/Foucauldian suspicion of religion, culture, and judicial processes. The story is based in part on an actual crime that occurred in Milledgeville, made famous by *Paris Trout,* a 1988 book-length treatment by Pete Dexter that some say is more like a nonfiction account than a novel. In O'Connor's rendering, a character named Singleton is confined to Quincy State Hospital for killing five distinguished men and the town drunk, an "innocent victim." The ne'er-do-well, called a "wastral" by an old man in town (CW 779), takes a bullet meant for the mayor, who bends down to pull on the tongue of his shoe at the moment Singleton fires (774).

Whereas Mary Grace has only her ambitious *Human Development* with which to oppose smug complacency, Mary Elizabeth, another intellectual outsider, has Calhoun, constitutionally her secret sharer and the main character. Identical in attitude, their "forms," as Calhoun says, "are different" (787). As the would-be novelist, he is interested in specific details, e.g., what Singleton looks like. "Life does not abide in abstractions," he condescendingly explains (788). Mary Elizabeth is the non-fiction side of suspicion, a self-proclaimed "thinker," a theorist. Calhoun is not interested in her abstractions, and she demeans his fascination with appearances, but they reach the same conclusion: Singleton is a scapegoat, a "Christ-figure," "crucified," "laden with the sins of the community. Sacrificed for the guilt of others" (787, 790, 783). Thus does O'Connor use these mirror-twins to parrot a Foucauldian analysis of the situation in Partridge.

For example, playing the role of critical theorist, Calhoun tells a "small white girl . . . with straight white hair" that Singleton is the Outsider (780). The little girl is hearing none of it. Representing the choral voice of Partridge, she has her tongue in the mouth of a Coca-Cola bottle (780). A white girl with white hair tonguing a bottle of Coke: one could hardly imagine a more compelling metaphor for the merger of eros, economics, and conventional morality. Twice in this short episode O'Connor refers to the *gaze* of the child watching Calhoun, and on the second occasion she has Calhoun equate the child's perspective with the community's way of seeing: "Her gaze might have been the depthless gaze of Partridge itself" (780). Calhoun's analysis is a simplistic parody of Foucault: "You people persecuted him and finally drove him mad" (781). He continues his critique of the communal rites of the town when he goes in for a haircut.

"He was an individualist," Calhoun tells the barber, "a man who would not allow himself to be pressed into the mold of his inferiors. A nonconformist. He was a man of depth living among caricatures and they finally drove him mad, unleashed all his violence on themselves" (783). It is the community that is guilty of the violence seemingly perpetrated by the nonconforming individual. Or as Foucault says, "[T]hrough the mediation of madness, it is the world that becomes guilty" (537).

We might think that Calhoun had been reading Foucault's book except for the fact that at the time O'Connor created the character, *Madness and Civilization* had not yet been published. During O'Connor's writing life, this fascination and celebration of madness was associated not with Foucault but with his forebear, Nietzsche, especially the Nietzsche of *Thus Spake Zarathustra*. And *Zarathustra* is one of the books that Mary Elizabeth gives to Singleton at the asylum. So we know that O'Connor was familiar with the notion that madness is a way of knowing superior to that of conventional bourgeois culture. During the 1950's the assertion of the superiority of madness was also associated with the Scotsman R. D. Laing, who in 1965 wrote an enthusiastic reader's report for Tavistock Publications strongly recommending *Madness and Civilization;* with the Herbert Marcuse of *Eros and Civilization;* and with the cast of characters somewhat confusingly identified as "existentialists" in William Barrett's 1958 book *Irrational Man.*[6] In the character of Calhoun O'Connor is consolidating much of this critical theory, some of which she heard espoused by her radical friend Maryat Lee.

So naturally Calhoun sees Singleton, as Foucault sees Sade and Artaud, as a Nietzschean *Ubermensch.* As "the pattern of [Singleton's] situation was borne in on [Calhoun]," he feels "a rush of empathy"; but there is nothing grand or glamorously sadomasochistic about this house of confinement (780). It is not a gothic dungeon but a simple outhouse, moved to the town square for the purposes of the Azalea Festival. Yet the romantic Calhoun imagines "himself flung in the privy" like Singleton and sees himself glaring "between the rotting planks at the fools howling and cavorting outside"; he understands that he is confined by "the spirit of the community" (780). The little girl explains the hermeneutic of the community elegantly and succinctly: "Six men was shot here. . . . A bad man did it. . . . He was a bad bad bad man" (780, 781). To Calhoun, identifying as he does with Singleton, this simple-minded explanation is absurd. His superior hermeneutics allows him to see the communal motive for assigning evil to Singleton, to expose the suppression of difference and abnormality in the name of law and order. Calhoun's theory allows him to see that what they call truth is a lie, that the resentful weak have found a way to imprison the independent Overman/Outsider. Singleton's murder of the six men does not make him "a bad bad man"; rather, the shooting is a symptom of a just and admirable rage. For his trouble, Singleton, the heroic resister, is hauled off to the nuthouse like Mary Grace so that the fearful community may preserve and instruct itself.

Mary Elizabeth, Calhoun's double, has a plan to write a piece that will reveal that the knowledge system of Partridge epitomized by the Azalea Festival is "false and rotten to the core"; like Mary Elizabeth, he intends to "finish it off in one swift literary kick" (785). Calhoun contrasts the deep colors of the azaleas and "the trees rustling protectively over the old houses," a sylvan, bourgeois scene, with the unjust imprisonment of Singleton, "who lay on a cot in a filthy ward at Quincy" (784). Like Mary Elizabeth, and Foucault for that matter, Calhoun is certain that his gnosis, superior to any collective episteme, transcends historical time and place; his way of knowing allows him to see an injustice while Partridge episteme is limited to the simplistic and self-serving perspective of the little white girl. Calhoun feels "in a concrete way the force of [Singleton's] innocence," just as Foucault asserts the innocence of the "tragic" heroes celebrated in *Madness and Civilization*.[7] The salesman who would be a writer sees it all so clearly and intends to compose his own critique of authorized confinement: "he would have to show, not say, how primary injustice operated" (784).

IV

"The Partridge Festival," of course, is not the first or only time that O'Connor has a go at the sentimental partnership of pity and theory. In "The Lame Shall Enter First," a story written and revised during the same twelve- to eighteen-month time period from late 1960 to early 1962, we see a similar innocence in the theory-ridden Sheppard, a "big tin Jesus" and know-it-all. He excuses Rufus Johnson's criminal activity as a compensation for his clubfoot; his alienation and house-breaking are a reaction to his religion-obsessed grandfather and the per-secution he suffers. Rufus Johnson's problem is one that can be fixed, Sheppard's theory goes, with tender-minded social work and a corrective shoe. His fate and that of his son constitute a terrifying rebuttal of the notion that criminal behavior and social alienation are problems that can be solved with contrarian sympathies and an abstract reversal of categories.

The climax of "The Partridge Festival" takes a similar, anti-Foucauldian, turn. Calhoun has been the absent-minded professor all along: preoccupied and dis-tracted, he walks "four doors past his aunt's house." Like any thinker abstracted from things in themselves, he needs "to turn and go back" to locate himself in space and time (784). Thinking without seeing is the bane of theorists generally, but the visit to Singleton at Quincy State Hospital focuses our attention again on the relationship of theory and confinement in O'Connor's work. The Christ figure imagined by Calhoun, when he appears in the story, is depicted not as innocent victim but stone killer. He is not a tragic hero but a thug, not a genius but a mundane exemplar of Hannah Arendt's banality of evil. Calhoun notices a "penetrating gleam" when the orderlies bring Singleton in—his eyes have "a slight reptilian quality" (794). When the madman's attention shifts from Calhoun to Mary Elizabeth, his predatory "glare" and demeanor become sexualized: "his eyes remained absolutely still like the eyes of a treetoad that has sighted its prey. His throat"—and doubtless other body parts—"began to swell. 'Ahhh,' he said as if he had just swallowed something pleasant, 'eeeee'" (794). Singleton makes "suggestive noises through his teeth" and propositions Mary Elizabeth, offering to make her a queen and put her on a float, an obvious allusion to the beauty contest to select Miss Partridge Azalea. He reaches out to fondle her, and when the orderlies attempt to restrain him, he breaks, races around the room, and begins to expose himself. "Look girl!" he shouts to Mary Elizabeth, and the demand to pay attention and *see* might as well be directed to any of us who romanticize madness. The two social theorists flee the old tree toad, scramble into the car, and speed away, shocked and exhausted. Yet even this encounter with intimidating eros and insanity is more campy than terrifying. Singleton is a stock comic character, the dirty old man. Our final image of him could hardly be further from the Marquis de Sade, Foucault's heroic, diabolical inmate.

If Singleton is no Sade, Quincy State is no Hôpital Général or teeming Bedlam. And here again, O'Connor's depiction of a modest house of confinement works counter to Foucault's grandiose history. The model for Quincy is Milledgeville State Hospital[8]—also the local source of the asylums in "Revelation" and *The Violent Bear It Away*, but used here in a very different way. The "center building" mentioned when Calhoun and Mary Elizabeth arrive is still the signature building at Milledgeville State Hospital; in 1907 its name was officially changed from "Center" to "Powell" to honor Dr. Theophilus Orgain Powell, who was superintendent from 1874 to 1907, but it was still often called the Center Building during O'Connor's life (Cranford 40, 55–56). The sounds of Quincy that Calhoun hears are sounds that Flannery would have heard driving through "The State," as it was known locally: "From one end of the building came a continuous mourning sound as delicate as the fluttering of owls; at the other end they heard rocketing peals of laughter" (793–94). O'Connor knew the asylum and referred to it as "the second largest insane asylum in the world," jokingly telling a potential visitor in a letter that it is one of the few things worth seeing in Milledgeville. The point for us is that O'Connor could have chosen to depict the massive buildings, the extensive food preparation facilities, the cultivated lands and working pastures that were all part of the sprawling "total institution" known as Milledgeville State Hospital. It was all part of her immediate experience, and more than most authors, that is what she drew on. But O'Connor is at pains to present the fictional asylum not as the huge city that Milledgeville State Hospital was, but as a collection of modest structures with patient nurses and "stupid but good-natured" attendants (792). Quincy's "cluster of low buildings" are "hardly noticeable" and rise with virtually no architectural impact "like a rich growth of warts on the hill" (791). What we see is an understated, functional campus. This house of confinement, unlike those described by Foucault, is hardly a grand temple attesting to the power of reason and the necessity of control.

Foucault would be disappointed with Quincy because only massive, intimidating buildings are a proper match for the potent madness that will eventually shatter them and with them, civilization. It is not surprising, then, that Foucault objects to Erasmus and other rationalist approaches to melancholy and mental illness because madness "is slowly disarmed" by such discourses (26). O'Connor gives a Quincy nurse a line that disarms madness even more thoroughly than Erasmus. Calhoun, waiting outside for Mary Elizabeth, is startled by "a gentle face, wrapped around with a green hand towel . . . smiling toothlessly but with an agonizing tenderness." The nurse tells the patient, "Get a move on, sweetie" (792), thereby domesticating the scene more effectively than "the whole humanist tradition," as Foucault disparagingly calls it (26). Like the unremarkable buildings themselves, the mental illness circulating within and between them is debilitating, mundane, and simply there.

"The Partridge Festival" is a different story of confinement, then, with an embedded self-critique lest the author and her readers become complacent themselves. With this story it is almost as if O'Connor is unwriting Mary Grace's incarceration in "Revelation," as if she is revising the story of "the perfidy" worked on Tarwater in *The Violent Bear It Away*. Maryat Lee and Flannery make their appearances again, not as innocent victims but as the romantic outsiders Calhoun and Mary Elizabeth. O'Connor neutralizes Foucault's depiction of madness as tonic and transformative by revealing the naïveté, nostalgia, and blind determination lurking within such a rendering. By associating a

William Monroe

Foucauldian perspective with Mary Elizabeth and Calhoun, and by extension with Calhoun's grandfather, O'Connor allows us to see Foucault's critique as the rhetorical contraption that it is, similar in ambition and abstraction to the houses of confinement it analyzes.

What O'Connor understands—and Foucault and other millenarian theorists ignore or even savor—is the hard fact that any social order, any episteme, however enlightened, however *critical,* requires victims who will seem to deserve their fates, new houses of confinement, new violence and force, administrative and otherwise. Perhaps that is the self-accusatory insight that Calhoun achieves at the close of the story. His resemblance to Singleton is not nearly so strong as his resemblance to his great-grandfather, and he imagines the old man's face and his reproductive potency as a "gift of life [that] had pushed straight forward to the future to raise festival after festival" (796). The vision, a nightmare one for Calhoun, is of an infinite repetition of festivals, a continuing cycle of rituals, each one establishing a new order or re-establishing an old, each one excluding and ostracizing the few as it invigorates the many. His Aunt Bessie gives him a miniature of the old man, "round-faced, bald, hands knotted on the head of a black stick," a tableau suggesting the capacity and willingness to exercise force. The implied threat of violence is underscored by the old man's expression: "all innocence and determination," a foreboding combination in any individual or group (774). Like Foucault, Calhoun's great-grandfather was a wordsmith and a theorist: his facile imagination is responsible for the town's motto, *Beauty is Our Money Crop.* His slogans no less than his methods "theorize" Partridge.

Calhoun's grandfather is called a "master merchant." Through his resemblance to Calhoun, O'Connor links him to influential masters of modern thought like Nietzsche, Laing, and Foucault. The similarity goes beyond appearance. Each summer Calhoun sets aside his penetrating critique and goes to live with his parents where he sells "air-conditioners, boats, and refrigerators," recreational and labor-saving devices, to middle-class buyers (776). Calhoun, we are told, could get by well enough without the "orgy of selling," but "in the depths of himself" he knows "he *enjoyed* selling." In the face of a customer, Calhoun "was carried outside himself; he was in the grip of a drive as strong as the drive of some men for liquor or a woman; and he was horribly good at it" (777). Here O'Connor eroticizes Calhoun's experience of selling, even pushing beyond eros to obsession and addiction. Like Foucault, Calhoun's conscious intention may be "to write something that would vindicate the madman" (776), but really he just wants to sell someone something. He even dreams the night before his visit to the asylum that he is "driving to Quincy to sell *Singleton* a refrigerator" (789, emphasis added). The erotic obsession with selling labor-saving contraptions to middle-class buyers—could this be an apt description of what goes by the name of "theory"? Is Foucault hawking Sade, Artaud, and Nietzsche in order to sell us a theory that pretends to resolve the intractable mystery of madness?

From 1938 to 1940, an optimistic and ambitious expansion program at Milledgeville State Hospital promised to solve the problem of insanity. The great expansion of the institution known locally as "the State" would significantly benefit not only society but the inmates incarcerated there. The impressive buildings were completed while O'Connor was at Peabody High School and were symbols of medical, social, and political progress. In Foucault's words, they were "dense symbols," architectural embodiments of "the civil equivalent of religion" (*The Foucault Reader* 139). As evidence of solved problems, those imposing brick structures, many of which are now surrounded with razor wire and incorporated into the Georgia State Penal System, represented a kind of secular Church Triumphant, houses of confinement declaring the arrival of yet another enlightened age. Unmasking the naïveté of a society that builds such institutions may be a most welcome corrective; but doing so with the notion that a more accepting knowledge/power system would make incarceration obsolete is equally sentimental. The emptying of America's huge asylums and state hospitals was initiated with another theory-driven reform, the Community Mental Health Centers Construction Act of 1963, part of John F. Kennedy's "New Frontier" legislation. It passed quickly and virtually without opposition; after Kennedy's death in November, 1963, community mental health initiatives became part of the Johnson Administration's pervasive efforts to solve social problems with scientific knowledge. Thus innocent theory built the houses of confinement, and theory equally naïve and millenarian emptied them.

For O'Connor, such a swift disposal of stubborn and mysterious affliction by literally the stroke of a pen—whether in the hand of a president, a governor, or a writer like Foucault—is reckless arrogance. Foucault's skeptical scrutiny of social institutions, truly fascinating and insightful, is finally also sentimental. It is, in O'Connor's formulation, innocent of the hard work of being and living in the world as it is. Foucault, like Calhoun's great-grandfather, can develop compelling slogans and tell a good story. He is indeed a master salesman. His dream of a world without administrative force or confinement, of Nietzschean excess in festival after festival, is visionary, apocalyptic, and eerily familiar. A world without restraint and confinement is never far to seek in human experience. Foucault's vision of such a world embraces without apology the violence and celebrates the destruction that would surely be its hallmarks:

Bosch, Brueghel, Thierry Bouts and Durer line up beside their silent images. For madness unleashes its fury in the space of pure vision. Fantasies and threats, the fleeting fragments of dreams and the secret destiny of the world, where madness has a primitive, prophetic force, revealing that the dream-like is real and that a thin surface of illusion opens onto bottomless depths. . . . the reality of the world will one day be absorbed into the fantastic Image, at that delirious moment between being and nothingness which is pure destruction. . . . all will flame up in a blinding flash, in the extremity of disorder that will precede the ordered monotony of the end of all things. (26)

Confinement now, apocalypse soon enough.

In Foucault's version of this romantic dream, the road to the monotonous end is one of glorious destruction, the madman a portentous sign of "primitive, prophetic force." "Through Goya and Sade," he writes in his conclusion, "the Western world rediscovered the possibility of going beyond its reason with violence" (*History of Madness* 535). Such a dithyramb to madness, as Miller describes the book, neatly avoids the shame of living in a world where confinement and other forms of administrative force create the personal security that make oeuvres like Foucault's, and O'Connor's for that matter, possible. The refusal to accept confinement and other punitive limits ends in a romantic embrace of annihilation, an apocalyptic story all too familiar in an age of terror. Like Foucault's theoretical hermeneutic, Calhoun's appliances are designed to make life in this difficult world simple, easy, convenient. And similarly, Foucault's reversal of criminality and citizenship is an example of what some friends in graduate school archly called "artificial intelligence": predictable critical theory promoted by smug salesmen, contemptuous of hard presence and real affliction, promising to make vexing mysteries vanish, all the while flashing "new, new, new" signs to a credulous audience.

Notes

1. Foucault develops the concept of *epistemes* as the unexamined knowledge systems of a society or an age in *The Order of Things: An Archeology of the Human Sciences*. The concept of the gaze (Sartre's *le regard*) precedes Foucault, but he elaborated the concept of the dehumanizing medical gaze in *The Birth of the Clinic*.

2. A readily available collection of Foucault's essays and interviews is entitled *Knowledge/Power*. His notion is the Nietzschean one that knowledge is always

purposive, and that that purpose is always self-interest. A way of knowing is not indicative of a simple will to truth; knowledge is a system of order and signification that reveals a will to power, a striving for superiority.

3. During the month of July, 2007, I had the opportunity to participate in "Reconsidering Flannery O'Connor," a National Endowment for the Humanities Institute at Georgia College in Milledgeville. During a weekend excursion to Savannah we visited the O'Connor Childhood Home.

4. In *Madness and Civilization,* Foucault, as storytellers do, draws on patterns, themes, and plots that were already in wide circulation. So we need not make the claim that Foucault read O'Connor, or vice versa. They were both paying attention, and their observations and insights overlap to a remarkable degree.

5. Karl-Heinz Westarp lists four versions of "Judgement Day" in his *Flannery O'Connor: The Growing Craft:* "The Geranium" (1946), "An Exile in the East" (completed in 1954), "Getting Home" (completed 1964), and "Judgement Day" (1964). Westarp makes the point that O'Connor worked on versions of a story about an exiled and imprisoned old man off and on throughout her writing life.

6. In *Eros and Civilization,* Herbert Marcuse elaborates Freud's insights in *Civilization and Its Discontents* that the orderliness and domestic demands of civilization require the repression of the libido. Unlike Freud, Marcuse imagines, John Lennon–style, a future Marxian world where such repression would not be necessary. Foucault's celebration of madness is apocalyptic rather than utopian, but his depiction of bourgeois civilization as repressive and fearful of the erotic mirrors Marcuse. Laing describes the 1965 English translation (*Madness and Civilization*) as "an exceptional book of very high caliber—brilliantly written, intellectually rigorous, and with a thesis that thoroughly shelves the assumptions of traditional psychiatry" (*History of Madness,* ii).

7. Foucault speaks of a "tragic consciousness" that is "visible in the last words of Nietzsche and the last visions of Van Gogh. . . . it is that same consciousness that finds expression in the work of Antonin Artaud" (28).

8. The Partridge Festival, likewise, is easily identified as the Milledgeville *Azalea Festival*—so easy, in fact, that Regina O'Connor urged her daughter not to publish the story with the title "The Azalea Festival."

William Monroe

Works Cited

Barrett, William. *Irrational Man: A Study in Existential Philosophy.* New York: Doubleday, 1958.

Cranford, Peter G. *But for the Grace of God. The Inside Story of the World's Largest Insane Asylum, Milledgeville!* Augusta, GA: Great Pyramid, 1981.

Donahoo, Robert. "Flannery O'Connor's Correspondence: Some Academic Issues." Roundtable contribution, American Literature Association, Long Beach, CA. 31 May 2002.

Foucault, Michel. *The Birth of the Clinic: An Archaeology of Medical Perception.* London: Tavistock, 1973.

———. *The Foucault Reader.* Ed. Paul Rabinow. New York: Pantheon, 1984.

———. *The Order of Things: An Archeology of the Human Sciences.* New York: Random, 1970.

———. *Madness and Civilization: A History of Insanity in the Age of Reason.* Trans. Richard Howard. New York: Random, 1965.

———. *History of Madness.* Trans. Jonathan Murphy and Jean Khalfa. London: Routledge, 2006.

Goffman, Erving. *Asylums: Essays on the Social Situation of Mental Patients and Other Inmates.* Garden City, NY: Anchor, 1961.

Miller, James. *The Passion of Michel Foucault.* Cambridge, MA: Harvard UP, 2000.

Monroe, William. "The 'Mountain on the Landscape' of Flannery O'Connor" (illus.). *The Chronicle of Higher Education* (Sec. 2, The Chronicle Review) Dec. 15, 2000: B14, 16.

O'Connor, Flannery. *Collected Works.* New York: Library of America, 1988.

———. Letter to Fred Darsey. 26 Dec. 1955. The Flannery O'Connor Collection. Emory University Manuscript, Archives, and Rare Book Library, Atlanta.

———. *Mystery and Manners: Occasional Prose.* Ed. Sally and Robert Fitzgerald. New York: Farrar, 1969.

Ricoeur, Paul. *Freud and Philosophy: An Essay on Interpretation.* Trans. Denis Savage. New Haven: Yale UP, 1970.

Westarp, Karl-Heinz. *Flannery O'Connor: The Growing Craft.* Birmingham, AL: Summa, 1993.

ON BELIEF, CONFLICT, AND UNIVERSALITY: FLANNERY O'CONNOR, WALTER BENN MICHAELS, SLAVOJ ŽIŽEK

Thomas F. Haddox

This is an essay born of exasperation, of the futility that I feel in confronting the interpretive impasse to which Flannery O'Connor drives me and, it would seem, just about everyone else who values her work. We all know, thanks to O'Connor's essays and correspondence, what her intentions as a writer were; we all know whether we are persuaded by her arguments; and we have probably decimated forests staking out our own often mutually exclusive positions. The distinguished company of readers who share O'Connor's theological premises, viewing her as a prophet who lashes our fallen world with the painful truth that Jesus died to save us, is matched by the distinguished company of readers, going at least as far back as John Hawkes, who hold that O'Connor is unknowingly of the Devil's party. And these two contending sides are joined today by historicist-minded critics from Jon Lance Bacon to Patricia Yaeger, who see neither salvation nor nihilism in her work but only the distorted reflections of the racist, sexist, class-obsessed, and Cold War–damaged culture that was the South of her lifetime. The situation has not changed much since 1992, when Frederick Crews complained that "there is never a shortage of volunteers to replace the original antagonists" (156) in the fundamental debates over O'Connor's work. Some of us ask, "Should we take O'Connor's Catholicism seriously or stow it away in a box marked 'false consciousness' or 'irrelevant window dressing'"? Others among us ask, "Should we condemn O'Connor for remaining silent before the racial injustices of her time, or praise her for registering some slight or partial resistance to them?"

These questions will outlive us, because they cannot be definitively answered as long as we continue to act as though O'Connor's literary corpus provides all that we need to answer them. Although we pride ourselves on having escaped the limitations of the New Criticism, and although we repeat the notion that there is no disinterested point of view so often that it has become a bromide, the protocols of academic discourse still require us to act as if our arguments were latent in texts themselves and only incidentally positions in which we happen to believe. When we approach O'Connor, however, such protocols get us nowhere, for at this late date, it should be clear that *all* of these contending positions are amply supported by textual evidence. There is no good reason to doubt the sincerity or the orthodoxy of O'Connor's beliefs, and once we know how these beliefs informed her fictional practice, we must acknowledge her consistency in applying them: there is no necessary contradiction, for instance, in the claim that the Grandmother's murder in "A Good Man Is Hard to Find," or Mrs. May's goring on the horn of the scrub bull in "Greenleaf," might simultaneously function as the salvation of these women.[1] Those who blanch at the ferocity of O'Connor's vision, and dispute that so violent and uncompromising a stance can be authentically Christian, need to read more both about the dogmas and the history of Christianity.

On the other hand, it is equally evident that if O'Connor was writing, as she maintained in a letter to Betty Hester, for "the people who think God is dead" (*HB* 92) and was seeking to shock them into a life-changing awareness of the Incarnation, then she failed at least as often as she succeeded. Early readers such as Josephine Hendin and Martha Stephens, who found O'Connor's fundamental premises (though not necessarily her fiction) repellent, were neither stupid nor ignorant of O'Connor's intentions, and while such readers might be guilty of the intellectual hubris that O'Connor loved to skewer in her fiction, one cannot charge them with willful misreading of the text. Their own beliefs may be wrong, but their arguments are based on an examination of O'Connor's fiction in good faith through the light of these beliefs.

Moreover, anyone who has taught O'Connor repeatedly knows that uninitiated students typically adore her work and are deft at generating interpretations, but they almost never arrive at those that O'Connor intended. My avowedly secular students, upon hearing of O'Connor's religious orthodoxy, are puzzled and sometimes intrigued by what they perceive as the exoticism of her position, but they then shrug and go on pursuing their own interpretations, not converted, not feeling the slightest need to argue with her. My Christian students, on the other hand—unless they have been taught O'Connor by a previous teacher—are usually shocked. I almost always receive papers arguing either that O'Connor's vision cannot possibly be Christian, or that her efforts to persuade are at best counterintuitive, at worst perverse, because she makes Christianity look depraved and unattractive. The first of these arguments is untenable; the second, however, is difficult to dispute. There is a corpse with three bullet holes at the end of "A Good Man Is Hard to Find," a body rendered dead by a man obsessed with Jesus. O'Connor tells us, famously, not to pay attention to it, but to "the action of grace" and the "lines of spiritual motion" (*MM* 113). Unfortunately, only the body is in the text; whatever grace and lines of spiritual motion there may be exist only in readers. To interpret the murder either as an unambiguous but highly entertaining horror, as secular readers might, or as a sign that the Grandmother has been saved by one of God's more mysterious ways, is to go outside the text, to refer to structures of belief rather than to simple, unproblematic evidence. The debate centers not on the interpretation of the text, but on the proper context to choose for the interpretation of the text—and as such, it is irresolvable.

The same is true of the debate surrounding O'Connor's relationship to racial justice. On the one hand, many readers have found much to praise in O'Connor's representation of black characters—Alice Walker famously notes her "distance . . . from the inner workings of her black characters" and praises her for the humility that made such distance possible (52), while Crews echoes many readers' sense that "the black characters in her fiction generally do come off better than the whites—more humane, more intuitively sensible, and of course markedly less susceptible to the status anxiety and self-aggrandizement that she loved to pillory" (157–58). There is also, of course, O'Connor's orthodox conviction that everyone, black and white, can be saved—a conviction expressed most ringingly in "The Artificial Nigger" and in "Revelation." On the other hand, there is little in O'Connor's fiction to indicate clear, unambiguous support for the civil rights movement, much distaste for those who participated directly in it, and much to suggest that such merely political matters are insignificant when viewed *sub specie aeternitatis*. Again, the debate is not about the interpretation of the text, since readers on both sides point to the same passages; it is about the priority of contexts of interpretation. What matters most—representational depth, declarations in support of racial justice, or the state of individual souls? Again, without a textually grounded way to adjudicate these competing claims, the debate becomes irresolvable.

Faced with these impasses, my own impulse has always been to change the subject. In my own writing on O'Connor, I have read "Parker's Back" as a critique of visuality that can be illuminated by the work of Lacan and Irigaray; I have invoked Jane Jacobs's theories of urbanism to account for the function of community in "A Stroke of Good Fortune" and "The Artificial Nigger"; and I have suggested that literary naturalism, especially in its theories of sexual determinism, might be a profitable lens through which to read *Wise Blood*. In pursuing these readings, my motivation has been to say something fresh, to draw attention to aspects of O'Connor's texts that have gone unnoticed, and, above all, to avoid the boredom of endless repetition. And yet I cannot escape the conviction that these readings, although not necessarily invalid—after all, they point to textual evidence and offer logical argument to make their cases, as any reading must—are ultimately beside the point. None of these readings challenges the fundamental debates about O'Connor's work; in fact, they can easily be pressed into the service of one side or the other. You can, for instance, be committed to a Catholic reading of O'Connor *and* think that O'Connor's stance toward vision has more in common with Lacan's than with Descartes'; there is no necessary contradiction here. You can reject O'Connor's Christian interpretation *and* believe that *Wise Blood* is best understood as a naturalist novel. My attention to differences has not made a difference.

In *The Shape of the Signifier,* Walter Benn Michaels suggests that what I have been trying to do—to multiply possible readings of O'Connor's work, to let a thousand flowers bloom—reflects a larger trend within academic writing, a move away from "disagreement" and toward "difference." The most obvious expression of this trend is the absolute commitment among many theorists and critics to the primacy of the subject position. As Michaels puts it, when we commit to subject position—to identity—as the key element that determines how we read a text, we thereby commit to a protocol in which "there can be no conflicts of interpretation, not because there can be no conflict but because there can be no interpretation. All conflict has been turned into conflict between those who speak one language and those who speak another or between those who wish to eliminate difference and those who wish to preserve it, and the act of interpreting what someone says has been reconfigured either as the act of saying the same thing or as the act of saying something else" (64). While I have not proposed my readings of O'Connor as the expression of my own identity (in the manner of the "As a [fill in the blank with an identitarian category], I maintain" readings that one sometimes encounters), I have valued them precisely because I saw them as introducing an element of difference into an arena marked by endless disagreement. To speak of disagreement is to speak about belief, about questions of what is true and what is false; to speak of difference is to speak about identity or taste, neither of which is subject to debate in any meaningful sense.

And yet, Michaels goes on to suggest, to speak of difference instead of disagreement cannot, in the end, be anything other than a dodge, for the distinction between difference and disagreement is also a clash of beliefs, not a choice, as my writing on O'Connor has sometimes implied, between beliefs and something else. The claim that difference qua difference matters is, after all, a truth claim, and it is just as contestable as the claims that either O'Connor's religious vision or her vexing position on southern race relations should be the starting point for whatever we say about her. And as a truth claim, it is necessarily exclusionary, despite its rhetoric of openness to multiplicity. It is, however, a claim that refuses to defend itself against direct challenges, and that smugly takes its refusal as a sign of unwarranted moral superiority.

I read Michaels's indictment of the way we in the academy argue—or, more precisely, refuse to argue—and I find myself justly condemned. The enjoyment I have derived from my readings of O'Connor has taken the form of one-upmanship, of a sense that while others go on vulgarly shouting at each other about Christianity or about racial justice, I have perceived, as Wallace Stevens might put it, "ghostlier demarcations, keener sounds" (106). I have been like the representative intellectual that Slavoj Žižek posits in the following passage from *The Puppet and the Dwarf,* one of his recent books on the Judeo-Christian tradition:

> When, today, one directly asks an intellectual: "OK, let's cut the crap and get down to basics: do you believe in some form of the divine or not?," the first answer is an embarrassed withdrawal, as if the question is too intimate, too probing; this withdrawal is then usually explained in more "theoretical" terms: "That is the wrong question to ask! It is not simply a matter of believing or not, but, rather, a matter of certain radical experience, of the ability to open oneself to a certain unheard-of dimension, of the way our openness to radical Otherness allows us to adopt a specific ethical stance, to experience a shattering form of enjoyment. . . ." (5–6)

Žižek then goes on to say: "What we are getting today is a kind of 'suspended' belief, a belief that can thrive only as not fully (publicly) admitted, as a private obscene secret. Against this attitude, one should insist even more emphatically that the 'vulgar' question 'Do you really believe or not?' matters—more than ever, perhaps" (6).

Žižek is correct here. Although his recent work has been rightly criticized by those who perceive its opportunism—his stated thesis is that Christianity and his own brand of atheistic dialectical materialism belong, so to speak, on the same side of the barricades—this opportunism does not invalidate what I take to be his more fundamental claim: that we are all *believers* of one kind or another, and that what divides believers in disagreement from believers in difference is merely that the first group takes both its beliefs and its antagonists seriously while the second group tries to disavow its beliefs or to prevent their emergence as points of contention. After all, you can argue with a belief; you cannot argue with a subject position. And you can only respond to claims of radical openness to experience by suggesting that the speaker is less radically open than he or she believes—which leaves unexamined the premise that radical openness is supremely desirable or even possible. To invoke such terms in the course of an argument is, in effect, to declare them off limits, to decline engagement with those who see interpretation as a function of something other than a mere reflection of identity, and to call our seriousness into question.

In an age when the general public knows little about our work as teachers and scholars, and derives much of what it does know from the inevitable stories in the media after each MLA Convention that portray it as a circus, Žižek's lesson demands attention. The commitment to difference among literary scholars is necessarily a commitment to novelty, and as such it reinforces the consumerist imperatives both of our late capitalist society and our profession. It is becoming difficult to avoid the conclusion that we value difference qua difference primarily because we need to go on publishing new things, and that our disdain for repetition differs little from the disdain of the consumer who, having purchased last year's model, now needs this year's lest he or she feel outclassed by hipper, more beautiful people.

For this reason, we in the field of O'Connor studies may have much to offer our colleagues in the profession as a whole. The record of O'Connor criticism shows that for all the different topics that we might focus on in her work, it is impossible to avoid coming back to or being co-opted by a few fundamental debates about significant matters. The profession would probably be healthier and its value more evident if all our academic debate were like debate about O'Connor, if we were less consumed with the pursuit of novelty and publication and more concerned with the proposal and defense of core beliefs in our interpretations. As Fredric Jameson observed twenty-six years ago in *The Political Unconscious:*

> Our object of study is less the text itself than the interpretations through which we attempt to confront and to appropriate it. Interpretation is here construed as an essentially allegorical act, which consists in rewriting a given text in terms of a particular interpretive master code. . . . I happen to feel that no interpretation can be effectively disqualified on its own terms by a simple enumeration of inaccuracies or omissions, or by a list of unanswered questions. Interpretation is not an isolated act, but takes place within

a Homeric battlefield, on which a host of interpretive options are either openly or implicitly in conflict. (9–10, 13)

O'Connor criticism certainly has been a Homeric battlefield, in which a few interpretive master codes have slugged it out. Secular, religious, and historicizing critics have jumped into the fray, and whatever their arguments, they have expressed their basic commitment to their beliefs in ways that remind me of the altogether admirable sentiment of Rufus Johnson in "The Lame Shall Enter First": "Even if I didn't believe it, it would still be true" (477). In other words, they have not shrunk from emphasizing the universality of their claims, the logical conclusion that claims that are true or false must be true or false for everyone, and that every genuine debate—as opposed to proliferations of difference—is a clash of competing universalisms.

Henry T. Edmondson III has recently argued that O'Connor's work urges a "return to good and evil" and a rejection of modern attempts (beginning with Nietzsche) to transcend these categories. His argument is correct, and it ought to be acknowledged as such even by those readers who reject the Christian (and particularly Thomistic) framework that he and O'Connor draw upon to define good and evil. It is correct not only because O'Connor did indeed believe in the distinction between good and evil and sought to make readers freshly aware of it (this is simply a fact about her intentions), but also because *everyone* who argues in good faith for the truth of his or her beliefs necessarily universalizes, necessarily combats those who reject them. Everyone, in other words, committed to the search for truth invokes definitions of good and evil. Even Nietzsche's claim to have transcended good and evil entails its own good and its own evil.

Many readers will find such a conclusion unsettling, because we have become accustomed to thinking of epistemic uncertainty and limitless tolerance as the highest virtues, as the indispensable preconditions for peace and justice. Many might point out that the world's most conspicuously militant universalism at the moment—a strand of Islamic fundamentalism with a very concrete notion of jihad—has turned to terrorism, religious warfare, and other forms of violent provocation in order to advance its cause. Does not my argument here suggest that firmly held convictions make violence inevitable, because in a pluralistic world, there is no other way to make one triumph over others?

I certainly hope that violence is not inevitable, and the banal fact that people sometimes do change their most firmly held convictions without having suffered coercion provides grounds for hope. Yet even if violence is not inevitable, conflict most certainly is, because even the attempt to reject certitude in the name of tolerance grounds itself in a universalist notion of the good, however it strives to deny that fact. What we need is a better account of how persuasion works, how conflicts about beliefs may come to an end without recourse to violence. How does one interpretation of a work of fiction prove more convincing than another, especially when it is not, as Jameson suggests, a question of asking which interpretation has the fewest inaccuracies, omissions, or unanswered questions, but of asking one to subscribe to a completely different worldview? How does one universalism triumph over another, particularly when the debate is couched not in the conventions of philosophy, but in the essentially rhetorical mode of fiction—a mode given as much to the cultivation of "mystery" (to use one of O'Connor's favorite words) as to rational argument?

I do not know the answer to these questions, and this is why O'Connor exasperates me. Perhaps if I could begin to answer them, I would feel less exasperated. Until then I am, like too many others in this historical moment, too easily bored, too ready to pursue novelty for its own sake, too peevishly frustrated by the fact that debates about the true and the good are, however important, however inescapable, also (for the foreseeable future, at least) irresolvable. The debates go on, world without end, and all of us in O'Connor studies—myself included—had better learn not merely to accept that fact, but to embrace it.

Notes

I would like to thank David Malone, Anthony Di Renzo, and Honor McKitrick Wallace for their discussions with me on this topic, which have improved this essay greatly.

1. How *effective* O'Connor was in her persuasive strategies is, of course, a different question, and even those who adhere to O'Connor's theology sometimes differ on this point.

Works Cited

Bacon, Jon Lance. *Flannery O'Connor and Cold War Culture.* Cambridge: Cambridge UP, 1993.

Crews, Frederick. *The Critics Bear It Away: American Fiction and the Academy.* New York: Random, 1992.

Edmondson, Henry T., III. *Return to Good and Evil: Flannery O'Connor's Response to Nihilism.* Lanham, MD: Lexington, 2002.

Hawkes, John. "Flannery O'Connor's Devil." *Sewanee Review* 70 (Summer 1962): 395–407.

Hendin, Josephine. *The World of Flannery O'Connor.* Bloomington: Indiana UP, 1970.

Jameson, Fredric. *The Political Unconscious: Narrative as a Socially Symbolic Act.* Ithaca: Cornell UP, 1981.

Michaels, Walter Benn. *The Shape of the Signifier: 1967 to the End of History.* Princeton: Princeton UP, 2004.

O'Connor, Flannery. *The Complete Stories.* New York: Farrar, 1971.

———. *The Habit of Being.* Ed. Sally Fitzgerald. New York: Farrar, 1979.

———. *Mystery and Manners: Occasional Prose.* Ed. Sally and Robert Fitzgerald. New York: Farrar, 1969.

Stephens, Martha. *The Question of Flannery O'Connor.* Baton Rouge: Louisiana State UP, 1973.

Stevens, Wallace. "The Idea of Order at Key West." *Collected Poetry and Prose.* New York: Library of America, 1997. 105–6.

Walker, Alice. "Beyond the Peacock: The Reconstruction of Flannery O'Connor." *In Search of Our Mother's Gardens: Womanist Prose.* San Diego: Harcourt Brace Jovanovich, 1984. 42–59.

Yaeger, Patricia. "Flannery O'Connor and the Aesthetics of Torture." *Flannery O'Connor: New Perspectives,* ed. Sura Rath. Athens: U of Georgia P, 1996. 183–206.

Žižek, Slavoj. *The Puppet and the Dwarf: The Perverse Core of Christianity.* Cambridge: MIT Press, 2003.

EVERYTHING THAT RISES DOES NOT CONVERGE: THE STATE OF O'CONNOR STUDIES

Robert Donahoo

> Let us leave behind the ABCs of Christ and not lay again
> a foundation of repentance from dead works, faith in
> God, teaching about baptisms, laying on hands, raising
> the dead, and everlasting judgment. But let us go on to be
> mature. We will do this if God lets us.
>
> —Epistle to the Hebrews 6:1–3, William F. Beck,
> *The New Testament in the Language of Today*

However odd some may find beginning a survey of literary criticism with such a doctrinal Christian epigraph, I cannot help but find this passage in Beck's translation highly appropriate to the state of O'Connor studies today, perhaps even offering us a bit of wisdom. More important, I find O'Connor using similar language about her own writing when late in her career she writes a long letter to Sister Mariella Gable, whom O'Connor once described in a letter as a writing teacher in St. Louis who had once been transferred from Minnesota to "some outpost in the Dakotas" for teaching *The Catcher in the Rye* (HB 453). Dated 4 May 1963, O'Connor's letter to Gable spends its first four paragraphs complaining about and chastising religious—specifically Catholic—readers, ending with a blunt assessment:

> I know that the writer does call up the general and maybe the essential
> through the particular, but this general and essential is still deeply embedded
> in mystery. It is not answerable to any of *our* formulas. It doesn't rest finally
> in a statable kind of solution. It ought to throw you back on the living God.
> Our Catholic mentality is great on paraphrase, logic, formula, instant and
> correct answers. We judge before we experience and never trust our faith to
> be subjected to reality, because it is not strong enough. . . . I think this spirit

is changing on account of the council but the changes will take a long time to soak through. (HB 516–17, my emphasis)

This passage throws a chill into my scholarly soul with its questioning of "statable kind(s) of solution" and its attack on thought by formula. After all, such things are our tools—though we call them not formulas but theories; not solutions but logical interpretations. Moreover, this challenge to reading by expectation is made more pointed for O'Connor scholars by the letter's discussion of O'Connor's fiction and what *she* sees as its failure to fulfill Catholic expectations. O'Connor goes so far as to state, "And if I set myself to write about the essence of Christianity, I would have to quit writing fiction, or become another person" (517). She then returns to her complaint focusing specifically on religious critics who search for fiction looking for "some ideal intention," and she implies an appreciation of secular critics when she adds, "In the gospels it was the devils who first recognized Christ and the evangelists didn't censor this information. They apparently thought it was pretty good witness" (517).

What shimmers into the visible spectrum in this letter, I think, is O'Connor at her most Henry Jamesian—a somewhat surprising stance given her tendency in essays and letters to either put James on a pedestal or make him an object of humor (see *MM* 47, 49, 76, 146; *HB* 68, 92, 99, 226, 258, 332). Nevertheless, she clearly desires a criticism but insists on her Jamesian "donee"—her artistic right not to be confined to some category, not to be required to write for others' expectations and, as a consequence, made relevant to only one type of critical approach. This, I argue, implies a criticism that grows and develops, even, possibly, taking dangerous risks rather than one that settles comfortably for the acceptable. O'Connor, despite the published pronouncements that too often see her trying to control her own interpretation (see, for example, Carol Shloss 102–3 and Keetley 74–75), seems willing to accept heathen or "misreadings" *if* it brings an awareness of the artistry in her work. Certainly, the often quoted paragraph of this letter to Sister Mariella makes plain that she felt some analogous impulse in her vision of her own work: "I appreciate and need your prayers," she writes in the penultimate paragraph. "I've been writing eighteen years and I've reached the point where I can't do again what I know I can do well, and the larger things that I need to do now, I doubt my capacity for doing" (518).

What does any of this have to do with the state of O'Connor studies? It strikes me as offering reasonable criteria and goals by which what O'Connor scholars have done can be measured as well as criteria and goals that may healthily if not always safely steer O'Connor scholars in the future. The criteria are these: (1) the ability to open up and deepen awareness of mystery in her work; and (2) the ability to be generative rather than mummifying. The measuring, at least, is clearly needed. After all, O'Connor studies have been "doing" and writing for over fifty years—if one will accept my view that Paul Engle and Martin Hansford's introduction to the collection of 1955's O'Henry award winners is the first serious, if brief, assessment of her work. But even if an earlier or later date for the start of O'Connor studies is preferred, surely we will all agree that O'Connor's own eighteen-year limit has been exceeded. Just what have we been doing and writing well and what are the "larger things" that challenge us?

Looking Back

Let me begin by a backward look focusing particularly on the idea of mystery. O'Connor, of course, used the term often but nowhere more powerfully than in her essay "The Grotesque in Southern Fiction," where she writes of characters in grotesque writing having "fictional qualities" that "lean away from typical social patterns, toward mystery and the unexpected" (40). The same essay picks up the term again as she discusses a certain kind of writer with which she identifies: "if the writer believes that our life is and will remain essentially mysterious, if he looks upon us as beings existing in a created order to whose laws we freely respond, then what he sees on the surface will be of interest to him only as he can go through it into an experience of mystery itself. His kind of fiction will always be pushing its own limits outward toward the limits of mystery, because for this kind of writer, the meaning of a story does not begin except at a depth where adequate motivation and adequate psychology and the various determinations have been exhausted" (41–42). Clearly, the concept must be taken seriously, but its exact meaning for O'Connor is clarified more by a passage from William Dean's book, *The American Spiritual Culture:*

> On certain rare occasions, people give themselves to a piece of music without reserve, so that the music sweeps them away, eradicating everything else. That music at that moment becomes entirely sufficient; nothing else matters and everything else is transcended. Even if it is sacred music, the idea of God, the ceremonies of the church, the dogmas of organized religion escape notice—along with the artistry of the performers and the particular structure of the composition. The secular performance of this music at this moment is entirely sufficient and nothing else is needed. But just as it

becomes everything, music's specific musical identity can fall away and become, in itself, nothing. At that point, ironically, the utterly secular hearing of pure music can become anything but that; it can open the listener to what feels sacred, dwarfing the music itself. (95–96)

Dean goes on to apply this concept briefly to O'Connor in the midst of a larger argument, but the fact that he even turns to O'Connor at all highlights one of the successes of O'Connor studies to date: that the importance of mystery in her work has been brought to the surface. Probably the most important pieces of scholarship in this vein are the textual work done by Robert and Sally Fitzgerald in collecting O'Connor's essays and then her letters—both providing valuable comments—including the one I quoted earlier—that have put scholars on the track of mystery in her fiction. Though neither *Mystery and Manners* or *The Habit of Being* are above reproach in terms of their scholarly editing— I'm particularly thinking about the choices made in combining manuscripts for the essays and in deleting unflattering references and language in the letters— no O'Connor scholar can or would want either work to disappear, and both tasks presented difficult editing challenges without the possibility of universally pleasing solutions.

Prior to the appearance of either the essays or the letters, criticism steered closest to the concept of mystery by taking theological approaches, taking as their point of contention early reviews of O'Connor's work that saw it as the latest representative of "southern" or "grotesque" schools of realism. Early scholars generally responded by creating the vocabulary of "grace" and "redemption" that would come to be familiar in O'Connor's work. Robert Fitzgerald's 1962 essay in *Sewanee Review,* as well as essays that year in *Thought* by Sister Bertrande Meyers and in *Xavier University Studies* by Sister Simon M. Nolde, offered interpretations of the fiction in theological terms that pushed it beyond established schools. Ted Spivey's two articles in 1964 also undertook to distance O'Connor from writers such as J. D. Salinger and Carson McCullers while linking her to European Catholic writers such as Georges Bernanos and François Mauriac, as well as writers of what he terms "Existential theology," such as Kafka and Dostoevsky. Louise Gossett's 1965 book *Violence in Recent Southern Fiction* made a clear attempt at reconciling the violence and horror on O'Connor's pages with theological aims while Lewis Lawson's essay in *Renascence* that year and Stanley Edgar Hyman's pamphlet *Flannery O'Connor* a year later made clear that O'Connor's theological themes could attract and sustain examination by major critics.

Nevertheless, in this same period the critical work that helped ensure the longevity and vitality of exploring mystery in O'Connor's work came not from a professional scholar or from someone with an orthodox religious perspective but from O'Connor's friend and fellow novelist John Hawkes. His essay "Flannery O'Connor's Devil," published in the *Sewanee Review* in 1962, claimed that "in the most vigorously moral of writers the actual creation of fiction seems often to depend on immoral impulse" (11). Looking closely at O'Connor style, especially in *The Violent Bear It Away,* and drawing from O'Connor's comments in letters to him, Hawkes argued, "the creative process transforms the writer's objective Catholic knowledge of the devil into an authorial attitude in itself in some measure diabolical. This is to say that in Flannery O'Connor's most familiar stories and novels the 'disbelief . . . that we breathe in with the air of the times' emerges fully as two-sided or complex as attraction for the Holy (13). Such claims drew heated response from several O'Connor critics anxious to remove a perceived blight on O'Connor's orthodoxy, but it's worth noting two facts about Hawkes's argument: (1) despite Hawkes's unorthodox approach, he is theological in his terms, taking O'Connor's theological statements seriously. He makes clear that one need not accept O'Connor's specific interpretations of her fiction in order to see either its theological content or its sense of mystery; and (2) in line with the ideas in her letter to Sister Mariella Gable, O'Connor's own responses to Hawkes are lacking in anger or alarm. Instead in a letter to Elizabeth Hester, to whom she sent a Hawkes letter in which he stated some of his ideas about her demonic voice, O'Connor writes, "I am not sure what he means by 'demonic' as he uses it; frequently he leaves me behind, but I think what he says is just & good" (355). And in 1960 O'Connor sent Hawkes himself a letter telling him of the publication of "The Comforts of Home," which, she says, "has a very interesting devil in it that might appeal to you" (416). In 1961, she wrote to Hester concerning her work on "The Lame Shall Enter First": "The thing I am writing now is surely going to convince Jack that I am of the Devil's party," (449), and in 1962 she wrote to Hawkes offering to send him a prepublication copy of that story for the article he was writing for the *Sewanee Review.* She states, "it will add fuel to your theory though not legitimately I think" (456). In short, far from fearing, detesting, or even reviling such criticism, O'Connor seems to have found it useful and worth encouraging.

Unfortunately, Hawkes's "misreading"—though interesting to O'Connor and possibly even generative for her fiction—has not consistently remained the norm for theological criticism. Both Josephine Hendin's *The World of Flannery O'Connor* (1972) and, even more strongly, Martha Stephens's *The Question of Flannery O'Connor* (1973) used O'Connor's theological ideas as a point of attack on the status of her writing as a whole rather than as a way of developing insight into her work. In addition, in a 1974 overview, published in the *Mississippi Review,* of O'Connor criticism, Stuart Burns, himself the author of several strong essays on O'Connor fiction, complained about the redundancy of O'Connor criticism and of the tendency to offer explications of individual works rather than develop original theses about the fiction. More than a decade later, Frederick Crews would add his complaint: "Where the religious critics go most seriously astray is in assuming that O'Connor must have chosen the bare ingredients of her artistry—her characters, settings, actions, and tone—with a didactic end already in mind" (162). Along these lines, I will always remember the response of Bernard Duffey at Duke University when I approached him during the mid 1980s about directing my dissertation on O'Connor: he emitted a long sigh and then told me, "OK, but nothing religious."

Such comments, ranging from the grand to the petty, suggest that the problem that has confronted and will continue to confront theologically oriented criticism is how to avoid offering simply another slightly rephrased argument that O'Connor is indeed Christian and Catholic. The bad news is that essays and articles committed merely to affirming these ABCs of O'Connor scholarship continue to be written and occasionally published. I see this in my own graduate students who work on O'Connor; I see it in some of the essays I'm asked to evaluate for the *Flannery O'Connor Review;* and I hear it often at academic conferences.

The good news, however, is that a number of theologically oriented critics have found ways to avoid rehashing the basics. From Miles Orvell's 1972 *Invisible Parade* to Rowan Williams's 2005 *Grace and Necessity,* scholars have addressed issues and ideas of faith and belief without denying the mystery in O'Connor's work, without turning her fiction into repetitive and lifeless tracts for Christian Orthodoxy. Interestingly, both Orvell and Williams do this by searching out O'Connor's literary and spiritual roots—Orvell the American romance and humor traditions; Williams the Catholic philosopher Jacques Maritain. Their approaches parallel those of scholars ranging from Richard Giannone in his work on the hermit fathers to Farrell O'Gorman in his work on the Catholic Revival movement. However, perhaps the most intriguing, at least for me, of the recent major theological examinations of O'Connor is Ralph C. Wood's 2004 *Flannery O'Connor and the Christ-Haunted South.* Wood once told me in a private conversation that the book was not intended as a traditional scholarly study of O'Connor's fiction and, though it is wonderfully erudite, it isn't traditional.

Rather it makes what should be recognized as postmodern moves in addressing O'Connor's fiction in personal and political terms. From its autobiographical preface to its chapters on preaching and its comments on abortion, this book, like Hawkes's essay, is a wake-up call to enter into debate with and about O'Connor's theological ideas—an attempt to stop reading O'Connor according to polite and expected patterns. Moreover, judging from comments I've heard from other scholars and from Sarah Gordon's powerfully written response in an essay for the *Flannery O'Connor Review*, it has been quite successful. In doing so, Wood helps highlight one of the goals for all future O'Connor scholarship: keeping her work alive in the ongoing debates of the academy.

Beyond Theological Readings

If such theological scholarship has seemed to dominate O'Connor studies, it is far from the full story. Bibliographies by Robert Golden and R. Neil Scott reveal that O'Connor's works have attracted commentary from various theoretical perspectives. For instance, as early as 1964, Bartlett C. Jones published a psychological reading of "Good Country People" in *Midcontinent American Studies Journal*—an article replete with Freudian psychological jargon current today: "neurosis," "a forbidden desire to view the parents' genitals," and even a perhaps unconscious reference to "gaze." A decade later, Claire Katz Kahane offered a more interesting and substantial psychological analysis in the journal *American Literature*. However, unlike Jones, her focus is as much on reading O'Connor's psyche as it is on establishing psychological patterns in the fiction—a fact underscored in 2005 when she offered a self-analysis in terms of her work on O'Connor ("The Re-vision"). More recently, James Mellard has offered two essays that address O'Connor's fiction in terms of the theories of Jacques Lacan. Mellard's "Flannery O'Connor's *Others*: Freud, Lacan and the Unconscious," published in *American Literature*, and his more approachable "Framed in the Gaze: Haze, *Wise Blood*, and Lacanian Reading," published in Michael Kreyling's collection *New Essays on* Wise Blood, both make clear that the theory movement could and should deal with O'Connor. Interestingly, however, though numerous studies have in places tried to probe O'Connor's mind, no full-length psychological study of any bent has yet been published. In part, this is surely due to O'Connor's own ambivalent ideas toward psychology and the social sciences. After all, she once wrote to Elizabeth Hester, "As to Sigmund, I am against him tooth and toenail but I am crafty: never deny, seldom confirm, always distinguish. Within his limitations I am ready to admit certain uses for him" (HB

110). Nevertheless, if a worthy goal of O'Connor studies is to confront the mystery of her work, surely psychological interpretation will yet play a more major role—especially if those knowledgeable about the links between religion and psychology begin to apply that knowledge to O'Connor's work and life.

Much more successful and flourishing have been rhetorical/stylistic approaches to O'Connor. Early in O'Connor studies this was often a point from which to attack her work, as William Esty does in a 1958 essay for *Commonweal,* criticizing her grotesque creations. But from at least James Farnham's response to Esty in an article for *America,* the grotesque has been taken with continued seriousness as an access point to O'Connor's craft and thought. More recently, Anthony Di Renzo in his 1995 *American Gargoyles: Flannery O'Connor and the Medieval Grotesque* continues to demonstrate the vitality of this concept, not only linking O'Connor to medieval folk art but also examining the social ramifications of her work in terms of the changing American South. More important than any one trope or theme, however, rhetorical and stylistic approaches have produced a number of crucial works in O'Connor studies. Frederick Asals's 1982 *Flannery O'Connor: The Imagination of Extremity* and Marshall Bruce Gentry's 1986 *Flannery O'Connor's Religion of the Grotesque* are two midpoint works in O'Connor studies that stand out. Each makes readers aware of characteristic aspects crucial to O'Connor's fiction: doubling in the Poe tradition for Asals, and the narrative voice for Gentry. Beyond the individual readings of specific works, these concepts have become part of the crucial knowledge of O'Connor students and scholars. Gentry's ideas have been further developed by scholars interested in the theories of Mikhail Bakhtin—especially Robert Brinkmeyer in his 1989 book *The Art and Vision of Flannery O'Connor* and, more recently, Sarah Gordon in her 2000 book, *Flannery O'Connor, the Obedient Imagination.* Most important, Gordon's book enters into direct debate with Brinkmeyer. Where Brinkmeyer undertakes the task of asserting that O'Connor's writing reflects the dialogic model that Bakhtin deems central to the novel, Gordon argues instead that O'Connor "embrace[s] . . . the 'female monologic' vision" and states, "O'Connor would not have apologized for this monologic vision" (45). When we are tracing the historical tradition, there is no reason to attempt to arbitrate between these arguments. Rather, we simply need to note that the debate is a sign of the health of O'Connor studies since it evidences the relentless way her work excites creative thought. At the same time, such debate suggests a further step that remains, to my knowledge, untaken: that of using O'Connor to evaluate and correct Bakhtin, particularly in the sense of his applicability for late-twentieth-century and twenty-first-century fiction. If Gordon is right, shouldn't O'Connor's success as a writer suggest amendments to a theory derived largely from the study of nineteenth-century European fiction? Or, from another angle, what might the monologism of O'Connor's short stories reveal about the applicability of Bakhtin to the short story form? In other words, one potential future step for rhetorical/stylistic approaches to O'Connor will be to move from using her as the subject of analysis to using her as a tool for theory creation. Given O'Connor's continued importance to short story writers both in America and abroad, such theorizing seems long overdue as well as offering a sign that rhetorical/stylistic approaches still have much to offer O'Connor studies.

The mention of Sarah Gordon's book raises the increasing importance of feminist studies to O'Connor scholarship. Though the value of work showing O'Connor's connection to other women writers, especially her connection to Caroline Gordon, became clear early in O'Connor studies, the first analyses likely to merit the label "feminist" are Claire Katz Kahane's "Gothic Mirrors and Feminine Identity," published in *Centennial Review* in 1980, and Barbara Wilkie Tedford's "Flannery O'Connor and the Social Classes," published a year later in *Southern Literary Journal.* However, though both these essays appeared a decade after Kate Millett's *Sexual Politics,* they keep, as their titles suggest, their feminism on the margins. Not until Louis Westling's *Sacred Groves and Ravaged Gardens: The Fiction of Eudora Welty, Carson McCullers, and Flannery O'Connor* appeared in 1985 did O'Connor's work receive a strong feminist critique. Though Westling has much to praise about O'Connor's artistry, she also sees it as ultimately supportive of patriarchy and punishing of aggressive females. For the next fifteen years, few attempts were made to counter Westling's conclusion, and both Sarah Gordon's *Obedient Imagination* in 2000 and Katherine Hemple Prown's *Revising Flannery O'Connor: Southern Literary Culture and the Problem of Female Authorship* published in 2001 reinforced the sense of O'Connor as complacent if not collaborative with an oppressive male patriarchy. Nevertheless, dissenting voices have been heard. For instance, two essays in Sura Rath and Mary Neff Shaw's *Flannery O'Connor: New Perspectives* (1996) made stabs in that direction. More strongly, Patricia Yaeger's 1995 essay in *New Essays on* Wise Blood and portions of her *Dirt and Desire: Reconstructing Southern Women's Writing* offered an alternative feminist reading. Yaeger's work sees O'Connor's fiction undermining the narrow southern conventions of female behavior and uncovering women's complex situation in southern culture. More recently, the

2004 collection of essays edited by Teresa Caruso, *"On the Subject of the Feminist Business": Re-reading Flannery O'Connor,* has further expanded the possibilities for feminist readings of O'Connor, though it seems likely this debate, like the debates among the "third wave" feminist scholars, will not soon be settled. In short, though a few cries of alarm are sometimes heard regarding the feminist Flannery, the gender approach has been generative of new scholarship even as it forces readers to confront the role of gender in O'Connor's creation of mystery.

Similarly, historical approaches, though more diverse than feminist ones, have expanded our understanding of O'Connor's fiction. A number of early pieces situate O'Connor in southern literary history, with Louis Rubin's essays published in the *Flannery O'Connor Bulletin* in late 1970s being among the most memorable, if only because they show a clear change from Rubin's initial focus on religion in O'Connor. In a totally different vein, J. O. Tate, in a series of articles published between 1979 and 1985, pioneered work connecting O'Connor to southern history, finding, for instance, sources for some of her stories in the Milledgeville newspaper and dealing with her use of southern military names. Meanwhile Marion Montgomery's 1981 *Why Flannery O'Connor Stayed Home,* while largely philosophical in orientation, also offered a close reading of O'Connor's library, giving particular stress to the ideas of historical philosopher Eric Voegelin. John Desmond's 1987 *Risen Sons: Flannery O'Connor's Vision of History* moved more deeply in this direction. It explored the connection between O'Connor's view of history and her theology. The 1990s saw the application of ideas from New Historicism begin to appear in O'Connor studies, with Thomas Hill Schaub's *American Fiction in the Cold War* chapter on O'Connor's *Good Man* collection and, more fully, with Jon Lance Bacon's *Flannery O'Connor and Cold War Culture,* as well as his essay in *New Essays on* Wise Blood, "A Fondness for Supermarkets: *Wise Blood* and Consumer Culture." Though far from completely mined, this vein of criticism has served well to show O'Connor's relation to the world around her and is working to challenge myths that stress her isolation physically in rural Georgia and intellectually in theological interests only.

Though it would be possible to review other approaches that have been used to discuss O'Connor's fiction, it's appropriate to stop and point out that, given my earlier criteria or goal for O'Connor criticism—an increasing awareness of the mystery in her work and a generative, rather than mummifying, impulse toward her work—that interpretative criticism is doing a good job. Yes, theology outweighs other types of criticism, often even overlapping with them; but then O'Connor's writing itself is steeped in theology—as is her region and her nation.

Wisely, however, O'Connor studies has not allowed itself to be limited to this one category. Moreover, despite the general tendency of academic interpretation to claim finality, there is as yet no sense of that having happened with O'Connor criticism. A study by Bernard Koloski presented at the 2005 American Literature Association found that between 1994 and 2004, the MLA Bibliography had listed 327 entries for O'Connor—a number equivalent to or exceeding the entries for such authors as Saul Bellow (313), Elizabeth Bishop (331), Robert Frost (294), Cormac McCarthy (295), John Steinbeck (281), and Eudora Welty (365). In short, O'Connor scholars still have much to say, and only a reader indifferent to the fate of O'Connor studies would wish otherwise.

Challenges

However, lest I sound like a politician running for reelection, let me note at least two major weaknesses or challenges confronting O'Connor studies. The first concerns the state of O'Connor biography. Though this is far better today than it was a mere five years ago, there is reason for concern. Jean Cash's *Flannery O'Connor: A Life* (2002), Paul Elie's *The Life You Save May Be Your Own: An American Pilgrimage* (2003), and even Melissa Simpson's book for high school students, *Flannery O'Connor: A Biography* (2005) all advance or make accessible narratives of O'Connor's life. But all are limited and sometimes erroneous in part due to an inability to gain access to relevant source materials and the hesitancy of some individuals to cooperate with research. At a time when highly competent biographies of such O'Connor contemporaries as Eudora Welty, Carson McCullers, and Katherine Anne Porter are in print—some for many years—no friend of O'Connor studies can be happy with this situation. There are hopeful signs on the horizon. Brad Gooch, the distinguished biographer of Frank O'Hara, had his *Flannery: A Life of Flannery O'Connor* successfully appear in February 2009—a year before this collection headed to press. Highly anticipated, Gooch's book has not only attracted new interest in the life that O'Connor once described as being "spent between the house and the chicken year" (quoted in Cash xiv), but has also garnered over ninety reviews and spent two weeks on the New York Times Bestseller List. William Sessions, O'Connor's friend and correspondent as well as the distinguished author of a biography of Renaissance poet Henry Howard, the Earl of Surrey, has stated publicly that he is near the completion of an authorized biography with the cooperation of the O'Connor estate—a relationship that should lead to access of previously unseen O'Connor materials. Already, Sessions has aided the study of O'Connor's biography by using his position as executor of the Elizabeth Hester papers to give scholars access to all Hester's unedited letters from O'Connor—those whose edited versions appear in *Habit of Being* as from "A." These letters held by Emory University are showing scholars sides of O'Connor's personality that will fuel many future discussions. On a less comprehensive level, Mark Bosco's recent work on O'Connor's relationship to Erik Langkjaer has proved highly insightful. Nevertheless, no book made with total access to all materials has yet appeared. The long expected authorized biography by Sally Fitzgerald remains in limbo: Will the portions she completed before her death be published? Will someone complete her manuscript? Rumors abound, but for the moment, the best biographical insight remains the published letters, which, as I mentioned earlier, are sanitized and edited more than befits the best scholarship. And they tell us little about O'Connor's early life—particularly her relationship to her father, her early education, and her formative years as a writer at the University of Iowa. In short, large gaps remain.

Problems with the letters point to the larger issue of textual scholarship on O'Connor. While there has been some work done on O'Connor's manuscripts and writing process, it remains incomplete. Most work centers on *Wise Blood* for which a large number of manuscripts exist and are available to scholars at the O'Connor Collection at George State College and University. Stuart Burns published an early essay, "The Evolution of *Wise Blood*," in 1970, but Katherine Hemple Prown's book *Revising Flannery O'Connor* makes the most extensive use of the manuscripts. Still, these are finally not textual studies. In the sense of true analysis of manuscript and published versions of texts, only one major example exists: *Flannery O'Connor: The Growing Craft* by Karl-Heinz Westarp. This synoptic variorum edition of four versions of the story best known as "Judgment Day" was published in 1993, though it is too seldom cited in scholarship—indeed my sense is that, too often, the various versions are not even acknowledged in scholarship. This is a situation O'Connor studies must remedy. O'Connor, as the *Wise Blood* manuscripts and her letters make clear, invested tremendous effort and time into revising her manuscripts, sending them to friends for comment and advice, and she published her stories in more than one venue, potentially sending them through various editing processes. Stephen G. Driggers, Robert J. Dunn, and Sarah Gordon's *The Manuscripts of Flannery O'Connor at Georgia College* is a highly helpful description of the holdings in a significant collection, but is not a scholarly edition or a complete description of the evolution of any one manuscript. In short, our knowledge of O'Connor's "texts" is limited.

Undoubtedly part of the explanation for limited textual study has come from limited access to materials. The O'Connor Collection in Milledgeville does an excellent job of providing access to its materials, and the collection of Elizabeth Hester materials, mentioned above, recently made accessible at Emory University seems likely to offer another valuable cache of documents. However, other, smaller collections too often remain unknown. Much to my chagrin, I wrote my dissertation on O'Connor at Duke University without ever finding a reference to the fact that a number of O'Connor's letters are located in Duke's manuscript collection. But 2002 brought a significant improvement in this situation with the publication of *Postmarked Milledgeville: A Guide to Flannery O'Connor's Correspondence in Libraries and Archives* complied by R. Neil Scott and Valerie Nye. This slim volume may well be the key to uncovering ignored riches in O'Connor studies, especially in revealing which libraries possess magazine archives for journals where O'Connor published. However, this is not a widely known book or one readily accessible outside of major research institutions. If O'Connor scholarship is to plow fresh fields, emerging scholars need to be made aware of such resources.

In addition, all in the O'Connor community need actively and consistently to encourage the O'Connor estate and others who own O'Connor materials to bring to light any yet unknown materials. The benefit from the publication of O'Connor cartoons and other juvenilia would be great, and that of yet unseen letters and journals even more so. The recent deaths of Robert Mann, his wife, Margaret Florencourt Mann—both invaluable in opening the O'Connor farm Andalusia to the public—and Catherine Florencourt Firth are sad reminders that the ranks of those with direct, living connection to O'Connor are fast thinning. Scholars need to work closely with those who remain to bring any lost materials to light.

Conclusion

As I hope this essay makes clear, the legacy of O'Connor scholarship is a rich one—rich in large part because it has fulfilled O'Connor's own best desires for a critical response that rejected the doctrinaire while allowing for a spectrum of interpretations. As the age of terrorism appears to settle in around us, an age rich in the certainties of numerous fundamentalisms, those of us convinced that O'Connor has much to say to such an age will need to continue to accept our own inability to reach final interpretations, being at least as open to generative readings and misreading as O'Connor herself was and carefully setting our priorities with a full awareness of work already done and a strong commitment to the much-needed work that remains to be done. In other words, we need to apply the advice of the author of Hebrews to our own discipline: leaving behind the ABCs of O'Connor studies, refusing to lay again the foundations so many have labored well to put down. This will free us to recognize further the mystery in O'Connor's fiction and her life, generate new readers and fresh readings—be they right or wrong—trusting in the writing and our fellow laborers in the field. Quoting again Beck's translation of the epistle, "We will do this if God lets us."

Acknowledgments

To acknowledge all the individuals who have enabled and encouraged my participation in the project would involve a long list of O'Connor scholars who never cease to prod and encourage efforts to add to our understanding of O'Connor's thought and writing. Four, however, stand out: Sura Rath, who first welcomed me into the circle of O'Connor scholars; Bruce Gentry, who has continually encouraged me to publish; Ralph Wood, who has provided a patient sounding board and a consistent measuring rod for my historical and heterodox musings, and Virginia Wray, whose insistence on originality and willingness to include friendship as a key element in being a scholar have proven a reliable guide.

On a more personal level, I also recognize that this book has a particular debt to my family. My wife, Anne, not only endured my long spiels of commentary at every step in the process of forming this book but also aided me in the thankless tasks of proofreading and indexing the book. In addition, her example of balancing her own career with family gave me a constant model for living each day. My children, Ben and Kate, gave me the great gift of being interested as well as time away from being Dad to get this brought to fruition.

And, of course, none of it would have been possible without the work of my co-editor, Avis Hewitt, whose lack of ego and abundance of drive kept us constantly moving forward and positive at all the slough moments.

Works Cited

Asals, Frederick. *Flannery O'Connor: The Imagination of Extremity.* Athens: U of Georgia P, 1982.

Bacon, Jon Lance. *Flannery O'Connor and Cold War Culture.* Cambridge: Cambridge UP, 1993.

———. "A Fondness for Supermarkets: *Wise Blood* and Consumer Culture." *New Essays on* Wise Blood. Ed. Michael Kreyling. Cambridge: Cambridge UP, 1995. 25–49.

Bosco, Mark. "Consenting to Love: Autobiographical Roots of 'Good Country People.'" *Southern Review* 41 (2005): 283–95.

Brinkmeyer, Robert H., Jr. *The Art and Vision of Flannery O'Connor.* Baton Rouge: Louisiana State UP, 1989.

Burns, Stuart. "O'Connor and the Critics: An Overview." *Mississippi Quarterly* 27 (1974): 483–95.

Caruso, Teresa, ed. *"On the Subject of the Feminist Business": Re-Reading Flannery O'Connor.* New York: Peter Lang, 2004.

Cash, Jean. *Flannery O'Connor: A Life.* U of Tennessee P, 2002.

Crews, Frederick. *The Critics Bear It Away: American Fiction and the Academy.* New York: Random House, 1992.

Dean, William. *The American Spiritual Culture and the Invention of Jazz, Football and the Movies.* New York: Continuum, 2003.

Desmond John. *Risen Sons: Flannery O'Connor's Vision of History.* Athens: U of Georgia P, 1987.

Di Renzo, Anthony. *American Gargoyles: Flannery O'Connor and the Medieval Grotesque.* Carbondale: Southern Illinois UP, 1995.

Elie, Paul. *The Life You Save May Be Your Own: An American Pilgrimage.* New York: Farrar, 2003.

Engle, Paul, and Hansford Martin. Introduction to *Prize Stories 1955: The O. Henry Awards.* Ed. Paul Engle and Hansford Martin. Garden City, NY: Doubleday, 1955. 9–12.

Esty, William. "In American, Intellectual Bomb Shelters." *Commonweal,* 7 March 1958, 586–88.

Farnham, James F. "The Grotesque in Flannery O'Connor." *America,* 13 May 1961, 277–81.

Fitzgerald, Robert. "The Countryside and the True Country." *Sewanee Review* 70 (1962): 380–94.

Gentry, Marshall Bruce. *Flannery O'Connor's Religion of the Grotesque.* Jackson: U of Mississippi P, 1986.

Giannone, Richard. *Flannery O'Connor: Hermit Novelist.* Urbana: U of Illinois P, 2000.

Golden, Robert E., and Mary C. Sullivan. *Flannery O'Connor and Caroline Gordon: A Reference Guide.* Boston: G. K. Hall, 1977.

Gordon, Sarah. *Flannery O'Connor: The Obedient Imagination.* Athens: U of Georgia P, 2000.

———. "Review of *Flannery O'Connor and the Christ-Haunted South.*" *Flannery O'Connor Review* 3 (2005): 102–9.

Gossett, Louise Y. *Violence and Recent Southern Fiction.* Durham: Duke UP, 1965.

Hawkes, John. "Flannery O'Connor's Devil." *Sewanee Review* 70.3 (1962): 395–407. Rpt. *Flannery O'Connor: Modern Critical Views.* Ed. Harold Bloom. New York: Chelsea, 1986. 9–17.

Hendin, Josephine. *The World of Flannery O'Connor.* Bloomington: Indiana UP, 1970.

Hyman, Stanley Edgar. *Flannery O'Connor.* University of Minnesota Pamphlets on American Writers: No. 54. Minneapolis: U of Minnesota P, 1966.

Jones, Bartlett C. "Depth Psychology and Literary Study." *Midcontinent American Studies Journal* 5 (1964): 50–56.

Kahane, Claire Katz. "Flannery O'Connor's Rage of Vision." *American Literature* 46 (1974): 54–67.

———. "Gothic Mirrors and Feminine Identity." *Centennial Review* 24 (1980): 43–64.

———. "The Re-vision of Rage: Flannery O'Connor and Me." *Massachusetts Review* 46 (2005): 439–61.

Keetley, Dawn. "'I forgot what I done': Repressed Anger and Violent Fantasy in 'A Good Man Is Hard to Find.'" *"On the Subject of the Feminist Business": Re-reading Flannery O'Connor.* Ed. Teresa Caruso. New York: Peter Lang, 2004. 74–93.

Koloski, Bernard. Handout. 2005 American Literature Association Conference.

Lawson, Lewis. "Flannery O'Connor and the Grotesque: *Wise Blood.*" *Renascence* 17 (1965): 137–47, 156.

Mellard, James M. "Flannery O'Connor's *Others:* Freud, Lacan, and the Unconscious." *American Literature* 61 (1989): 625–43.

———. "Framed in the Gaze: Haze, *Wise Blood,* and Lacanian Reading." *New Essays on* Wise Blood. Ed. Michael Kreyling. Cambridge: Cambridge UP 1995. 51–69.

Meyers, Sister Bertrande. "Four Stories of Flannery O'Connor." *Thought* 37 (1962): 410–26.

Montgomery, Marion. *Why Flannery O'Connor Stayed Home.* La Salle, IL: Sherwood Sugden, 1981.

Nolde, Sister Simon N. "*The Violent Bear It Away:* A Study in Imagery." *Xavier University Studies* 1 (1962): 180–94.

O'Connor, Flannery. *The Habit of Being.* Ed. Sally Fitzgerald. New York: Farrar, 1979.

———. *Mystery and Manners.* Ed. Sally and Robert Fitzgerald. New York: Farrar, 1969.

O'Gorman, Farrell. *Peculiar Crossroads: Flannery O'Connor, Walker Percy, and Catholic Vision in Postwar Southern Fiction.* Baton Rouge: Louisiana State UP, 2004.

Orvell, Miles. *Invisible Parade: The Fiction of Flannery O'Connor.* Philadelphia: Temple UP, 1971.

Prown, Katherine Hemple. *Revising Flannery O'Connor: Southern Literary Culture and the Problem of Female Authorship.* Charlottesville: UP of Virginia, 2001.

Rath, Sura, and Mary Neff Shaw, eds. *Flannery O'Connor: New Perspectives.* Athens: U of Georgia P, 1996.

Rubin, Louis. "Flannery O'Connor's Company of Southerners or 'The Artificial Nigger' Read as Fiction Rather Than Theology." *Flannery O'Connor Bulletin* 6 (1977): 47–71.

Schaub, Thomas Hill. *American Fiction in the Cold War.* Madison: U of Wisconsin P, 1991.

Scott, R. Neil. *Flannery O'Connor: An Annotated Reference Guide to Criticism.* Milledgeville, GA: Timberlane, 2002.

Scott, R. Neil, and Valerie Nye. *Postmarked Milledgeville: A Guide to Flannery O'Connor's Correspondence in Libraries and Archives.* Milledgeville: Georgia College and State U, 2002.

Shloss, Carol. *Flannery O'Connor's Dark Comedies: The Limits of Inference.* Baton Rouge: Louisiana State UP, 1980.

Simpson, Melissa. *Flannery O'Connor: A Biography.* Westport, CT: Greenwood P, 2005.

Spivey, Ted R. "Flannery O'Connor: A Tribute." *Esprit* 8 (1964): 46–47.

———. "Flannery O'Connor's View of God and Man." *Studies in Short Fiction* 1 (1964): 200–206.

Stephens, Martha. *The Question of Flannery O'Connor.* Baton Rouge: Louisiana State UP, 1973.

Tate, J. O. "A Note on O'Connor's Use of Military Names." *Flannery O'Connor Bulletin* 14 (1985): 99–102.

———. "O'Connor's Confederate General: A Late Encounter." *Flannery O'Connor Bulletin* 8 (1979): 45–53.

Tedford, Barbara Wilkie. "Flannery O'Connor and the Social Classes." *Southern Literary Journal* 13.2 (1981): 27–40.

Westarp, Karl-Heinz. *Flannery O'Connor: The Growing Craft.* Birmingham, AL: Summa, 1993.

Westling, Louise. *Sacred Groves and Ravaged Gardens: The Fiction of Eudora Welty, Carson McCullers, and Flannery O'Connor.* Athens: U of Georgia P, 1985.

Williams, Rowan. *Grace and Necessity: Reflections on Art and Love.* Harrisburg, PA: Morehouse, 2005.

Wood, Ralph C. *Flannery O'Connor and the Christ-Haunted South.* Grand Rapids, MI: Eerdmans, 2004.

Yaeger, Patricia Smith. *Dirt and Desire: Reconstructing Southern Women's Writing, 1930–1990.* Chicago: U of Chicago P, 2000.

———. "'The Woman without Any Bones': Anti-Angel Aggression in *Wise Blood.* *New Essays on* Wise Blood. Ed. Michael Kreyling. Cambridge: Cambridge UP, 1995. 91–116.

CONTRIBUTORS

Jon Lance Bacon is the author of *Flannery O'Connor and Cold War Culture* (1993), an interdisciplinary study published by Cambridge University Press. Bacon has taught at Vanderbilt University, where he earned a Ph.D. in English, as well as Belmont University and North Carolina Wesleyan. He currently works as a writer and director for Dagtype Films, a production company he co-founded in Raleigh. In 2009 he completed his first feature film—a murder mystery called *Foresight*.

William Brevda is professor of English at Central Michigan University, where he specializes in modern American literature. His publications include *Harry Kemp: The Last Bohemian* (Bucknell University Press, 1986) and journal articles on Poe, Faulkner, Fitzgerald, Dos Passos, West, Chandler, Hammett, Algren, and other American writers. He is currently writing a critical study of Jack Kerouac and completing a book on the electric sign in American literature.

Doug Davis is associate professor of English at Gordon College in Barnesville, Georgia. His research interests include Cold War cultural studies and science and technology studies. In addition to publishing essays on Flannery O'Connor, he has published essays on Tim O'Brien, the pedagogy of science fiction, the culture of the nuclear threat, and the metaphoric origins of impact-extinction theory. He is currently working on his book manuscript, "Strategic Fictions," a study of the interrelations of future-war storytelling and national security.

Anthony Di Renzo teaches classical rhetoric and professional writing at Ithaca College. His major critical studies include *American Gargoyles: Flannery O'Connor and the Medieval Grotesque* (Southern Illinois University Press, 1993) and *If I Were Boss: The Early Business Stories of Sinclair Lewis* (Southern Illinois University Press, 1997). An ordained cantor, lector, and Eucharistic minister, he is also a scholar of Catholic history and doctrine. Cited in *Best American Essays,* his creative nonfiction has appeared in *Alimentum Journal: The Literature of Food, The Normal School, River Styx,* and *Voices in Italian Americana.* His collection "Bitter Greens: Essays on Food, Politics, and Ethnicity from the Imperial Kitchen" is being considered for publication.

ROBERT DONAHOO is president of the Flannery O'Connor Society and past editor of *Cheers! The Flannery O'Connor Society Newsletter*. He has published articles on O'Connor in journals including *Flannery O'Connor Review*, the *CEA Critic*, *Literature and Belief*, and the *Journal of Contemporary Thought*, as well as in several essay collections on O'Connor. In addition, he has published essays on postmodern American science fiction, Tolstoy's novel *Resurrection*, and the plays of Horton Foote, as well as one on Foote's adaptation of "The Displaced Person." A graduate of Baylor University and Duke University, he is currently professor of English at Sam Houston State University.

MARSHALL BRUCE GENTRY is professor of English at Georgia College & State University in Milledgeville and editor of the *Flannery O'Connor Review*. He is the author of the book *Flannery O'Connor's Religion of the Grotesque*, published by the University Press of Mississippi. His articles on O'Connor's works appear in *Flannery O'Connor's Radical Reality*, *"On the Subject of the Feminist Business": Re-Reading Flannery O'Connor*, *Flannery O'Connor: New Perspectives*, and the *Southern Quarterly*. Publications by Gentry on other American fiction writers include *Conversations with Raymond Carver* (for which Gentry was coeditor) and articles in *Contemporary Literature*, *South Atlantic Review*, *The CEA Critic*, *Shofar*, and *South Carolina Review*. Gentry was co-director for "Reconsidering Flannery O'Connor," a 2007 NEH Summer Institute for College and University Teachers, and he occasionally hosts O'Connor conferences at Georgia College and State University.

THOMAS F. HADDOX is associate professor of English at the University of Tennessee. He is the author of *Fears and Fascinations: Representing Catholicism in the American South* (Fordham University Press, 2005). His articles on southern and American literature have appeared in *American Literature*, *Modern Language Quarterly*, *Mississippi Quarterly*, *Mosaic*, *Flannery O'Connor Review*, *Southern Quarterly*, and other journals. His current work in progress includes a coedited volume on the limits of historicism as literary-critical method and a monograph with the working title "Hard Sayings: The Rhetoric of Christian Orthodoxy in Contemporary Fiction."

AVIS HEWITT is associate professor of English at Grand Valley State University in Allendale, Michigan, where she teaches both survey and period courses in American literature, a genre course in fiction, and a capstone survey of literary theory, as well as major-authors courses on Flannery O'Connor. She earned her B.A. at the College of Wooster and her M.A. and Ph.D. at Ball State University and taught at Campbellsville University and Northern Arizona University before moving to Michigan. She has published essays on Mary McCarthy, Denise Levertov, John Updike, and Flannery O'Connor. Along with a group of outstanding graduate students, Rebecca

Karnes, Ruth Reiniche, and Christina Triezenberg, she organized "Flannery O'Connor in the Age of Terrorism," the 2006 conference in Grand Rapids, Michigan. She currently serves as the editor of *Cheers! The Flannery O'Connor Society Newsletter.*

CHRISTINA BIEBER LAKE is associate professor of English at Wheaton College in Wheaton, Illinois, where she teaches classes in contemporary American literature and literary theory. She earned her B.A. at Princeton University and her Ph.D. at Emory. She is the author of *The Incarnational Art of Flannery O'Connor* (Mercer University Press, 2005). She is currently investigating the role of fiction in shaping ethical questions about what it means to be human in an increasingly posthuman world.

J. RAMSEY MICHAELS is a professor of religious studies emeritus at Missouri State University, Springfield, specializing in New Testament studies, including books on the Gospel of John, the Epistle to the Hebrews, the First Epistle of Peter, and the book of Revelation, with occasional forays into church history and (not least) into O'Connor studies. He is currently serving as an adjunct professor of New Testament at Bangor Theological Seminary, Portland, Maine.

WILLIAM MONROE is professor of English and Abendshein Professor and Dean of the Honors College at the University of Houston. His monograph, *Power to Hurt: The Virtues of Alienation* (1998), was selected as an outstanding academic book of the year by *Choice* magazine and nominated for the Phi Beta Kappa/Christian Gauss Award. His other publications include the play *Primary Care,* which deals with end-of-life issues related to Alzheimer's disease, and articles on Cather, Eliot, Nabokov, and O'Connor. He teaches in "The Human Situation," the Honors College great books course, directs the Common Ground Teachers Institute, and founded the Medicine and Society Program at Houston. His current book project is "The Vocation of Affliction: Flannery O'Connor and the Myth of Mastery."

LINDA NARANJO-HUEBL is currently assistant professor of literature at Calvin College in Grand Rapids, Michigan, where she teaches Women and Literature, American ethnic literatures, and American literature. She is also on the board of Consistent Life, an umbrella organization dedicated to the protection of human life and the promotion of nonviolence. Her research interests include nineteenth- and twentieth-century women writers, psychological approaches to literature, and American ethnic literatures. She has published essays on various women writers, including E.D.E.N. Southworth, Harriet Jacobs, Harriet Beecher Stowe, Susan Warner, Denise Chavez, and American feminist essayists.

FARRELL O'GORMAN is the author of *Peculiar Crossroads: Flannery O'Connor, Walker Percy, and Catholic Vision in Postwar Southern Fiction* (Louisiana State University

Press, 2004) and of recent articles in the *Cormac McCarthy Journal, Flannery O'Connor Review,* and *Critique: Studies in Contemporary Fiction.* He is assistant professor of Catholic Studies at DePaul University in Chicago.

W. A. SESSIONS, Regents' Professor of English Emeritus at Georgia State University, received his B.A. from the University of North Carolina at Chapel Hill and his M.A. and Ph.D. from Columbia. He is a poet, a critic, a writer, and a playwright. His third play, *Words without End,* was produced as a Gateway Performance production in 2002. He has authored or edited seven books and more than seventy-five essays, book chapters, and reviews on such figures as Francis Bacon, Edmund Spenser, William Shakespeare, John Milton, and on early modern English literature. His most widely acclaimed work in Renaissance Studies is *Henry Howard: The Poet Earl of Surry* (1999). With regard to Flannery O'Connor, not only has he already published extensively on her work, but he was her friend, correspondent, and a frequent visitor to Andalusia during most of the two decades of her writing life. He appears numerous times in *The Habit of Being* (1979) as "Billy." He serves on the board of directors of the Flannery O'Connor–Andalusia Foundation and is completing her authorized biography. He was also selected by Elizabeth (Betty) Hester (revealed in 1998 to be O'Connor's longtime correspondent "A.") to serve as her literary executor.

JOHN D. SYKES JR. was educated at Wake Forest University (B.A. Philosophy and English), the University of Chicago (M.A. Divinity), and the University of Virginia (M.A. English, Ph.D. Religious Studies). His teaching career has included appointments at Wake Forest University and Austin College. Currently, he serves as professor of English at Wingate University. He has published two books on the literature of the American South, *The Romance of Innocence and the Myth of History: Faulkner's Religious Critique of Southern Culture* (1989) and *Flannery O'Connor, Walker Percy, and the Aesthetic of Revelation* (2007). His academic articles have appeared in such periodicals as *Mississippi Quarterly, Renascence, Modern Theology, Flannery O'Connor Review,* and *Religion & Literature.*

RALPH C. WOOD, university professor of theology and literature at Baylor University in Waco, Texas, holds B.A. and M.A. degrees from Texas A&M University–Commerce, as well as M.A. and Ph.D. degrees from the University of Chicago. From 1971 to 1997 he taught on the faculty of Wake Forest University, in Winston-Salem, North Carolina, where he was the John Allen Easley Professor of Religion. At Baylor, he teaches in both the Great Texts program and the Department of Religion. He serves as an editor-at-large for the *Christian Century* and as a member of the editorial boards of the *Flannery O'Connor Review* and *VII: An Anglo-American Literary Review.* His major book, first published in 1988 and still in print from the University of Notre Dame Press, is *The Comedy of Redemption: Christian Faith and Comic*

Vision in Four American Novelists (Flannery O'Connor, Walker Percy, John Updike, and Peter De Vries). He is also the author of *Contending for the Faith: The Church's Engagement with Culture* (Baylor University Press, 2003); *The Gospel According to Tolkien: Visions of the Kingdom in Middle-Earth* (Westminster John Knox, 2004); *Flannery O'Connor and the Christ-Haunted South* (Eerdmans, 2004); and *Literature and Theology* (Abingdon Press, 2008).

INDEX

spirit 68, 104; sacred violence, 64; sense of Christian vocation, 125–26; utter goodness of creation, 55; view of natural world, 152, 154, 160

—view of history: formative impressions of WWII and the Holocaust, 98–99; WWII and nihilism, 107, 128–29, 132–40, 152, 154, 160, 161, 163, 169–70, 172, 174–76, 179, 180, 189–94, 198, 201–11, 213–18, 220, 221, 222, 224–26, 227, 232, 233, 238n, 241–42, 243, 245, 247

—writing: depiction of the asylum, 224–27; grotesque, as "semiotic switchboard," 172; her plot quarantines of the odd and unwanted, 220–22; imagery, 179; influences, Kierkegaard, 117; irony, 121–23; Poe, 89; reading noir, 114; sources of writing style, 113; symbol, 128–29; theoretical lenses applied to her writing, 247; views of characters, 28; the writer and mystery, 243

O'Connor, Flannery, works of

—essays

Mystery and Manners "The Catholic Novelist in the Protestant South," 143, 172–73

"The Grotesque in Southern Fiction," 143, 243

"Introduction to *A Memoir of Mary Ann*," 26; "The Nature and Aim of Fiction," 9

"Some Aspects of the Grotesque in Southern Fiction," 143

—novels

Wise Blood, ix, 7, 61, 62, 66, 74, 89–90, 92, 94, 99, 100, 103–4, 105, 117, 123n1, 129, 131–32, 145–46, 147, 151, 176, 177, 183n1, 197–98, 233, 234, 247, 249, 250, 252; Mrs. Flood, 62, 89, 94, 102, 132, 151; Asa Hawks, 7; Hazel Motes, ix, 12, 18, 52, 61, 62, 74, 89–90, 94, 102–4, 128, 129, 132, 145–47, 151, 176–77, 179, 183n1, 193, 197, 206; Layfield, Solace, ix, 18; Hoover Shoats (aka Onnie Jay Holy), 123n1

The Violent Bear It Away, 6, 18–20, 27, 28, 29, 44, 59–68, 89, 92, 99, 102–3, 123n1, 134, 144–46, 154–58, 163, 197, 213, 219–20, 224, 225, 245; Bishop, ix, 19,

20, 28, 29, 52, 59, 60–63, 64, 65, 68n, 144, 156, 157, 159; Lucette Carmody, viii, 19, 22, 64; Cherokee Lodge, 63, 65; Buford Munson, 64, 65–66, 68, 69n9; Rayber, 6, 19, 21, 28, 61, 63–65, 68n1, 144, 154, 155–56, 157, 160, 220; Francis Marion Tarwater, ix, xiv, 18–20, 28, 29, 52, 59–68, 68n, 89–90, 92, 102–3, 146, 147, 155–57, 197, 219; Tarwater's friend/rapist, 63–64, 89, 146, 155; Mason Tarwater, 6, 19, 60, 62–66, 68, 68n, 102–3, 146, 156, 157, 163, 190, 219–20, 225

—short story collections

A Good Man is Hard to Find, 89, 207, 250; "The Artificial Nigger," xiv, 69n, 129, 132–34, 136–38, 140, 196–97, 220, 233; Mr. Head, 53, 131, 132, 134–36, 137, 138, 197, 220; Nelson, 53, 131, 132, 134–35, 137, 138, 196–97; "A Circle in the Fire," 17, 42, 195–96; Powell Boyd, 17, 195; Cope, Mrs., 17, 52, 195–96; Cope, Sally Virginia, 42; "The Displaced Person," 17, 29, 92, 99, 134, 194; the Judge 89, 102, 190; Mr. Guizac, 17, 52, 128, 192, 193, 194;, Mrs. McIntyre, 51, 52, 102, 194; Chauncey Shortley, 52, 102; Mrs. Shortley, 17, 29, 51, 92, 99, 193, 194; Sulk, 194; "Good Country People," 42, 92, 123n1, 207, 247; Hulga/Joy Hopewell, 42, 51, 52, 92, 123n1; Pointer, Manley, 51, 52, 108, 118; "A Good Man is Hard to Find," xiv, 27, 42, 90, 113, 114, 116, 119–20, 128, 132, 134, 144–45, 149–50, 152, 232–33; the grandmother, ix, 52, 113, 116, 118, 119, 120, 122, 128, 132, 144, 149–50, 232, 233; ; John Wesley, 90; June Star, 42, 90; the Misfit, ix, 18, 27, 52, 104, 113, 115–22, 132, 144–45, 148–53, 160, 206; Red Sammy Butts, 114, 190; "The Life You Save May Be Your Own," 92, 148, 169–74, 176, 177–82, 183n3; Mrs. and Ms. Lucynell Crater, 169, 171, 177, 179, 180, 181–82; Tom T. Shiftlet, 92, 93, 148, 169–74, 177–82, 183n7; "The River," 17, 63, 123n1, 132, 145, 152, 154, 158–59; Ashfield, Harry/Bevel, ix, 17, 52, 63, 132, 158, 159, 160; Mrs. Connin,